SURMOUNTABLE

SURMOUNTABLE

HOW CITIZENS FROM SELMA TO SEOUL CHANGED THE WORLD

BY **BRIAN GRUBER** & **ADAM MONIER EDWARDS**

Designed by Adam Monier Edwards. Cover photography credits:
Mountaineers, Westend61/Alun Richardson. The first picket
line, photographer unknown, public domain from the Library
of Congress, February 1917. Bonus Army in front of U.S. Capitol,
Harris & Ewing, public domain from the Library of Congress, 1932.
Abernathy children on front line leading the Selma to Montgomery
march for the right to vote, public domain from the Abernathy
Family, March 1965. South Korea candlelight vigils, AP Photo/
Lee Jin-man, November 2016.

ISBN 978-1-7361185-1-1

From Adam

in memory of my father and stepfather,
who expanded my understanding of history beyond
what was taught in school,
and to my brother,
who opened my eyes to a bigger world

From Brian

to Silas Alder,
the little man with the big blue eyes

ACKNOWLEDGEMENTS

Too many people live their entire lives and yet are never able to follow through on their ideas. That is not a criticism; it is a fact of life. Day jobs are consuming and many can be stressful just to keep. Some people have night jobs as well. Or families to support. Or health issues to battle. Or disasters to rebuild from. Or dangerous situations to flee. Just overcoming these challenges is enough to put us in awe of the stories told in the forthcoming pages.

One small change in that eternal struggle has been the advent of crowdfunding platforms. This book would not have been possible without one. Brian funded a previous book on Kickstarter, which Adam found online and chose to support. After continued correspondence and eventually meeting in person, Adam asked Brian if he would like to collaborate on a future book. Many late night discussions ensued, ironing out Adam's initial concept into a full-fledged joint proposal. Ultimately, we were able to fund travel to 15 cities through our own online campaign as well. Had crowdfunding not been available, *Surmountable* likely never would have happened.

So thank you to our 80+ backers who helped make *Surmountable* a reality, especially Adam Bohn, Alexandra LaGuardia, Kanako Shirasaki, Karma Edwards, Michele Geller, Jeremy Winterson, Bill O'Luanaigh, Chris & Jennifer Gibson, Dale Larson, Joan Cainan, Lou Borrelli, Sean Cullen & Tanya Nam, Spencer Nassar, Stacy Nunamaker, Patrick Laird, Eric Gruber, Cyrus Semmence, Cat Hamilton, Eugene Lee, Garry Golden, JiYoung Kim, Joel Ficks, Justin Giddings, Khaing Sithuu Tindianos, Kristi VandenBosch, Lia Alexander, Maggie Chin, Mike Paschall, Nicole Maron, Piet Holten, Roberto Alcazar, Steven Herman, Terry Rich, and Yvonne Wong. Our gratitude also goes out to our 40+ interviewees who selflessly gave their time, and then some, to this endeavor. Heartfelt thanks to Dr. Nick De Bonis as our intrepid editor for going the extra mile in researching important context, as well as Dr. Susan De Bonis for her early contributions to the direction of the book.

Finally, profound admiration to many of the people profiled herein. In an age when many billionaires inherit their wealth or celebrities are famous for being famous, history will not forget those who achieved something tangible.

TABLE OF CONTENTS

INTRODUCTION

Surmountable \sər·moun′tə·bəl\, adj.

1. capable of being overcome or conquered despite the challenges ahead

2. the opposite of insurmountable

On February 15, 2003, millions of protesters take to the streets in more than 50 countries to stop the United States-led invasion of Iraq, claiming that the military action is based on a string of deceptions and would cause irreparable, catastrophic harm in the region and beyond.

Demonstrators fail in achieving their objective, though their claims are proven correct. The conflict lasts longer than World War II, causes more than one million Iraqi casualties, drives 10 million from their homes, destabilizes the Middle East, facilitates the rise of ISIS, and costs U.S. taxpayers over $2 trillion, before interest. No weapons of mass destruction are found, and the tenuous connection of Iraq to the 9/11 attacks, promoted by the George W. Bush administration to the public and the troops, proves to be false.

In recent years, many have watched these and other large political rallies in exasperation. They seem futile or, worse, delusional. And the movements, by and large, fail to hold leadership accountable in subsequent elections.

In late 2018, we spent some weeks exploring that phenomenon, while also asking whether something more was happening, the gradual erosion of American institutions, the neutering of aspects of American political life, defined by the country's founders as vital.

To wit,

- Just over half of us vote during presidential elections, well under half in most midterm congressional races, and, in local and state off-year contests, *fuhgeddaboudit*.[1]

- We are awash in a tsunami of digital information, increasingly uninformed. Most Americans can't list the freedoms in the First Amendment, can't list the three branches of government, can't name their own members of Congress – nearly half don't know that each state has two senators – and most can't name a single Supreme Court Justice.[2]

- We are increasingly, hopelessly divided. Members of Congress used to cast 60 percent of their votes along party lines, the rest according to the interests of their districts, constituents, and personal convictions; now it's over 90 percent, their votes carefully calibrated so as not to offend donors and lobbyists.[3]

Underlying our problems is the slow death of active and effective citizen engagement. A growing number of Americans believe voting is a waste of time, believe that the system is so saturated with money that activism is futile, and believe that upward mobility, and access to quality health care and education, are out of reach.

Throughout our history, Americans have encountered seemingly insurmountable obstacles, then fiercely engage to move mountains on causes that mattered, on big ideas. Protest and citizen activism aren't uniquely American, but they are uniquely part of our founding documents, our political DNA, our creation myth.

Thus, the *Surmountable* project is born, in pursuit of the answer to a simple question: What works? As we enter the third decade of the third millennium CE, what does it look like to protest, to engage, to move the government, the system, effectively?

With support from over 80 Kickstarter crowdfunding patrons, and a set of inquiries researched and designed by Adam, Brian travels around the United States, then around the world to scenes of iconic protests to harvest fresh narratives from witnesses to history, activists, thought leaders, and those who imagined the big ideas that brought the country's founding vision alive.

Snowbound days are filled at the Standing Rock Lakota Sioux Reservation with LaDonna Brave Bull Allard, the warrior who inspired tens of thousands to become Water Protectors. He shares Austin barbecue with Gregory Watson, the man who single-handedly added an amendment to the United States Constitution. Brian talks with tech thinkers about privacy, social media, and copyright, and chats with *Adbusters'* Kalle Lasn about co-creating the Occupy Wall Street movement.

He walks the Edmund Pettus Bridge in Selma and wanders the White House of the Confederacy in Montgomery, spending evenings at bars with activists and citizens on both sides of the Alabama racial divide. He visits the Alice Paul Institute in New Jersey, talks with visionaries across the political spectrum in Washington and New York. And meets with heroes of Kyiv's Euromaidan revolution, activists from the first days of the Arab Spring in Tunis, and South Korean cooks, journalists, professors, and monks who help overthrow a president.

Every era has its crises, with urgent declarations that the sky is falling. We believe this is a unique, critical moment in the history of the nation and of the species. Progress in human liberties; the embrace of democratic government of, by, and for the people; the inclusion of all genders, religions, and ethnicities in the pursuit of wealth, justice and power; environmental protection – they are all at risk.

There is an endless amount of academic and literary work on the subject, but none fully answer our questions. With the full knowledge that this is not a complete history of protest, rather a gathering of vital stories, *Surmountable* hit the road to ask:

- Is there a checklist, an effective playbook for the modern activist, even as heroic fourth quarter wins are often unpredictable, astonishing, and subject to serendipitous external forces?

- How is success – and failure – measured?

- How universal are the values in the U.S. Constitution?

- What can we learn from those who act outside the U.S., who may be outperforming us in the fierce pursuit of freedom, justice, and prosperity?

Surmountable is the story of what we learned.

Adam Monier Edwards   Brian Gruber
New York, New York   Koh Phangan, Thailand

1. PROMISES TO KEEP

Heroes are exalted for their courage and grand achievements, for noble, even superhuman qualities. In Greek lore, Hero is a priestess of Aphrodite, whose lover Leander swims the Dardanelles strait each night to be with her.

Mythologist Joseph Campbell, in his best-selling classic *The Hero with a Thousand Faces*, identifies a universal theme of adventure and transformation that runs through the world's mythic traditions. The hero leaves a safe harbor, the "Ordinary World," ventures into unknown territory, the "Special World," enduring certain trials, then returns home, in triumph.

The term "superhero" is used as early as 1917, according to Mike Benton's *Superhero Comics of the Golden Age*. But it emerges in popular culture with Superman, first as a DC comic book targeted at kids, then a radio serial and, in 1952, a hit show in the emerging medium of television. A superhero harnesses abilities beyond those of ordinary people, using superpowers to fight villains, to help the world become a better place.

Superman is a celestial refugee from the planet Krypton's violent upheavals. He is raised as an adopted orphan in a loving Midwestern American home, then moves to the big city when he comes of age, choosing journalism as his profession. And, while he has superpowers – *faster than a speeding bullet, able to leap tall buildings in a single bound* – what's most interesting is his purpose, made famous in the intro to the '50s-era series starring George Reeves:

Superman – who, disguised as Clark Kent, mild-mannered reporter for a great metropolitan newspaper, fights a never-ending battle for truth, justice and the American way.

Fundamental to the "American way" is the First Amendment to the Constitution of the United States, the first of the Bill of Rights. It codifies five historically important liberties that enable citizens' unfettered pursuit of truth and justice.

The Founding Fathers apply their considerable intellectual skills to construct an entirely new way of organizing society, putting their lives at risk in declaring independence from their British overlords. Embedded in their founding documents is a view of the citizen as hero, with the entire enterprise of liberal democracy resting on an informed, engaged citizenry.

Knowing their fragile system is subject to subversion by autocrats and aristocrats, by powerful, moneyed interests, they entrench in the First Amendment an expectation, if not requirement, that American citizens will regularly raise hell.

After all, the United States of America was born of protest.

The founders who drafted and affirmed the Constitution know what it means to be denied their rights. They are raised as British subjects, many not born in the colonies. Thousands of British colonists, including Major George Washington, fight for king and country in the French and Indian War. But by 1765, most resent the Parliament-approved Stamp Act, a direct tax on printed materials. To demonstrate their outrage, the clandestine Sons of Liberty, led by Samuel Adams, engage in protests ranging from boycotting British goods and burning buildings to publicly tarring and feathering local officials. Samuel's cousin, John Adams, along with 26 others from nine colonies, seek to compose a more formal response to the reviled legislation. They assemble in New York City as an unsanctioned Congress to petition King George III with a Declaration of Rights and Grievances stating their opposition to "taxation without representation," as framed by James Otis, Jr.

While petition has been a guaranteed right of British subjects since the Magna Carta in 1215, assemblies can be deemed unlawful and thus punishable by fine and imprisonment.

Both the assembled petitioners and protesters risk a great deal to defy the Crown. The Stamp Act is ultimately revoked, largely due to pressure from British merchants who suffered commercially. It proves a pyrrhic victory for the colonial protesters; Parliament passes the Declaratory Act, which refutes the petitioners' core position and reasserts the legal right of Great Britain to enact any and all legislation over the colonies without American representation.

Resentment grows into insurrection. From September 5 through October 26, 1774, delegates from 12 of 13 colonies meet in Philadelphia as the First Continental Congress to organize resistance to the British Parliament's Coercive Acts. It issues a declaration of "immutable" rights of the North American colonies, ideas later threading through the Declaration of Independence, the Articles of Confederation, the Constitution of the United States and the Bill of Rights.

The Declaration and Resolves of the Congress state that "assemblies have been frequently dissolved, contrary to the rights of the people, when they attempted to deliberate on grievances; and their dutiful, humble, loyal, and reasonable petitions to crown for redress, have been repeatedly treated with contempt, by his Majesty's ministers of state... That (the inhabitants of the English colonies in North-America) have a right peaceably to assemble, consider of their grievances, and petition the king; and that all prosecutions, prohibitory proclamations, and commitments for the same, are illegal."[4]

The extralegal assembly formalizes previously ad hoc boycotts, including the Boston Tea Party, and sends another petition to the king. It, too, is ignored. After the battles of Lexington and Concord, the Continental Congress reconvenes to discuss a common defense and on June 12, 1776, appoints a committee of five to draft a Declaration of Independence. Thomas Jefferson crafts the original draft. Independence is formally declared on July 2nd, with the final text approved on July 4th.

Congress soon begins discussing governance of the colonies should Great Britain be defeated. Two competing systems are proposed: federalists support a strong union, while anti-federalists want a confederation of largely independent states. The latter believe a republic the size of the thirteen colonies would not adequately answer to the local needs of citizens and would devolve into tyranny.

After six drafts, the Articles of Confederation are adopted by the Continental Congress, the first constitution of the United States, on November 15, 1777. It creates a loose confederation of sovereign states and a weak central government, leaving most of the power with the states. Virginia is the first state to ratify, Maryland the 13th in February 1781, eight months before Cornwallis surrenders at Yorktown ending the Revolutionary War. The Peace of Paris treaties officially ending the war are signed on September 3, 1783.

The Continental Congress soon proves ineffective.

For example, it is unable to raise the funds to pay the massive debts from the Revolutionary War both to French and Dutch allies as well as reimburse domestic suppliers and veterans. So, the Congress invites a new set of delegates to Philadelphia to revise the Articles of Confederation in February 1787.

Recognizing the flaws in the confederation, attendees emerge after a summer of heated debate with an entirely new Constitution.

It officially designates the country as the United States of America, served by three branches of government – executive, legislative, and judicial – with a system of checks and balances to equally distribute authority among them.

The final draft is signed on September 17. Five states of the required nine ratify the Constitution quickly. Others, particularly Massachusetts, oppose the document, claiming it lacks protection of basic civil liberties and does not entrust further power to the states.

Holdouts are assured that amendments to address their concerns would be immediately proposed after passage. The compromise convinces the remaining states to join in ratification. The new government commences on March 4, 1789, with George Washington inaugurated as president on April 30.

To fulfill the compromise, Representative James Madison (VA) introduces 19 amendments to the Constitution. Twelve are adopted by the new Congress on September 25, 1789, and are sent to the states for ratification. Ten of the amendments are ratified and, thus, become part of the Constitution on December 10, 1791. Known as the Bill of Rights, they guarantee individuals certain basic protections as citizens. It delegates remaining functions not mentioned in the Constitution or enacted by the federal government to the states and, where not prohibited, to the people. The most popular and influential of these is the First Amendment, which defends five civil liberties including the freedoms of speech, religion, and the press. Less well-known within the First Amendment are the equally important and hard-won rights to peaceably assemble and petition the government for a redress of grievances.

> Congress shall make no law respecting an establishment of religion, or prohibiting the free exercise thereof; or abridging the freedom of speech, or of the press; or the right of the people peaceably to assemble, and to petition the government for a redress of grievances.

Were the freedoms codified in the Bill of Rights revolutionary ideas in their time?

"They were absolutely revolutionary," according to Dr. Todd Gitlin, professor and Ph.D. program chair at the Columbia University Graduate School of Journalism. "And before the American Revolution, before the overthrow of the crown, a number of the colonies adopted guarantees of the freedoms."

The American colonies derive most of their constitutional and legal systems from England, including the selective freedoms granted to white male landowners. Most of the original colonies include a declaration of fundamental rights and liberties in their constitutions.

"When you ask people what's in the First Amendment, they've heard of freedom of speech, of the press, of freedom of religion," Gitlin says. "They don't know the right of the people peaceably to assemble and to petition the government for redress of grievances." Gitlin, author of numerous books on the history and dynamics of protest, refers to his emphasis of the issue in *Occupy Nation*. "There is so little jurisprudence, there's so little even legal discussion either in the courts or among the law schools about this phenomenon of the right to assemble, it's really quite extraordinary. I mean, it's like it there's an actual collective forgetting."

The idea of petition comes from the Magna Carta, a charter of rights agreed to by King John of England in 1215. Heavy burdens in blood and treasure were imposed on barons to fund foreign wars and they revolted, capturing London and forcing the king to negotiate at Runnymede. The most famous clause, still codified in English law, gave "free men" the right to justice and a fair trial, though most citizens were unfree peasants, chattel lorded over by landowners.

"I don't think there's anything in the Magna Carta about assembly," points out Gitlin. "There is about petition. The law professor Ronald Krotoszynski, of the University of Alabama, wrote a smart, important piece about petition; the nobles, and eventually the commoners, had a right to actually go and deliver the petition to the king. It's a face-to-face operation."

"When cities hosting political conventions started sequestering demonstrations like in Boston – a compound was set up far away from the (2004 Democratic National Convention) arena – he stated that should be held unconstitutional, that defies the spirit of petition. Petition is like serving you with papers. And if you put me in a cage a mile away, that won't pass muster. A very interesting notion. And we don't have much conversation about this."

Norm Ornstein, author and resident congressional scholar at the American Enterprise Institute (AEI), says protest and activism were essential aspects of the founders' vision of being American, of the American way.

"They wanted a republican form of government, but they also wanted to have a direct line from the people to the government. It's certainly very much a part of our DNA. Protest itself is not an unknown phenomenon in other places around the world, it's just that in most other governments, it's not enshrined in their constitution."

Underlying these revolutionary legal rights lay something deeper, drawn from Enlightenment-era philosophy about what it means to be human, what it means to live with others in a social compact, explains Colleen Sheehan, Villanova University political science professor, Heritage Foundation scholar, former Republican state legislator, and the author of numerous books and articles on James Madison.

"There's one right that Madison really wanted in the Bill of Rights, what he considered the most sacred of all of our rights," insists Sheehan, "and that's the right of conscience. It's the only right that's pure and inalienable. First Amendment freedoms are all connected with, and are to some extent derivative of this idea of the right of conscience. It's our conscience that we have to answer to, first and foremost, and the other rights are the expression of our opinions."

Why is James Madison important to you?

Sheehan thinks of Madison as the father of the United States Constitution. "He was the one who prepared most out all the delegates to the Philadelphia convention, prepared most for the upcoming convention, studying ancient modern confederacies, ancient and modern republics and wrote about a piece called *License of the Political System of the United States*, looking at all the weaknesses under the Articles of Confederation, trying to think about what could be done to fix those problems.

"Here was the challenge in Madison's mind, that free government, or what they called 'small r' republican government (a state in which supreme power is held by the people and their elected representatives, with an elected president), had never succeeded in the history of humankind. And Madison's challenge, Madison's goal was to find a way to make it possible for people to govern themselves."

A radical notion that existed in practice meaningfully nowhere on the planet at that time.

"England is a constitutional monarchy. It utilizes what Madison calls the mechanism of representation; he talked about this in *Federalist 14*, that the English sort of discovered a mechanism to collect the public voice in the modern world. There's some debate about whether there was such a thing as representation in the ancient world or not. Madison talks about his research of the ephors (council leaders) in Sparta and the archons (civil/judicial officers) and the tribunes (political and military officers) in Rome. So, it's not a radical new idea to have representation. What's new and different is this idea of extending the republic, extending the territory and encompassing a large variety of interests and religious sects, and that somehow in this large republic, you could have people governing themselves. The traditional view on this was, in any large territory, it would necessarily lead to despotism."

What was unique about this experiment at that time?

"Madison put it this way, in a little piece he wrote in 1792 called *Spirit of Governments*, 'Such is the government for which philosophy has been searching, and humanity been sighing, from the most remote ages. Such are the republican governments which it is the glory of America to have invented, and her unrivalled happiness to possess.' He's talking about the way America designed this new republic, and it has to do both with structure, but also the purpose of the structure, in Madison's mind to 'refine and enlarge' public opinion, so that the majority will actually rule."

Historian Stephen Schlesinger, author of *Act of Creation, the Founding of the United Nations*, points to U.S. founding documents as inspiration for numerous fledgling democracies. "The opening sentence of the American Constitution, 'We the people,' was actually adopted in the UN (United Nations) Charter. Behind that were the values that had come from the American Revolution, the whole idea of human rights and free elections, free assembly, the notion of individualism, individual civil rights, and so on.

"We were a revolutionary nation, and new nations that overthrow bad governments often want to articulate those values around the world. There was an impulse to spread democracy and, at the same time, a reluctance to get entangled in alliances abroad, George Washington and Thomas Jefferson warning against getting involved in overseas activities that would betray our values."

Americans like to think of some of the ideas embodied in the First Amendment as exceptional. How exceptional were they at the time of their drafting?

"I think they were exceptional," says Schlesinger, "in the sense that when we became a union and set up the American Constitution, we were the only democracy on the face of the globe. That alone made us unique, and the fact that we've kept that democracy for over 200 years is quite an extraordinary record. Most countries have democracies; they lose them and they get it back, and it goes back and forth.

"You have to be bedazzled by the founders. They understood both the virtues and the depths of infamy of human nature, and they were able to balance one against the other and create a tripartite system, so we had a balance of powers within the government itself."

Professor Sheehan agrees. "I think Madison saw the right of petition as part of control over the government. Not veneration, but watching over the government, that they're your servants. And so, the free flow of opinion, free communication is always paramount in Madison's thought, particularly between the people and the representatives."

Madison and other drafters of the Constitution drew pieces of their ideology from Enlightenment thinkers such as Jean-Jacques Rousseau, author of The Social Contract. "Man is born free, but he is everywhere in chains." What was Madison's view of the obligation of a citizen in the social contract?

"The person I think best understands Madison, in terms of 20th century people, is Robert Frost. If you look at his commencement address at Sarah Lawrence College, 1956, he just nails it. And in another, at his alma mater, Dartmouth, he talks about the social compact. That beautiful poem by Frost that everyone knows, *Stopping by the Woods on a Snowy Evening*. How does it go?"

Whose woods these are, I think I know, his house is in the village though.

"You know, he stops and the only sound is the wind and the tinker of the horse's bell. And he says, whenever I say this poem, somebody always asks me, 'What does it mean?' What are these promises? 'But I have promises to keep, and miles to go before I sleep.' And he says, one is the promise that I myself made to others, the other is the promise that my ancestors made for me in the form of a social compact, a social contract. He's talking about how this fellow is in the woods, and he got this perfect freedom, but there's this village calling, the society, and he has promises to keep.

"Madison said we have a certain debt to our ancestors through this social compact. A kind of tacit consent, an obligation to uphold these promises, because we not only have rights and property, but we have a property in our rights.

"And then, the free communication of our opinions. See, this is critical to Madison, this idea of communication and the kind of deliberation that comes from it, to make what he calls 'the reason of the public.' We have a pledge that we make, each citizen to every other citizen in this social compact. These are all the obligations we owe each other as human beings and Frost captured that in that poem. He just gets Madison."

Is there anything unique about American freedoms? Other countries have freedoms.

"American exceptionalism. I'm going to quote Frost once more. In the poem he wrote for John F. Kennedy, for the inauguration, called Dedication, Frost explains we were the first to get rid of this divine right of kings. He said, our job in the world is to teach others how democracy is met, to serve as an example; we have a responsibility to ourselves and to others to get this right. And it's a continuing experiment. We don't know if it's going to work. We somehow got over a Civil War. And right now, we're facing another crisis that I don't know if we will get over."

You say in your writing that the nation is at a critical juncture with the future of popular self-government in peril. Practically speaking, what does the social compact require of the modern American citizen?

"That's the process part, the civic participation," says Sheehan. "And Madison was very much about activating people to get them to express their opinion, to have influence, and change the course of the administration. It's voting, but it's not just voting, it's in between voting: expressing your views, petitioning for grievances, running for office, engaging with your representative, etc. There's also a substantive part of responsibilities. And that has to do with the fundamental principles in the Declaration of Independence, the recognition of human equality. And that means respecting each other's rights, not just claiming your own. Madison calls this a pledge that we make in the social contract. And that's what's Frost is talking about in terms of promises to keep. The government is not part of it. There is no such thing as a government, the compact creates a constitution, which then creates a government."

In your writing and in Madison's, an informed citizenry is critical to the life of a republic. This idea of the settled opinion of the community. So, a two-part question: one, is that true? And second, when you look at the lack of knowledge that Americans have about their government, the Constitution, and public issues, do we have a problem here?

"The answer is yes and yes. Yeah, Madison said, liberty and learning lean on each other. And one without the other is a prologue to a farce or a comedy or both."

A popular government without popular information
or the means of acquiring it is but a prologue to a farce
or a tragedy, or perhaps both. Knowledge will forever
govern ignorance: And a people who mean to be their own
Governors, must arm themselves with the power which
knowledge gives.

"It's a farcical comedy that just falls apart," says Sheehan. "And that's why he works with Jefferson, who founded the University of Virginia; the importance of education in a free nation is critical. And if you don't know how to play the game, just, you know, be a citizen, it's going to fall apart. So, there's a problem today. It's not only that we don't have civics education and that people don't even know what century the Civil War was fought.

"Somebody did a study out in Chicago, and asked people about the Bill of Rights. And they said that the people have a right to own a car. Hardly anyone could name the five rights in the First Amendment. But here's my favorite one. A lot of people said that one of the rights in the First Amendment is the right to plead the Fifth."

A minority of Americans can name the three branches of
government, around 30 percent can't name one. I mean, a
lot of this is comical on one level, and – let's be fair – people
are busy, but here's the other alarming quote of yours, 'But
today, many Americans don't believe in the central ideas
that animated the revolutionary and founding generation.'
Doesn't that mean we're doomed?

"That's even more critical than naming the three branches of government, right? How can we be one people, if we don't have the most fundamental of ideas in common?"

Superman's physical feats are impressive, but can largely be replicated by technology. Some superheroes, such as Batman and Iron Man, possess no superhuman biology. Superman is heroic, we're told, because of his never-ending pursuit of truth, justice, and the American way.

Superhero tales often feature a process of transformation. Scientist Bruce Bannon turns into the Incredible Hulk. Timid Petey Parker becomes Spiderman. Doctor Strange morphs from wealthy New York surgeon to sorcerer defender of the Earth.

Many of the activists introduced in this book transform the world after their own moments of personal alchemy. Their stories are often tinged with a metaphysical tone, a revelation. From the ordinary, mundane life to the harnessing of internal and external forces. Alice Paul's Quaker 'concern,' LaDonna Brave Bull Allard's call to resist, Gregory Watson's disappointing class grade, Martin Luther King Jr.'s vision of the promised land, citizens thrust into leadership roles in Tunis, Kyiv, and Seoul.

The hero leaves a safe harbor, the 'Ordinary World,' ventures into unknown territory, the 'Special World,' surmounts impossible challenges, then arrives home, in triumph.

They have promises to keep.

Stopping by the Woods on a Snowy Evening
by Robert Frost

Whose woods these are I think I know.
His house is in the village though;
He will not see me stopping here
To watch his woods fill up with snow.

My little horse must think it queer
To stop without a farmhouse near
Between the woods and frozen lake
The darkest evening of the year.

He gives his harness bells a shake
To ask if there is some mistake.
The only other sound's the sweep
Of easy wind and downy flake.

The woods are lovely, dark and deep,
But I have promises to keep,
And miles to go before I sleep,
And miles to go before I sleep.

2. SUFFRAGE: ALICE PAUL AND ORDINARY EQUALITY

The term 'feminism' has become a political Rorschach test, though its essential idea remains constant. French utopian socialist Charles Fournier first used 'féminisme' in 1837 when describing advocacy of women's rights. Its earliest known usage in the United States is 1910, the year Alice Paul returned home from England after three years of study and activism with Emmeline Pankhurst and daughters Christabel and Sylvia of the suffragette Women's Social and Political Union (WSPU).

Alice Paul, who drove the successful campaign to get women of the United States 'suffrage' or the right to vote, ratified on August 18, 1920, stripped the idea down to two words: ordinary equality. Equal treatment under the law.

In a December 28, 1922 Washington Times (no relation to the current publication) feature, Paul was asked what effect "modern feminism would have on the lives of women in 2023." She answered, with certainty, that it would not take 100 years to elect a woman as president, but that women "would participate equally in the direction of life," in the control "of government, of family, and of industry."

Alice Paul was a champion and trailblazer of nonviolent resistance. Mohandas K. (Mahatma) Gandhi was himself deeply affected and impressed by the strategy and vision of the suffragettes while visiting London to lobby for Indian rights in South Africa. 'Suffrag-ette'

originated as a term used by British newspapers
to belittle the fierce drive of suffrage activists, but
militants took on the name as a badge of honor. Gandhi
had mixed feelings about what he saw, as evidenced in
his journal writings.

He first visited London in 1906, describing street
protests in a November issue of his *Indian Opinion*.
"Today the whole country is laughing at them, and they
have only a few people on their side," wrote the eventual
liberator of India from British rule. "But undaunted,
these women work on steadfast in their cause. They
are bound to succeed and gain the franchise, for the
simple reason that deeds are better than words." That
last phase possibly pinched from Emmeline Pankhurst's
battle cry, *"Deeds not words."*

Gandhi was moved by their acts of civil disobedience
and, as a barrister and son of a provincial chief minister,
was impressed that many activists came from prominent
families, risking much. He wondered if Indians in South
Africa would "consider gaol (jail) a palace and readily go
there" in their fight against racial discrimination.

In a 1909 return visit, he wrote in *Indian Opinion*, "Some
of these ladies have suffered in health (during prison
hunger strikes), but they do not give up the struggle.
Every day a number of them keep standing the whole
night near Parliament gate with the intention of
handing in a petition to Mr. (Prime Minister) Asquith.
This is no ordinary courage... We can learn quite a few
things and draw much inspiration from it."

He had one reservation. The Pankhursts considered
unjust laws unworthy of submission. They asked
nicely, then firmly, then began throwing bricks through
windows. Christabel Pankhurst famously spit in the
face of a police officer at a Liberal Party event, spending

a week in jail for the privilege. "There is no room for impatience in satyagraha," claimed Gandhi, referring to his philosophy of non-violent resistance, 'fighting with peace,' used to great effect in his native India.

The "franchise is nowhere in sight," he noted, "but they refuse to accept defeat and go on fighting... Only, we should avoid imitating them in their use of physical force. We may be sure that no good will come out of it."

The Pankhursts were not so sure. Emmeline, like Gandhi, spent stretches in jail, and, there, used hunger strikes as a public relations weapon. She saw what Paul would later come to realize, that political leaders were resistant to change and committed to protecting the interests of those with power and money and, in pre-suffrage Britain, women had little of either. Pankhurst disdained objections to her fierce tactics by male journalists and authorities. At her first public address after getting out of prison on October 17, 1912 in London's Royal Albert Hall, known for its concluding call to action, *"I incite this meeting to rebellion,"* she places a distinction between smashed windows on Bond and Regent Streets and the acts of political and military violence perpetuated by male leaders.

> It always seems to me when the anti-suffrage members of the Government criticize militancy in women that it is very like beasts of prey reproaching the gentler animals who turn in desperate resistance when at the point of death. Criticism from gentlemen who do not hesitate to order out armies to kill and slay their opponents, who do not hesitate to encourage party mobs to attack defenseless women in public meetings – criticism from them hardly rings true.

Pankhurst insists that her street demonstrators, by contrast, would never recklessly endanger human life, then adds,

> There is something that governments care far more for than human life, and that is the security of property, and so it is through property that we shall strike the enemy. From henceforward the women who agree with me will say, 'We disregard your laws, gentlemen, we set the liberty and the dignity and the welfare of women above all such considerations, and we shall continue this war, as we have done in the past; and what sacrifice of property, or what injury to property accrues will not be our fault.'

Emmeline Pankhurst became masterful at garnering attention over time, believing, "You have to make more noise than anybody else, you have to make yourself more obtrusive than anybody else, you have to fill all the papers more than anybody else. In fact, you have to be there all the time and see that they do not snow you under." And as cinema – and newsreels – grew into a mass medium, reaching 20 million each week, the British suffragettes strategically provided news cameras choice positions at rallies and marches.

ALICE PAUL IN ENGLAND

Alice Paul moves to England in 1907 to become the first woman to study commerce at the University of Birmingham, after earning her biology degree from Swarthmore College – the Quaker school co-founded by her grandfather – and a master's degree in sociology from the New York School of Philanthropy (now Columbia University). And it was there, at the age of twenty-two, during a speech by an also young (28) Christabel Pankhurst, that she has what Quakers call a 'concern,' an epiphany.

The American Quaker mystic Thomas Kelly describes a concern as "the Life of God breaking through into the world." Not as in 'being concerned about something,' rather, an obligatory call to action. Acting under 'concern' for a Quaker is acting in accordance with one's 'inward light.' Theology aside, it's a story common to historic fighters for social justice, the alchemical transformation from observer to principal actor, from indifference to the willingness to put one's body on the line.

"She pointed to that moment where she heard Christabel speak, and, suddenly, everything converged," says Lucienne (Lucy) Beard, Executive Director of the Alice Paul Institute (API), located at the 'Paulsdale' farmhouse in Mount Laurel, New Jersey. "Born here in this house in 1885, the air she breathed was different, born and raised in an atmosphere where she was equal to her brothers. Her mother served on the Education Committee that decided who taught the children and decided how the schools would be run."

How old was the Quaker movement at the time?

"The Quakers started in the 1600s in England," says Beard, preparing for an evening program on race and the suffrage movement, "and they were radical. They were standing up to the Church of England, saying, 'No, you are not an intermediary between me and God.' That was a radical notion coming from Catholicism, that you could have a direct relationship with God.

"They would strip themselves of clothing. We think of them as stodgy; they were not back then. They came to America to escape persecution, a lot of them directly from jail, and those were Alice Paul's forebears. She could trace her lineage back to the 1600s, to the earliest Quakers to come to America, and there was a direct line between her and William Penn and other Quaker leaders.

"She was born thinking men and women were equal, and, another basic Quaker tenet, that you had a duty to work for social justice. She was born into a more activist branch of Quakerism. There was a split in the Quakers in the 1800s (1827), and both sides of her family were followers of Elias Hicks, from Long Island (New York).

"While all Quakers believed that men and women were equal, the Hicksite Quakers got involved in suffrage. Susan B. Anthony was a Hicksite Quaker; as was her father. While all Quakers believed slavery was an abomination, the Hicksites did the Underground Railroad (the protection and transport of slaves). There was a real sense of activism there that ran through her bones."

THE ALICE PAUL INSTITUTE

Local women's rights activists founded The Alice Paul Institute seeking a tangible way to memorialize the suffrage champion. They place a marker on her (previously unmarked) grave and found the Alice Paul Centennial Foundation. After they stage the first Equality Awards in 1985, the owners of the old Paul house ask if they might be interested in doing something with it in Alice Paul's honor. One is the librarian at the local Quaker school that Alice attended and is a Paul fan.

"They saved the house and turned it into a living, breathing legacy," explains Beard, "to teach future generations and give them the skills that would help create equality. They became preservationists, and started a national movement to preserve women's historic sites. The idea being, we save what we value.

"There are close to 3,000 National Historic Landmarks, and less than 100 of them honor women and their achievements. Yet, it's women who've been at the forefront of the preservation movement."

A SHORT HISTORY OF THE FIGHT FOR WOMEN'S SUFFRAGE

Women's suffrage starts as one of a number of reform groups taking hold across the United States in the 1820s. The Seneca Falls Convention in 1848 is the first organized national event for women's rights. More than 300 attend (mostly women), including former African-American slave and activist Frederick Douglass. Participants endorse the principle that women are "autonomous individuals who deserved their own political identities," and "better opportunities for education and employment."[5]

The delegates approve a "Declaration of Sentiments," an edited version of the beginning of the second paragraph of the Declaration of Independence written by Elizabeth Cady Stanton: "We hold these truths to be self-evident: that all men and women are created equal..." Implicit is the belief that women should have the right to vote.[6]

The idea is widely mocked in the press. Stanton and Lucretia Mott persist and go on to stage more women's rights conferences, attracting the support of Susan B. Anthony and other activists.

Twenty-one years later and after the Civil War, Stanton and Anthony form the National Woman Suffrage Association (NWSA) in 1869 to drive a federal constitutional amendment for women's right to vote. On December 10, 1869, the Wyoming Territory becomes the first place in the world where women are explicitly given the right. Between 1869 and 1887, the territories of Utah, Washington, and Montana also accord women full voting rights.

The 15th Amendment is ratified in February 1870, delivering the right to vote to anyone regardless of race, color, or previous condition of servitude. This phrasing allows states to continue to deny suffrage to women, who were told it was not their time despite their participation in the abolition movement.

In January 1878, Senator Aaron Sargent from California introduces a resolution drafted by Anthony and Stanton for a women's suffrage amendment to the Constitution for the first time: "The right of citizens of the United States to vote shall not be denied or abridged by the United States or by any State on account of sex." His wife, Ellen, is a friend of Anthony. The Senate's first vote on the suffrage amendment fails 34-16 in 1887.

The NWSA and the American Woman Suffrage Association (AWSA) merge to form the National American Woman Suffrage Association (NAWSA) in February 1890, and elect Stanton as president. The group decides to focus its advocacy for women's suffrage at the state level. Wyoming is admitted to the Union on July 10 and its constitution establishes the state as the first to allow women to vote.

Anthony dies in March 1906. Her last words are, "Failure is impossible." Nearly six decades after Seneca Falls, women have won suffrage in only four states: Wyoming, Colorado, Utah, and Idaho.

SETBACKS AND CULTURE

There were many movement losses before suffrage was gained. Most men believed women shouldn't have the right to own property, much less vote. Women could be jailed for being sympathetic to the cause. As with most social movements, the message to suffragists was, hey, not now.

What was the thinking of men at the time who believed that women should not have the right to vote?

"The popular-culture idea, out there in the cartoons and all, was, she will get corrupted, that politics was a dirty place, or she already runs the show," says Beard. "She has a vote through him and she can tell him how to vote. And just the idea that she's smaller; her head is smaller and her brain is smaller; she's not as capable.

"But the money behind it, and that's really what counts, was the liquor companies, who knew that if women got the vote, Prohibition (the legal prevention of the manufacture, sale, and transportation of alcoholic beverages) would pass, because it was such a popular movement among women. That is, in fact, what happened: The Eighteenth Amendment was Prohibition and, once that passed, the liquor companies folded their tents and went home, and suffrage passed five months later."

So, the liquor industry opposed suffrage. Southern whites didn't want black women to get the vote. Party bosses feared women would resist their control. Manufacturers worried about improved labor laws. A friend, a Ph.D. in political philosophy, recently said, "I think women are too emotional and probably shouldn't have been given the right to vote." In what way have those attitudes evolved? More interestingly, in what ways have they not?

"I think the very fact that we can sit here and laugh about it means they have evolved," asserts Beard. "And I think a sign that they've evolved is that people hesitate before they say those kinds of things out loud. They kind of know they will be perceived as wrong. A hundred years ago, they wouldn't have been perceived as wrong. But then, I think there's still a lot of it there, and among women as well as men, really."

In the constellation of the great suffragists of the past, what's Alice's position compared to some of the others, some of whom might even be more well-known?

"Susan B. Anthony didn't have children," remarks Beard, but, in 1920, her group considered Alice Paul her heir. "They gave her Susan's desk, because they felt that she was following most closely in Susan's footsteps."

"They were having some successes – they won the vote in 10 states by 1912 when Alice was getting involved – but she did the math and figured out that, at that rate, it would be well into the 21st century before all women had the vote. She just said, no, I'm not working for grandchildren, I'm working for this generation to get the vote.

"She was considered a radical by many people. She was using what they considered radical, unseemly tactics for a woman in the public sphere, but I think at moments like that, it's radicals that push the mainstream and made that more acceptable. Some of their tactics, the more I read about them, I feel awed. It was really in your face, (protests like) burning (President Woodrow) Wilson's speeches out in front of the White House.

"They were starting to throw these women in jail just for walking out in the street. They came back from one session in jail to find that their offices had been broken into by the police and their stuff had been dragged out on the street. It was really something, the buttons they pushed on people."

A CONVERSATION WITH BIOGRAPHER MARY WALTON

Alice Paul biographer Mary Walton joins the conversation, arriving in time for a small group dinner and the Institute's evening event. Walton's highly regarded *A Woman's Crusade: Alice Paul and the Battle for the Ballot* is written after retiring from *The Philadelphia Inquirer*. What about Alice Paul's story motivated her to want to do the book? "I'm a journalist by training," she explains. "It's a story with a beginning, a middle and a happy ending, if you will." She was encouraged to write it by former *Inquirer* editor Gene Roberts. "It was the power of the story."

Lucy Beard is discussing Institute videos and images showing angry male hecklers during suffrage pickets and parades. "We do have to remember that it was thanks to the votes of men that women did honorably win the vote," points out Walton. "I always think of it as a power issue, whether it was whites versus blacks or men versus women; men didn't want to give up power. We had a very interesting talk in this (Alice Paul Institute speaker) series – tonight's the third one – where the speaker talks about how it was part of the culture, where women's 'place' was and men's 'place' was. Men were out in the world, and women were in the home. For women to step outside of those boundaries was terribly threatening to them and to their world, the world of power and authority."

The movement had been around for some decades. Was there a point at which Alice felt that it needed new strategies, including the public spectacle of the parade?

"Her new strategy," says Walton, "was to focus on a federal amendment, because the approach at that time by the National American Women's Suffrage Association was to go state by state. The Women's Christian Temperance Union was pro-suffrage, and so the liquor lobby was against it and poured money into fighting suffrage state-by-state.

"Also, when you think about it, it took a vote by the state legislature to get a measure on the ballot – all men voters – so it was very slow, and Alice just thought of a federal amendment. The whole country over was the way to go. That was certainly her strategy."

Beard explains, "When Alice Paul came along in 1912, she brought back the idea of the Constitutional Amendment campaign (after it had been abandoned with Anthony's death). NAWSA made her their 'Congressional Committee,' a position that had been empty for several years, and sent her to Washington with her own budget of $10 and told her she would have to raise her own support. So, the strategy had been mothballed with Anthony's death and was only brought out again when Alice Paul joined the group with the intention of pursuing it." Ten dollars would equate to roughly $260 in 2020, inadequate for the mantle she assumed.

NAWSA president Carrie Chapman Catt is frustrated by Paul's refusal to channel the monies she is raising through the organization's treasury. "Money is power," states Beard, "and no way was Alice going to give that up. She was not eager to go it alone. She liked having NAWSA's imprimatur. She wiggled around their demands, trying to look like a good girl. But she did not wiggle when it came to the question of the money that she had raised without any help from NAWSA."

One colleague later describes her as having "all the attributes of a corporation president, and by that I mean praise, because she ran the organization with great precision, single minded devotion, pared-down economy, and with an uncanny gift of getting the most out of what she had in limited resources, human and financial."[7]

"The easiest way to collect money," Paul tells CU (Congressional Union) organizer Margaret Whittemore, "is to aim at a definite sum and take a very short period in which to get it ... Once an expense is incurred, it is next to impossible to get anyone to donate for it."[8]

Beard adds, "Alice Paul was always chasing money and often went on long road trips to visit donors. She used direct asks in letter and in person. She saw the value in lots of donations from small donors and big donations from a few. She was very good at cultivating very wealthy supporters as well as attracting working class women to their ranks... They also ran a tea shop and café in their headquarters as a way to raise money."

TRIAL AND ERROR

"Alice Paul and her group were masters of branding," claims Beard, "something we hear a lot about these days. They picked colors for the movement (purple, white, and gold). They staged events. They were considered frighteningly radical in their day, though by today's standards they seem tame."

One month after Woodrow Wilson wins the November 1912 election, Paul is inspired by the 1910 suffrage parade in New York City and convinces the NAWSA board to endorse the first-ever event of its kind in the capital for the eve of Woodrow Wilson's inauguration.

The parade down Pennsylvania Avenue in Washington, D.C., is the first major "suffrage spectacle" organized by NAWSA. Paul rents a room on I Street in Washington, D.C., with a NAWSA fundraising list that is hopelessly out of date; most of the contacts have died or left the city. Yet, in January, she rallies over 100 women to attend the first meeting to organize the event.[9]

"The only other social protest parade in Washington was in 1894, Jacob Coxey," declares Walton. "That was really the only precursor to Alice's parade in 1913; (the city) was isolated by design, and so, it was not a natural venue for protests and parades.

"Paul was very influenced by her time in England and her service with Emmeline Pankhurst and they had a couple of very large parades. She was really worried that people wouldn't come. Her idea was that, if it wasn't going to be a big parade – New York had had 10,000 people marching and she couldn't get those numbers – she was going to have a beautiful parade, and it was beautiful."

Labor lawyer Inez Milholland, "a celebrity whose fame is one-part movie star Mary Pickford and one-part anarchist Emma Goldman,"[10] leads the parade on her horse, Gray Dawn, dressed in a white cape, gloves and a crown. "There were beautiful floats and she organized the women according to their professions, and they had caps and capes in different colors. She only had just over two months to organize it."

Conservative estimates for the Woman's Suffrage Procession on March 3, 1913, are 5,000-8,000 marchers and 100,000 spectators. The parade is attacked by a mob, and hundreds of women, unprotected by the police, are injured.

"There were a lot of things they tried and abandoned," adds Beard, but they considered (the parade) pretty successful."

"There was this four-year period between 1913 and 1917 when a lot happened, but not much to advance the amendment," discloses Walton. "There were other parades. She sent people, young volunteers out west to campaign in 1914 and 1916 against Democrats. She broke with the National, so that she was on her own, and she organized her own organization, the Congressional Union for Woman Suffrage, and started a newspaper."

Was the newspaper important for fundraising?

"She brought Alva Belmont into the (Congressional Union) movement," relates Walton, "and a lot of it was Alva's money. The purpose of *The Suffragist*, their weekly newspaper – they're all upstairs in bound volumes – was always about that federal amendment; she felt the newspapers weren't covering its progress. It was to keep her members and whoever read it informed about what was going on, what was planned, what would have been achieved, what they needed to do."

Distraught following her husband's death, Belmont seeks solace in working for the advancement of suffrage. Seeing little progress in America, she attends the Fifth Conference of the International Woman Suffrage Alliance in London in April 1909. She returns home inspired to finance the campaign to gain the vote for women and founds the Political Equality League. She opens an office on Fifth Avenue in Manhattan and convinces NAWSA president Anna Howard Shaw to move their headquarters there from its previous modest – and remote – home in Warren, Ohio.[11]

Belmont is active in numerous political causes. The New York shirtwaist strike of 1909, also called the 'Uprising of the 20,000,' had mostly women workers demanding a 20 percent pay raise, a 52-hour workweek, and overtime compensation. More than 20,000 workers from 500 factories walk out. Belmont (whose first husband was William Vanderbilt) arranges rallies and fund-raising events, and bails out arrested strikers.

"There was a sense of noblesse oblige among wealthier women," adds Beard. "This is what you did. You helped the less fortunate. Alice Paul did it socially. When Alice Paul was first coming out of college, this was exactly when they professionalized social work. It was becoming a profession. It was becoming an academic discipline with degrees and certifications. It was a new outlet for women who had so few professional outlets, if she didn't want to be a teacher, a librarian, a nurse, etc."

MANAGING A HOSTILE PRESS

The New York Times was antagonistic.

"Always," claims Walton, "even after it passed Congress, it was like, we'll just see if they can ratify this."

Was there an organized press outreach over time, a way that they mitigated those negative attitudes?

"The National (NAWSA) had a better relationship with the press," replies Walton. "But Alice was good for news. Hers was a regular stop when things were hot. In fact, she set up this tea room in the second big headquarters, to bring influential people in Washington; you would see her serving, she would never ask people to do something she wouldn't do.

"(President Woodrow) Wilson got control of the press – this was in the picketing era – and when he didn't like the coverage that the women were getting with regard to pickets and arrests, the press agreed not to print more than their names and where they were from; none of the details of their treatment."

Strikes had only become legal nationwide in 1914 as a result of the Clayton Antitrust Act, signed into law by Wilson, so peaceful picketing has newly won protections on top of the constitutional right to peacefully assemble. But once the U.S. enters WWI in April 1917, Wilson uses censorship in the form of the wartime Committee on Public Information (CPI) to keep suffragists out of the news.

Paul's prior refusal to funnel funds she raises through headquarters, her "unladylike" tactics, and previous antagonism toward Democrats convince NAWSA to conspire privately with the CPI – impeding the struggle for suffrage in an attempt to maintain control of the movement.

"I think that most people think that it's easier to compete than to collaborate," admits Beard. "Collaboration means you will have to compromise, highlight another's priorities over your own, give up something of importance. There is also the constant struggle to raise money. An organization has to stress to potential funders how it is unique, different from the others, more effective than the others, in order to attract financial support."

The schism between the two organizations ultimately lead to Paul's inadequate legacy when compared with her contribution to both American and women's history overall.

"The people who wrote the official history of the suffrage movement were commissioned by Carrie Chapman Catt, leader of NAWSA in 1920. Catt gave them strict orders to minimize any role of Paul or the NWP," Beard laments.

WINNING THE DC FIGHT

In June 1916, Paul, Belmont and Lucy Burns disband the CU and establish the National Woman's Party (NWP) with the additional strategy of influencing elections. Paul and Burns are longtime friends, learning militant protest tactics together while in England, such as picketing and hunger strikes. Arrested seven times and jailed three, Paul goes on a hunger strike in one imprisonment in England and is force-fed by nasal tube twice a day for four weeks.

The NWP fails to unseat Wilson as president, but their influence forces him to make a concession to bolster his chances at reelection and maintain majority party status in Congress. For the first time, both the Republican and Democratic Party platforms support women's suffrage. Jeannette Rankin (R–MT) becomes the first woman to win a Congressional seat, while Wilson ekes out reelection by fewer than 4,000 votes in California – the deciding factor in a very close Electoral College contest.

Burns leads a "suffrage school" to teach women how to maintain composure in the face of constant hecklers and physical threats. Beginning in July 1917, nearly 500 women are arrested, 168 serving jail time. Many are beaten and abused at the Occoquan Workhouse in Virginia, while enduring horrendous conditions, including worm-ridden food and filthy bedding and water. Paul goes on hunger strike and is violently force-fed, then is transferred in early November to the District Jail's psychiatric ward. The jailed suffragists are eventually released from prison with an appellate court ruling that the arrests were illegal. Their treatment in jail, once publicized, generates public sympathy and outrage.

Because Paul was careful to recruit women from across the country, she is able to get around Wilson's national censorship by appealing to local newspapers covering treatment of their residents.

The Nineteenth Amendment to the U.S. Constitution, which grants women suffrage, passes the U.S. House with a two-thirds vote, but loses by two votes in the Senate on January 11, 1918. On September 30, President Woodrow Wilson addresses the Senate – only the second president to appear before the body – and urges it to pass the amendment. "(World War I) could not have been fought... (without) the services of...women."[12]

The NWP begins 1919 by lighting and guarding a "Watchfire for Freedom." Party members burn copies of Wilson's speeches on democracy in urns outside the White House and other public buildings, often alongside banners accusing the president of hypocrisy. The bold acts of political theater bring more interest, arrests, and counter demonstrations. In March, the New York Times profiles Maud Younger who manages NWP lobbying efforts, ensuring her team uses and regularly updates an extensive file on every member of Congress.

The watchfires are maintained until the Nineteenth Amendment passes the Senate on June 4. Now a committed supporter of the amendment, Wilson agrees to use his power to politically twist arms in state houses across the country for the ratification process.

On August 18, 1920, Tennessee becomes the 36th state to ratify the 19th Amendment and make it law. With the presidential election looming, the state is a fierce battle ground for pro- and anti-suffrage advocates. The state senate votes in favor of ratification, but the state house of representatives is deadlocked, with a motion to table the amendment defeated in a 48-48 tie.

Harry Burn, a 24-year-old representative elected two years prior as the youngest member of the state legislature, arrives to vote wearing a red rose in his lapel, a symbol of opposition to women's suffrage. Burn, though, receives an urgent message from his mother. "Hurrah, and vote for suffrage!" Phoebe Ensminger Burn implores, known to friends as Miss Febb. "Don't keep them in doubt. I notice some of the speeches against. They were bitter. I have been watching to see how you stood, but have not noticed anything yet." She ends the note instructing her son to "be a good boy and help Mrs. (Carrie Chapman) Catt put the 'rat' in ratification." To the shock and outrage of his anti-suffrage colleagues, he casts the deciding vote in favor.

The 19th Amendment to the Constitution is certified into law by the United States Secretary of State on August 26, 1920, using the same language as Senator Sargent's original bill more than 40 years earlier:

> The right of citizens of the United States to vote shall not be denied or abridged by the United States or by any State on account of sex. Congress shall have power to enforce this article by appropriate legislation.

THE AMERICAN WOMAN AT THE TURN OF THE CENTURY

Describe what an American woman's life would be like in the early-1900s in the years preceding the right to vote, prior to the gradual adoption of certain legal protections and privileges.

"They were still homebound," expresses Walton. "You were beginning to see women becoming professionals, doctors and lawyers, but in very limited numbers. Though they could attend state universities and there were women's colleges. A lot of this was thanks to Stanton and Anthony who had worked hard on revising state laws. Widows, especially widows who had inherited husbands' business, had more status in the laws. They couldn't vote, but they could own property in their own names as they were widows."

Walton details the results of a 1902 NAWSA survey on legal barriers to equality in her biography.

> ... a wife could own property in three-quarters of the states and in two-thirds she could keep her paycheck. The doors to most public universities had swung open. The holdouts were largely in the South, a bastion of prejudice against women. In Georgia, husbands no longer had the right to whip their wives, but the state university was one of just four (all in the South) that didn't admit women. In Alabama, women could not practice law or medicine or serve as ministers. In Louisiana, with the exception of mothers and grandmothers, women, classed with idiots and lunatics, could not be appointed guardians. Despite advances in family law, in all but nine states and the District of Columbia a father still had sole custody and control of minor children.[13]

"But women, by and large, did not go out into the (world)," adds Walton. "There were large numbers of immigrant women, who worked in factories, but they were still very constrained by poverty, and so they didn't they didn't have power and they weren't active in the public sphere. Upper-class women like Alva Belmont belonged to clubs and did good works."

Was there a phenomenon during World War I similar to the Rosie the Riveter campaign in WWII where, suddenly, women were in new visible work roles with men at war? And did that have an impact on the suffrage vote?

"World War I, absolutely, that had an impact," believes

Walton. "Women were running New York City. They were running trains, doing physical labor, and they worked in the munition factories. There was the Women's Land Army, a private effort. It was very big in New Jersey, where women went out in the place of men in the fields; they loved it, too. You can see pictures, all just happy.

"I give a talk on Alice Paul from time to time and I would have those photos, and I always say at the end, when Wilson reversed (his willingness to support suffrage), there were three factors.

"One is the trend in Western democracies for giving women the vote. The Prime Minister of Canada tells him it's coming there and in England. Wilson tells a Congressional delegation from Congress other great democracies are giving women the vote, which is the language of the pickets."

Wilson was saying we wanted to "make the world safe for democracy."

"The second was the accusations of hypocrisy against Wilson," relates Walton.

Pickets antagonize Wilson with a banner using a paraphrase from his 1913 book, *A New Freedom: A Call for the Emancipation of the Generous Energies of a People*: "Liberty is a fundamental demand of the human spirit; and, we are interested in the United States, politically speaking, in nothing but liberty."[14]

The women later hold up a sign using text from an April 1917 speech: "We shall fight for the thing which we have always held nearest our hearts – for democracy, for the right of those who submit to authority to have a voice in their own governments."

The strategy is likely inspired by British suffragette Marion Wallace Dunlop. In 1909, she posts a passage from England's 1689 Bill of Rights in the House of Commons: "It is the right of the Subject to petition the King, and all commitments and Prosecutions for such petitioning are illegal." After her arrest, she is the first to practice the hunger strikes that so impress Gandhi and influence Paul.

"The third was the work that women did in the war," Walton goes on. "How were they going to turn them down? They weren't just making bandages. Women were running major systems in the country. I don't know really why World War II got all the attention and they were doing this in World War I."

What work is there still to be done, as we celebrate the 100th anniversary of the 19th Amendment in 2020?

"Let's pass the ERA just for openers," suggests Walton, "and then just let's keep doing what we're doing, just constantly pushing for more women in the corporate world, more women in government. Women already outvote (men) now by 10 percent."

After passage of the 19th Amendment, Alice Paul drafts the original Equal Rights Amendment in 1923 then revises it in 1943. The National Organization for Women (NOW) later takes up the fight and helps pass the Amendment in the U.S. House and Senate in 1972. Virginia becomes the required 38th state to ratify it in 2020, but it hasn't been certified or made law by Congress due to legal challenges; opponents question the validity of the ratification due to the passage of time and the subsequent rescindment by some states.

Why do you think that certain women today still resist the idea of the Equal Rights Amendment, the idea of feminism, the idea of legislation for protecting women's access to employment or equal pay?

"Many of them think we have equal rights," opines Walton. "Many believe that the Equal Rights Amendment was passed. I talked to a big group at Swarthmore. One woman at the end raised her hand and said, 'What is the ERA?'"

Most Americans can't name the three branches of government.

"No, but Swarthmore? But, anyway, yes, it beats me. They don't understand that such rights as we have in legislation can be reversed in court decisions. Not until you get it into the Constitution do you have solid footing."

THIS IS A LONG ROAD

Lucy Beard has been affiliated with the Institute in one form or another since 1995. She serves on its first professional staff, also as a board member and volunteer. She helps raised money to restore the house, and is on the committee that hires the first executive director. Beard establishes and directs Institute programs, then, after a five-year hiatus, she is hired as executive director in 2012.

At the Institute's evening program, Beard mingles with founders and Institute leaders. *Joining the Parade: Women of Color Challenge the Mainstream Suffrage Movement* is presented by Dr. Cathleen Cahill, a professor of history at Penn State University and social historian who explores the everyday experiences of 'ordinary' women, exploring how identities such as race, nationality, class, and age have shaped them. During her talk, she discusses the ways in which race and racism impacted women as they worked and organized for the right to vote.

Barbara Haney Irvine, the Institute's founding president, sits in the front row. The Alice Paul Archives are contained in a women's history library at the Institute in her name. Irvine chaired the first national conference on women's historic sites in 1994 at Bryn Mawr College.

"She's really the one who saved that house and created this whole idea," reveals Beard, "instead of turning it into storage space. 'What's the best use of this property?' she asked. Everyone said, 'Listen, she didn't leave stuff. Don't make it a house museum. That's not what she would want. Make this a place to continue her work.' She will always deflect and say that it was a group effort, but – and I say this with great respect for all of the women – the group as a whole did not have Barbara's vision and energy to see it through.

"We started the girls' leadership programs in the '90s. There was all this research about what happens to girls in adolescence, self-esteem problems, academic-performance problems. We decided to focus on middle school.

"We worked in Camden, New Jersey schools and did workshops. Everything we learned with focus groups led to a new curriculum, a retooling. Once the house was restored, the mission has always been to get people there, doing workshops there, the idea being the power of place.

"Now, there are 75 girls in the Girls Leadership Council. They hear about it and they want to join. They identify as feminists. Out of those 75, I'd say, 15 to 20 are rock stars in their schools. They're leaders. The other 50 are interested, these things matter to them, and there's no place in school to go talk about them. We moved up to senior high, though we still do in-school programs for middle school girls."

What are their priorities in terms of political or social issues?

"These girls can speak quite well about the Equal Rights Amendment," claims Beard, "and legal equality being a key to getting full equality. They care about pay equity. Most of them come from two-income homes, and they see their moms working double and not getting paid at those jobs.

"A study just came out. In the average two-income home, Dad now devotes about 12 minutes a day to housework – they're getting somewhere – and Mom, two and a half hours a day. It's a real hot-button topic for them. They learn a lot about different international issues like genital mutilation, child marriage."

Why do people oppose the ERA? What is the pushback?

"They did a survey four or five years ago. Something like 98 percent answered yes to the question, 'Do you think that the Constitution should guarantee gender quality?' You can't get that percentage for 'Do you think we need the ERA?' It's really something; 87 or 89 percent think it's already in there. They don't know the ERA didn't pass. So, there's this extra hurdle of educating people about the actual ERA. There is the fear of the breakdown of the family, the 'natural' order; we're in a mess right now and it's because homes are unstable, because women aren't in them.

"We don't have civics. What people don't understand is that something like Title IX (1972) – which has given so much equal access to education, to sports – can be unfunded, can be overturned in one session of Congress.

Beard sits on the ERA coalition national steering committee that sought advice from the marketing firm that branded the same-sex marriage movement. "I can hear the guy's voice on the phone now. 'Listen, we messed around for several years with the argument that it's about equality. Everyone should have equal access to marriage. Finally, we landed on the right line – it's about love.' Who can argue that?' He said, 'You need to find that. You need to find that line. What is it?'

"We agreed that it's about dads, the husbands and the brothers, and do they really want their daughter, their wife or their sister to not get paid the same amount of money? Do they really want her to be subject to violence against women? Which is unfunded continually now. We have to fight for those things to be enforced."

During Cathleen Cahill's presentation, there was an emotional moment with an African-American woman in the front row. Dr. Cahill was leading a conversation about racism in the suffrage movement, decisions to decouple white women's voting rights from those of black and Native American women, the initial refusal to let (NAACP co-founder and suffragist) Ida B. Wells march in the 1913 parade with her Chicago delegation. Attendee Karen Abdul Malik said, to paraphrase, "No judgment. They were trying achieve something in that moment."

"Yes. I don't want to deny that they were racist. But does that shut down looking at what they did? A woman on a panel I was on last week was very forceful about it, 'I want everyone to understand that a constitutional amendment gave every woman the right to vote. It was states that took it away, not that constitutional amendment. So, we're blaming the people who got that done for how it was interpreted.'

"Now, it is true that after all women got the vote, Alice Paul did refuse to turn her energies to enforcing it, to making sure that women everywhere had equal access.

She moved on to something else, which she identified as being more important. If that was out of racism, I can't touch. She would say, no, she did not perceive herself as a racist."

When you are around these girls, which must be inspiring, how do you try to pass on the legacy that they are bringing forward?

"I try to cast things in terms of keeping your eyes open," concludes Beard, "and traveling as much as you can, that you're going to learn more from travel than anything else you do; that you have to be prepared for a long life and you're going to have many careers, so don't freak out at age 15 about not knowing what you're going to do because, at age 50, you'll be doing something different.

"I try to get across to them that this is a long road, and you're going to be in charge of it, and you have to take charge of it. Hold the party in power responsible. (Have a) willingness to risk all for the cause, laser focus on the central concept, and allow no distractions or dilution of that concept."

3. THE BONUS ARMY: NOW GET IN THERE AND FIGHT

The 1918 Spanish flu pandemic, one of the deadliest public health crises in human history, isn't Spanish at all. Overcrowded World War I medical camps and filthy hygienic conditions in the trenches accelerate the spread of the disease. It is attributed to neutral Spain by the press as military censors in France, the United States, Germany, and the United Kingdom prevent mention of the disease among combatants, seeking to minimize its effects on morale. The flu infects over 500 million people and is responsible for between 50 and 100 million deaths, three to five percent of the world population. In the United States, 12 percent of the population die.

World War I is a nightmare stain on Western civilization. On June 28, 1914, Bosnian Serb nationalist Gavrilo Princip assassinates the Austro-Hungarian heir Archduke Franz Ferdinand in Sarajevo. Alliances between European powers, driven by imperial egos and colonial ambitions, transform the incident from a dispute among Balkan powers to one involving the Triple Entente, or Allied, powers of France, Russia, and Britain on one side, and Central Powers Germany, Austria-Hungary, and the Ottoman Empire on the other. The war spreads to include Japan, Italy, Bulgaria, Romania, and many others, including colonial and Commonwealth nations such as Australia and India. The war brings over nine million dead combatants, seven million dead civilians, many times more impaired physically or mentally for life. It displaces millions of families and turns large swaths of cities and countryside into moonscapes from relentless artillery shelling.

President Woodrow Wilson pledges to keep the United States out of the war, "impartial in thought as well as in action." But three principal factors move him to change his mind.

The first is German U-boats attacks on U.S. ships, frequently carrying munitions to allied forces. The second is a January 1917 telegram from German Foreign Minister Arturo Zimmerman to the German Minister to Mexico proposing an alliance against the United States, which outrages Wilson and the American public.

The third reason is likely the critical driver. Massive debts to American banks and corporations incurred by the Allies might go unpaid if the Central Powers prevail. So, just as millions of French and German boys are sent to unspeakable horrors – living in filth and vermin, shell-shocked from hundreds of thousands of artillery assaults, gassed with lethal phosgene, mustard, and chlorine chemical weapons – with no personal stake in the disputes of colonial monarchs and empires, American boys are asked to accept a similar fate.

Wilson declares, "It is in no sense a conscription of the unwilling, it is rather selection from a nation which has volunteered its mass."

However, when asked to volunteer, only 70,000 American men answer the call, far short of the one million required. So, at Wilson's behest, Congress passes the Selective Service Act of 1917, which requires all men between the ages of 21 and 30 to register for military duty. Those who fight make a $1.25 a day, roughly one-tenth the daily wage of those employed back home.

More than 116,000 American soldiers die during WWI, of which 63,000 lose their lives to the influenza pandemic. Over 200,000 are wounded, many more suffer lifelong health effects from being gassed, shelled and otherwise traumatized.

At the end of *They Shall Not Grow Old*, Peter Jackson's impressive colorized documentary of life in the WWI trenches, returning veterans describe their welcome home. No one, outside their wartime mates, could understand their experience, so they largely keep their stories to themselves.

In the early 1920s, momentum builds nationally for the federal government to compensate World War I veterans for the broad differential in pay between military and civilian jobs. Congress approves a "bonus" bill in 1922, but it's vetoed by President Warren Harding. In 1924, Congress again approves "Adjusted Compensation" and overrides President Calvin Coolidge to enact it. Compensation is set at $1.25 for each day served overseas and $1 for each day served in the States. Veterans owed $50 or less are paid immediately. All others are given an adjusted compensation certificate with four percent interest and an additional 25 percent upon payment. The certificate isn't redeemable until 1945.[15]

The pre-eminent book on the subject is *The Bonus Army: An American Epic*, co-authored by Paul Dickson and Thomas B. Allen. Dickson, based in the Washington, D.C. area, is an inveterate storyteller and esteemed historian, weaving tales about area characters and homes en route to lunch at Garrett Park, Maryland's Black Market Bistro. The Victorian-style building abuts the railroad tracks that thousands of Bonus Army veterans ride to their date with destiny at the nation's capital. The moniker is shorthand for the Bonus Expedition Force, a wordplay on the American Expedition Force sent to liberate France.

LOBBYISTS, NOT PROTESTERS

"I think the major lesson about the Bonus Army," instructs Dickson as he leans into his elegantly presented hamburger, "is found in two key actors. Not the presidents, who uniformly failed the veterans, Roosevelt and Wilson as badly as Herbert Hoover.

"One is Washington D.C. police chief Pelham D. Glassford, another is Walter Waters, a self-taught factory worker who becomes fascinated by Gandhi and nonviolent resistance. After World War I, Waters sees big companies like US Steel and DuPont getting war reparations."

A compromise for an immediate, albeit reduced, payout is suggested in 1931 by General Electric official Owen Young. Members of Congress such as John J. Cochran (D-MO) support the idea, pointing to the adjusted claims of war contractors.

With the onset of the Depression, Waters' small business efforts fail and he survives as a "fruit tramp," a migrant fruit-picker, before landing in Portland. The worst year of the Depression is 1932. Three thousand banks fail. Unemployed, Waters takes easily to public speaking, promoting the idea of a veterans' march to present the demand to Congress.

"He starts in Portland, Oregon (in March of 1932)," says Dickson, "goes down to the Veterans of Foreign Wars post, and starts talking about a bill that keeps being tabled in Congress to pay a bonus, promised to the veterans."

"In the war," Dickson points out, "a guy got a dollar a day, overseas service a buck and a quarter. But out of that dollar, he had to buy his own uniform. He was also expected to buy bonds, he was expected to finance the war. These guys just made nothing. A similar individual

in a shipyard or defense plant was probably making 10
to 15 dollars a day and could go home and sleep in their
own bed."

*As opposed to a trench, getting gassed, shelled, or
slaughtered. How did the protest get started?*

"Representative Wright Patman (D-TX), a veteran,
starts this movement to pay the bonus immediately.
Patman was severely impacted by the dollar a day thing,
because he was trying to support his parents. At the end
of the day, he couldn't afford a movie, 10 cents. He kept
bringing it up for immediate payment and kept getting
tabled. Wright Patman, a great 20th century populist."

Patman points to Treasury Secretary Andrew Mellon's
negotiation of the suspension of European war debts.
Justified as necessary to speed recovery from the worldwide
depression, it further antagonizes bonus payment
supporters. Patman asks why this substantial financial
concession is economically feasible, while the bonus is not.

"And so, Waters," continues Dickson, "an unemployed
cannery worker – fought in the Mexican War, fought in
World War I – he's reading the papers about Patman,
he decides he's going to get a bunch of people together
(Waters' original 'brigade' from Portland starts with
300 veterans). He's going to get on a train, he's going to
Washington, and, just like DuPont or US Steel, they're
going to demand their lot."

*It's estimated more than two million Americans live on the
road at the time. Paint a picture, what does that mean, to get
on a train?*

"Well, they were hobos," says Dickson. "They jumped.
But they were allowed to do it because almost all of the
railroad detectives, as well as the police in D.C., were

World War I vets. These weren't bums. This was not a march on Washington in the sense that they were going to go in with placards and sticks. Instead, they were going to go in and lobby."

American Legion posts provide the vets coffee and snacks along the way, and railroad employees allow them to ride in empty boxcars. Waters leads his men across the continent, gaining national press coverage.

"So, when they get here," Dickson explains, "Waters and his other commanders run this thing extraordinarily well. And they tell these guys every morning to wash their shirt and put on a tie. Now, maybe, they have one shirt, a white shirt, and it's got holes in it, and they wash it in the river. Then they go off to Congress, sit in the office of their representative, and talk about the bonus. They claim they're not protesting, there's no sit-ins, there's no disruption of the public. *They're lobbyists*, and they're there to petition for a redress of grievances."

How did their experience during the war and the Depression form their politics and motivation?

"One of the problems is the right over the years tried to cast them as a sort of red-led protest, which it wasn't at all, just the opposite. In fact, when we were working on the book, and we found guys still alive, they told us they had to learn to not talk about it because they had been so vilified by the (Wisconsin Senator Joseph) McCarthy-ites when their protest was painted as a communist tactic.

"All over the world, veterans of World War I were rising up and overthrowing their governments. So, the fear by (four-star General and Army Chief of Staff Douglas) MacArthur and many other people was that these guys were going to get violent.

"MacArthur had spies in their camps," says Dickson, intelligence he and his co-author obtain via the Freedom of Information Act. "They would go to a meeting and see there were blacks and Jews; hence, they're communists."

The veterans are only after the immediate payout of their bonus, not political change. This attitude is reinforced at stop after stop across the country when Waters meets with police chiefs, who sympathize with their cause and refuse to imprison anyone for riding trains without paying a fare.

"Radio is just coming into its own and '32 is the worst year of the depression. Everything's really a mess. And the radio stations are looking for heroes. All of a sudden, you have these guys, Medal of Honor winners, officers. You cannot get in the camp unless you show proof that you were a veteran. As they cross the country, they pick up people, they start coming from New England, South Carolina, all over the country."

It's cinematic imagery – 17,000 guys, many with families, jumping freight trains and massing in the capital.

"Unbelievable," explains Dickson. "There's phenomenal footage." There is a public television (PBS) documentary on the subject, featuring Dickson and Allen. Several movie options have been taken on the book.

"Basically, they jump on a train, a few hundred bucks between them. In Washington, the police chief is waiting for them, Pelham D. Glassford, a brilliant man, a Brigadier General during World War I. He rides around in a blue Harley. The first time Glassford's name appears in *The Washington Post*, it's for an art exhibit he has at the Corcoran Gallery. He teaches (future president Dwight D.) Eisenhower to paint at West Point.

"Glassford forever changes the way protesters are received in Washington – he leads them into the city. He's built a whole camp, marked out with assigned street numbers, the streets named for the states. The veterans show up and Glassford gets chefs from the top hotels and creates this huge feast on the Mall. It's a symbolic gesture, they're fed this wonderful meal. He's this charismatic guy, who basically partners with Waters. By the end of the summer, there's at least 65,000 people coming in and out of that camp."

Just to clarify the politics, Congress passed this as a benefit payable in 1945, which was called the 'tombstone benefit' because most would be dead by then.

"That was the whole point," insists Dickson, "the fact that they had to die to get the benefit. A lot of these guys were gassed, they know they are dying. So, they come to Washington and establish this village. They have boxing matches. The music is unbelievable. There is a huge number of blacks involved, a huge racial component, probably one of the reasons they were driven out."

One of Waters' biggest challenges is keeping the veterans fed. Glassford petitions Congress for food in order to keep the peace. They decline, so he recruits boxing promoter Jimmy Lake to organize matches in Griffith Stadium; a record crowd of 15,000 raises $3,000, allowing a food budget of 7 cents per veteran.

"(Future civil rights leader) Roy Wilkins comes down from New York," says Dickson, "is working for the NAACP (National Association for the Advancement of Colored People) magazine. He can't believe his eyes. He sees tents with two sets of feet sticking out, one black, one white. A lot of blues singers wrote songs about the bonus. A friend of mine ran a jazz radio show and I asked, 'Did you ever find any songs about the bonus?'

"Sure."

"I said, 'What do you think the bonus was?'"

"He said, 'Of course, it's sex.' I learned there were about 18 bonus songs, and if you listen to them without knowing what the bonus was about, it's sort of, 'Give it to me, bonus, give it to me now.'"

And the pitch by the drafters of the bill was, these guys are suffering. We paid them poorly. We owe this to them. We're going to pay it to them eventually, they need it now. It's the right thing to do. Let's take care of our veterans.

"That was the pitch by the veterans," corrects Dickson. "Give them their bonus now, as promised, they could turn in their bonds with interest. But Congress wasn't that smart. These guys have become national heroes, because everybody else is suffering. And here these guys come, heads erect, smiling. The crime rate in the city goes down. Veterans would get thrown out of the camp if they were caught panhandling. The big agitators are kept out. The communist hierarchy comes down from New York, they can't even get in the camps. Every newspaper in America has written about them. H.L. Mencken, Sinclair Lewis, up and down the line."

The House of Representatives passes the Patman bill for veterans' relief on June 15, 1932, and there's a jubilant celebration in the House Gallery. "But it is defeated (by a wide margin) in the Senate," says Dickson. "The senators have to escape in the tunnels under the Capitol. They (the veterans) are all assembled on the Capitol lawn, and there's talk of becoming violent.

"Then, a newspaper woman gets up, realizing these guys are really furious, they're really getting restless, and she says, let's sing *America*. So, they sing *America*. And she says, 'Time to go back to the camp.'"

Many disillusioned veterans leave for home. But several thousand refuse.

"They don't want to leave," conveys Dickson. "Next day, Waters gets up and tells them Congress offered them money to get back home. But Congress didn't understand, they didn't have a home to go to. A lot of them came with families. And the train fare would come out of their bonus.

"Some people were starting to get sick. Tensions were rising, and Hoover did not want anything to do with them. And, finally, it becomes violent. There are a couple buildings downtown, the police come to evict them, one of the guys throws a brick, and a cop shoots two of them."

SMEDLEY BUTLER AND THE SOLDIER CLASS

Retired Major General Smedley Butler is at the time the most decorated Marine in United States history, one of only 19 men to twice receive the Medal of Honor. Over three decades, he participates and often leads military actions in the Philippines, China, Central America, and the Caribbean, and serves in World War I.

Representing the Veterans of Foreign Wars (VFW), he speaks to the Bonus Army vets, imploring them to persist with the same righteous fervor they had carried overseas. In a speech that reflects his views on war and the disposability of soldiers, subsequently made famous in a book on the subject, Butler frames the issue in terms familiar to his audience.

> When you got ready to go to war to lick the Hun, what did you do? You first learned how to fight.

We are divided, in America, into two classes: The Tories on one side, a class of citizens who were raised to believe that the whole of this country was created for their sole benefit, and on the other side, the other 99 per cent of us, the soldier class, the class from which all of you soldiers came. That class hasn't any privileges except to die when the Tories tell them. Every war that we have ever had was gotten up by that class. They do all the beating of the drums. Away the rest of us go. When we leave, you know what happens. We march down the street with all the Sears-Roebuck soldiers standing on the sidewalk, all the dollar-a-year men with spurs, all the patriots who call themselves patriots, square-legged women in uniforms making Liberty Loan speeches. You go down the street and they ring all the church bells. They promise you the sun, the moon, the stars and the earth, anything to save them. Off you go. Then the looting commences while you are doing the fighting. This last war made over 6,000 millionaires. Today those fellows won't help pay the bill.

It is only this damned Tory class that doesn't want... the veteran class cared for. Don't you realize that when this country started out, it wasn't worth more than 2.5 cents, and that every damned bit of land we have we took at the point of a gun? The soldiers took it.

The only trouble with you veterans is that you still believe in Santa Claus. It's time you woke up - it's time you realized there's another war on. It's your war this time. Now get in there and fight.

THE ARMY ATTACKS ITS VETERANS

On July 28, 1932, 11 days after the Senate rejects the Patman bill, President Herbert Hoover directs his Secretary of War to drive the protesters from the encampments. The main "Hooverville" is set up by Glassford just two miles from Congress, within easy walking distance.

General MacArthur commands the operation. He calls the protesting vets traitors, "bent on overthrowing the government," declaring, "Pacifism and its bedfellow communism are all around us."[16]

Major George S. Patton's Third Cavalry spearheads the eviction. Patton instructs his troops on how to deal with the vets. "If you must fire, do a good job. A few casualties become martyrs, a large number an object lesson… When a mob starts to move keep it on the run… Use a bayonet to encourage its retreat. If they are running, a few good wounds in the buttocks will encourage them. If they resist, they must be killed."[17]

MacArthur's special assistant is Major Dwight D. Eisenhower. "Believing it wrong for the Army's highest-ranking officer to lead an action against fellow American war veterans, he advised MacArthur against taking any public role: 'I told that dumb son-of-a-bitch not to go down there,' he said later. 'I told him it was no place for the chief of staff.' Despite his misgivings, Eisenhower later wrote the Army's official incident report that endorsed MacArthur's conduct."[18]

When Waters asks if campers would be given the opportunity to form in columns, salvage their belongings, and retreat in an orderly fashion, MacArthur replies, "Yes, my friend, of course."[19]

"MacArthur feels he's got to go in and drive them out," explains Dickson. "His Chief of Staff Eisenhower says, 'No, no, don't do it.' He tells Eisenhower to go home and put his uniform on. And then he orders the troops to burn them out. And the news people go ahead and said, 'No, you got to let us get the people out first. Because he was going to burn it to the ground.' Hoover said don't cross the bridge. Eisenhower seconded that and said, 'No, you can't cross the (Anacostia, now Eleventh Street) bridge.'

"The veterans are attacked in the streets; soldiers open fire, tanks are coming up. The imagery of the tank smoke coming up Constitution Avenue, led by Patton, is so severe, when that starts showing on the newsreels, they're booing MacArthur; they're pulling for the guys who were in the war."

Newsreels are a primary source of information in the 1930s, well before the advent of television, and the only source of video news for most Americans. They're shown prior to films in movie theaters, an integral part of the movie-going experience. Pathe News clips show soldiers, some on horseback, moving in formation, some dragging or carrying soldiers out of buildings.

The soldiers, under MacArthur's orders and in violation of the president's warning, cross the bridge. Shacks are set ablaze. One scene frames the United States Capitol in trees and foliage and billows of smoke. Soldiers brandish weapons, some charging at protesters, many wearing gas masks. One Pathe headline declares, "Bonus Army 'Routed: Troops, tanks and tear gas used to evict 8,000 veterans in Washington.'"

Hospitals are overwhelmed with casualties; an estimated 1,000 veterans suffer gas-related injuries.

"Hoover is terrible to the veterans. Roosevelt comes in and is also terrible. He cuts money for veterans. There are suicides at veterans' hospitals. Roosevelt feels they have already been paid."

HEMINGWAY AND THE HURRICANE

"The veterans come back again (in March 1933) and Roosevelt sends a lot of them to work camps in Florida. That's what turns things.

"The bill passes both houses of Congress for the first time, but Roosevelt vetoes it. It passes again in '35. Roosevelt says, 'I'm going to veto it again.' But he wants Congress to overrule him. He's begging them to get them out."

Why doesn't he just approve it?

"He was virulently opposed to it. Nobody could ever figure out why he had this colossal antagonism for these guys. The guys in Florida are killed in the hurricane. And Hemingway writes an article called, Who Murdered the Vets. And the answer is FDR."

Acclaimed novelist Ernest Hemingway is living in Key West and, witnessing the carnage, asks in the September 17, 1935 issue of New Masses, "Who sent nearly a thousand veterans, many of them husky, hard-working or simply out of luck, to live in frame shacks on the Florida Keys in hurricane months?"

He describes bodies floating in the ferry slip, "face down and face up in the mangroves. They didn't all let go at once but only when they could hold on no longer."

Hemingway describes how he'd gotten to know many of them "at Josie Grunt's place," some punch drunk, some smart. "… some had been on the bum since the Argonne almost and some had lost their jobs the year before last Christmas; some had wives and some couldn't remember; some were good guys and others put their pay checks in the Postal Savings and then came over to cadge in on the drinks when better men were drunk; some liked to fight and others liked to walk around the town; and they were all what you get after a war. But who sent them there to die?"

THE LEGACY

Congress passes the Adjusted Compensation Payment Act in 1936, allowing for the immediate payment of the $2 billion in bonuses. They override President Roosevelt's veto of the measure. The bonus distribution becomes a significant economic stimulus during the Great Depression, overcoming significant race-based resistance.

"The white Southerners were as angry as the black Southerners," says Dickson. "One of the reasons it wasn't passed was racial. Six hundred thousand blacks fought in World War I. They realized they were both being exploited by the same system.

"There was a fear of giving money to all these black people. And part of the reason the expulsion was so violent was the fact that they were integrated. MacArthur hated that, didn't believe that blacks should be in the Army.

"And what happens when they finally get paid in 1935 is, it fuels Roosevelt's economy. People are bumped from nowhere to the middle class. We talked to a former

Marine, whose parents bought a house in Brooklyn.
For the first time, the black newspapers ran ads from
Lincoln and Cadillac. A lot of them could buy houses for
the first time because they're given this chunk of money,
with interest. And in the depths of the Depression,
black newspapers come alive, because all of a sudden
people are advertising, right?

"It was a bond, came to four or five hundred dollars, in
a lot of cases. You buy a brand-new car for that. In the
rural South, if you had $500 in your pocket, you could
afford a small house.

"The biggest effect was on World War II," Dickson
apprises, "on the GI Bill, which passed on the day of the
D-Day invasion. After World War I, they turned all these
guys out a month or two after the war. No provision for
housing, nothing to help them catch up economically.

"And the guys in the American Legion, who wrote the
GI Bill, were watching. Everybody is watching. There
are so many more people fighting (in WWII) who will be
so much angrier because they've been fighting a longer
war, a two-ocean war. They will literally be a threat to
overthrow the country. They basically decide to correct
everything that they did wrong with the bonus guys.
Promise them money, promise them an education."

Dickson argues that the GI Bill, formally the
Servicemen's Readjustment Act of 1944, benefits a huge
generation of Americans, extending to every level of
society. It provides low-cost mortgages, low-interest
loans for new businesses, a year of unemployment
compensation, and tuition and living expenses for high
school, vocational school, or college. Within a decade of
the end of WWII, nearly eight million veterans use its
education benefits. Historians and economists generally
agree it was a major contributor to the expansion of the

American middle class and to the nation's long-term economic growth.

Why did this story appeal to you?

"Because it is a great American story that has never been told," says Dickson. "Beyond that, it was the largest protest of the Depression. It was the biggest nonviolent expression in American history.

"I think countries all over the world treated veterans like scum. They forgot about them. They might have had a job at a sawmill, but there was no protection. Only the wounded ones got some benefits. There's nobody who said, hey, we will help you find a job. I think what motivated them most is, they were just sort of left out there in the cold.

"There was one great hero, Joe Angelo, who saved Patton's life in the war. He becomes the sort of typical patriot who quits his job in a shipyard, where he is getting 12 bucks a day, and joins the Army where he gets paid nothing. When he approaches Patton in the field where they burn down the camp, Patton tells a soldier, 'Get this man away from me.' A reporter from the Baltimore Sun watches this and writes that Angelo is betrayed, puts in in biblical terms."

So why did they succeed?

"They ran the camps with rigid rules," explains Dickson, "you couldn't just be some bum dropping in, you had to prove (you were a veteran) with your ID. They were well organized. They refused to be infiltrated, either by fascists or communists, which they both regarded as not indigenous to their cause. They didn't care if you're a Republican or Democrat.

"They realized there was a difference between protesting and lobbying," he continues. "And that was the Gandhian influence. No drinking, no drugs, so, discipline, but also not becoming a threat. And there are thousands who weren't even in the camps. They were in boarding houses, and there were huge numbers just coming over the weekends, from Baltimore, from Philadelphia, who had jobs, who wanted to show their solidarity.

"They really knew about public relations, they put out their own newspaper, a brilliant thing. How many professional ballplayers are in the army? How many boxers? They made it all integral.

"And they posed this to people, 'Look, you asked us to go to war.' It was not screaming at a senator getting out of his car. They'd walk up to the senator, politely shake his hand and say, 'Can I have five minutes? I'm going to talk to you about our issue.' I think that was what made it work."

4. SELMA TO MONTGOMERY:
THE ARC OF THE MORAL UNIVERSE

The State Capitol of Alabama is within walking distance of a milieu of intersecting themes. Montgomery's evangelical churches extol the urgent virtues of the prince of peace, Jesus of Nazareth. Civil rights museums and monuments document the horrors and heroic civic transformations that bring the end of the "Jim Crow" segregation era. A plaque memorializes Alabama's early history as the home of the Creek tribe, the state itself named after its indigenous Native American forbears.

Montgomery is nicknamed the "Heart of Dixie," and the state's coat of arms, adopted in 1923, declares *"Audemus jura nostra defendere,"* Latin for "We Dare Defend Our Rights." The Capitol, listed on the National Register of Historic Places as the First Confederate Capitol, is known as the Cradle of the Confederacy.

On these steps, ignoring threats of assassination, the Reverend Doctor Martin Luther King Jr., the son and grandson of Christian pastors, gives an epochal address that alters the course of American history. It is the site of the dramatic culmination of the Selma to Montgomery March, framed as a voting rights protest in a county where only one percent of African Americans are registered (allowed) to vote, ultimately forcing the establishment of the national Voting Rights Act of 1965, one year after passage of the Civil Rights Act.

> Now it is not an accident that one of the great marches of American history should terminate

in Montgomery, Alabama. (*Yes, sir*) Just ten years ago, in this very city, a new philosophy was born of the Negro struggle. Montgomery was the first city in the South in which the entire Negro community united and squarely faced its age-old oppressors. (*Yes, sir. Well*) Out of this struggle, more than bus desegregation was won; a new idea, more powerful than guns or clubs was born. Negroes took it and carried it across the South in epic battles (*Yes, sir. Speak*) that electrified the nation (*Well*) and the world.[20]

The Civil Rights Act of 1964, originally advocated by President John F. Kennedy then signed into law by successor Lyndon Baines Johnson (LBJ), bans segregation in public places, from lunch counters to bus stations, as well as employment discrimination on the basis of race, color, religion, sex, or national origin. It is the seminal achievement of the civil rights movement.

The Voting Rights Act of 1965, in some ways an extension of the 1964 Act, prohibits racial discrimination in voting, securing the right to vote for racial minorities, especially in the South where disenfranchisement was at epic proportions. It is passed August 6, a few short months after the (March 21-25) Selma to Montgomery March, itself a few days after the nationally televised Bloody Sunday spectacle of state police brutally beating protesters on Selma's Edmund Pettus Bridge. Southern members of Congress fiercely oppose both pieces of legislation.

Discussions of race and civil rights are rife with canards; one is that southern Democratic, not Republican, legislators were in the vanguard of protecting white privilege. They were. But after a Democratic president pushed through those two bills, southern white voters shifted to the Republican Party en masse. White Alabama voters have voted overwhelmingly Republican ever since.

EVERYTHING'S DIVIDED

Directly across the street from the Capitol is the carefully maintained First White House of the Confederacy, home to the secessionist first president Jefferson Davis. It's a beautiful 19th century home, genteel, lovingly maintained, curated by professionals skilled in the art of restoration and preservation.

Walk in and you are greeted by Bob, a personable fellow, steeped in history and hospitality, quick to answer any and all questions about this meticulously restored room or that slice of memorabilia.

He is asked how modern Alabamans look at Jefferson Davis, and the Confederacy. He pauses, the home frequented by tourists most interested in the museum-quality maintenance of a grand 19th-century home, perhaps while silently reveling in its history, then exhibits the grace and good manners of which Alabamans take great pride.

"States' rights and free trade," responds Bob. "Slavery of course. Small elements of what's called the Lost Cause are still here. Yeah, there's probably a UDC (United Daughters of the Confederacy) chapter that meets once a month, little old ladies, there's 10 of them."

There are beautiful exhibits here. The issue of race, the Civil War, the century of segregation would be imbued somewhere in a consideration of Jefferson Davis, or the Confederacy. Are your visitors proud of that, ashamed of that, or, hey, it's the past?

"I went to graduate school in Mississippi," declares Bob, born up North. "So, I would be in the barber shop, would love to go to the real Bubba shops. Guys that talked about girls, oil on their boots, working offshore twice a week, 'Who's East Central playing next week?' 'Oh, they are playing Jackson Prep. That's my Academy.' Simply what they did is, they withdrew. They don't go to public school in the city. They'll go to church Sunday."

When you say 'they,' who do you mean?

"Alabamans. Black churches over there, a very different worship style, white churches over there. I am Presbyterian. My African American workers in here (sings, *'Every blessing...'*); 'That's how you worship?' 'Oh yeah!' I wouldn't want anything to do with it of course. Yeah, everything's divided."

Upstairs is a gift shop, with a range of symbolic memorabilia. "Our Heroes and Our Flags," honoring Confederate leaders and fighters. A newspaper article titled, "Jefferson Davis: An American Patriot." A map of the Confederate States of America.

The gentleman behind the counter loves his work, fields all questions with thoughtful enthusiasm, and has devoted a good portion of recent years to the study and ready articulation of matters regarding the Confederacy. Nathan is careful in his exposition on sensitive subjects, and defensive of the long way Alabamans have come in their embrace of civil rights.

The best-known of all Confederate insignia is the battle flag, erroneously confused with the national flag of the Confederacy. It features the cross of St. Andrew (the apostle of Jesus, brother of St. Peter, martyred on an X-shaped cross), commonly called the "Southern Cross." Andrew is the patron saint of Scotland, and a large part of the early 18th century Southern population was of Scottish and Scots-Irish ancestry. The stars represent the eleven states of the Confederacy, plus border states Kentucky and Missouri, both of whom eventually joined the secession.

The Alabama state flag flying high across the street, a diagonal crimson cross on a white field, seems to have some graphic relation to the Confederate memorabilia on display. Is the Alabama flag signifying the saltire, the *crux decussata* on which Andrew perishes at Patras, Greece? Nathan thinks it has Welsh origins, but he is reminded of the St. Andrews golf course and college and looks it up. Yes, the national flag of Scotland.

"In the 1830s and 1840s, there were a lot of Irish (in the South) and there was a feeling that the North was becoming too secular." He explains it goes back even further, to the founding years, to two founders in particular, Alexander Hamilton and Thomas Jefferson.

"So, the North is very much Hamilton," says Nathan, "very nationalist, very secular. The South is very Jeffersonian, they're clinging to Christianity, but also the idea that it's the people who change the government, who have the power, not the government. Lincoln in 1861, his cabinet asked him about secession, and he's like, well, you know, going to war is unconstitutional. Because the South has the right to secede. 'Why are you militarily forcing the South back in the Union?' He immediately said, he didn't care. As long as he wins the war, it is not going to matter. With Hamilton, the government is first and the preservation of the government is paramount.

"I think we're still divided today, the same way. It still goes back to 1787, the two worlds that have been fighting against each other; there's no middle ground."

A short walk from the Capitol offers a rich potpourri of scenes and experiences. Across from the Southern Poverty Law Center is The Civil Rights Memorial, honoring those who gave their lives for the cause. It's surrounded by a curving black granite wall with the inscription, "Until justice rolls down like waters and righteousness like a mighty stream." A black granite disc with water flowing over its surface displays the names of those who lost their lives in the fight.

The Dexter Avenue King Memorial Baptist Church dates from 1877, built on a slave trading site. Reverend King serves as its pastor from 1954 to 1960. The Hank Williams Museum boasts the country music legend's powder-blue 1952 Cadillac, his guitars and stage attire; a Hank statue is a short walk away, near the riverfront.

The Rosa Parks Library and Museum is located near the site of the seamstress' arrest for refusing to give up her seat on a segregated bus, launching the historic Montgomery bus boycott.

The protest lasts from December 5, 1955 to December 20, 1956, when the federal *Browder v. Gayle* ruling takes effect, leading to a United States Supreme Court decision that declares unconstitutional Alabama and Montgomery laws that segregated buses. The City of Montgomery then passes an ordinance authorizing African-American bus passengers to sit anywhere they choose. The year-long boycott establishes Dr. King as a national voice for civil rights.

The Freedom Rides Museum at the former Greyhound bus station on South Court Street commemorates May 20th, 1961, when an integrated group of college students step off a bus to a violent assault by white protesters. They are riding through the South, from Washington, D.C. to New Orleans to test *Boynton v. Virginia*, a case in which the Supreme Court of the United States declares

segregation in bus terminals unconstitutional. The
television and newspaper images of the vicious attacks
on the riders stun the nation and motivate the Kennedy
administration, perhaps for the first time, to publicly
side with civil rights protesters. The exhibits are modest
but heart-rending, with the station restored to its 1961
look and feel.

The Legacy Museum is located on the site of a
former warehouse where black people are enslaved
in Montgomery in the early 19th century.[21] Tens of
thousands of slaves are trafficked off the nearby river
dock and train station. By 1860, Montgomery is the
capital of the slave trade in Alabama, one of the two
highest-volume slave-owning states in the country.

Nearby is the National Memorial for Peace and Justice,
a field with 800 monuments, each representing a county
where a lynching took place; each marker engraved
with victims' names. Equal Justice Initiative staff
visit hundreds of lynching sites, collecting soil, and
memorializing the racial terror that drove millions of
black residents north as "refugees and exiles."

THE NEWSOUTH

Walk two hundred yards from the bus stop that
launches a revolution and you'll come across a
surprising sight. A specialty bookstore seems an
intrigue in this neighborhood dotted with aging,
sometimes abandoned storefronts. The NewSouth
inventory features an eclectic, carefully assembled set
of categories directly or indirectly related to the art of
politics, to the history of USA race relations, to notions
of justice and civil rights. A sign from San Francisco's
City Lights Bookstore proclaims, "A Kind of Library
Where Books Are Sold."

Randall Williams and his partner Suzanne La Rosa are the most prolific publishers in Alabama. The next-door Village Place pub has not yet opened, so Williams borrows a small table and two chairs stacked out front, and calls up to La Rosa for a bottle of red wine and glasses. As an author, an editor and publisher, a bookstore owner, and a community leader-activist, he's had a front row seat to the ebb and flow of Montgomery politics and the evolution of the city and state's race relations. As cars and tour buses shuttle down South Court Street, he considers whether the act of protest is fundamental to American patriotism.

"It's really sort of the fundamental deal, isn't it?" declares Williams. "It's the underpinning of the whole country and the structure of what we do. The founding fathers, imperfect though they may be, were protesting the system they found themselves in and it led to change. Some of the founding fathers believed in the need to continue to protest. Jefferson famously said that every country needs a new revolution every now and then."

Bringing the conversation "closer to home," he continues, "the civil rights movement existed because there had been slavery and a Civil War (1861-65), and Reconstruction (1866-77) was an unfulfilled promise. Then we had that dark, almost 100 years of Jim Crow segregation, and what brought that down was continual protest. It wasn't just, suddenly, one day... how did Julian Bond put it? The myth is that 'Rosa sat down, Martin stood up, and the world changed.' Of course, we know that's not the way it happened. We know that there were decades of protest going on, back from the black women who participated with the suffragists and were left out in many ways.

"Then, the anti-lynching campaign, the campaign to try to abolish the poll tax. Then, of course, right in this place, the great protest, the (1955 Rosa Parks-initiated) bus boycott. Then it was just one domino after another, culminating in the Civil Rights Act of '64 and the Voting Rights Act of '65. All of those people were troublemakers in the eyes of the folks who wielded power and held power, and they *were* troublemakers. Thank goodness, they were."

What brought activists of that era on buses from cities around the country, to say, I may get beaten up and I may die, but I want to do this anyway?

Williams answers, "It's their ultimate patriotic act, isn't it? If you believe in what the country is supposed to stand for and you think it's not being upheld, and you say, 'By God, I'm going to put myself on the line,' that exhibits to me a lot of faith in what the country is supposed to mean.

"Folks who marched from Selma through Dallas County in 1965 were confronting power. They were confronting injustice, and they were doing it in such a way that it might make a substantial difference.

"Then, of course, what has happened after the change came is, they have voting power in all the Black Belt (named for the region's rich black topsoil) counties, but they have not been able to do a damn thing about economic power, and the schools remain abysmal.

"When the Selma to Montgomery March happened," Williams reminisces, "I was 14. Had I been older, there's no question to me, I would have been more likely to be out in the mob, beating James Reeb (a white pastor from Boston killed by white segregationists during the Selma protests), because I grew up in a straight racist culture. That's what I'd do. The N word, that's all I knew until I was older.

"I assume a lot of white Alabamans have changed since 1961, but I assume a lot of people have not changed all that much. The change has been both enormous and miniscule at the same time, because when the laws changed, white people with rare exception were really hardcore haters, the Klansmen, the neo-Nazis, all that kind of stuff. There remain the exceptions, but for the most part, when the laws changed, white people accepted it pretty easily. Some things took a little longer, interracial dating and marriage, but now interracial couples go anywhere. Nobody bats an eye.

"Yet, the institutional racism, people are still holding on to that, and they don't socialize for the most part. The definition of a white liberal in Bullock County today is they no longer believe in slavery."

You were with the Southern Poverty Law Center. Were you there in the beginning?

"Not at the very beginning," answers Williams, "but pretty close. It started in '71 and I started there in '76, and was there for a decade. I started the Klanwatch Project."

La Rosa returns to continue the conversation inside the now closed bookstore. In the back is a cozy nook with an old weathered couch.

"Johnnie Carr was the fifth president of the Montgomery Improvement Association (formed in 1955 to lead the bus boycott)," says Williams. "(Martin Luther King, Jr.) was first. (Ralph) Abernathy was second. She became the president in 1968 and held that office until she died at age 97, eight or nine years ago. She gave us the couch you're sitting on. She was gonna get rid of it and Suzanne had the good sense to say, 'We want that couch.' It was in her living room. We can't document that Martin Luther King sat on it..."

La Rosa interjects, "We can."

Williams continues, "… but we know that John Lewis, Julian Bond, Ralph Abernathy, Solomon Seay. E.D. Nixon, Rosa Parks, and all these other people had sat on this couch."

Williams and La Rosa are getting ready to republish a book, with a photo taken by a famous civil rights photographer at "the integration of Lanier High School."

"As the blacks were walking into the school for the first day," says Williams, "all the white students were lined up over here, and there was this row of white girls that were 17 or 18 years old, their faces were so contorted with hatred. It's an amazing photograph.

"I have wanted for years to track and identify these women. I have wanted to go interview them and pull out that photograph and ask, 'What were you thinking there, by the way? What was going through your mind then?' (Williams does a short search of the store shelves and finds the book)."

What is the grievance of these women?

"Their grievance," says Williams, "is that their way of life is threatened, and that's it."

SELMA

The meandering Alabama River connects Montgomery and Selma, an hour's ride on US Business Route 80, but Greyhound's intercity service turns out to be a manic female entrepreneur who runs a minibus with a shot suspension system, careening down country roads well above the speed limit, picking up and dropping off patients at elder care facilities, an unadvertised personal side business. The harrowing two-hour journey leaves one off at Broad Street, down the street from the Edmund Pettus Bridge. Nearby is the Brown Chapel AME Church, gathering ground for voting rights protesters in 1965.

The Edmund Pettus was built in 1940, its antecedent a two-lane wooden swing bridge designed for transporting mule loads of cotton. The steel through arch bridge has a central span of 250 feet, the Alabama swirling 100 feet below its apex. As you cross the bridge, heading east from Selma, the National Voting Rights Museum & Institute lies on your left, "the cornerstone of the contemporary struggle for voting rights and human dignity."

Sam Walker, resident historian, is there at each of the early stages of the museum's development. From the fundraising event featuring former King aide Reverend Jesse Jackson to the opening in 1993, from the move to this side of the bridge in 2009 to the launch of new exhibits in 2011.

"We have a second museum," informs Walker in his measured, vigorous speaking tone, "the Slavery and Civil War Museum. Miss Annie Pearl Avery operates that. She was an actual foot soldier and part of the Bloody Sunday March."

Tribute to the foot soldiers is a theme of the exhibits, both visually and conceptually. The Museum gathers over 3,000 oral histories, according to Walker, "to identify and document the foot soldiers of the voting rights struggle."

On October 7, 1963, more than 300 African-Americans gather to register to vote at Selma's Dallas County Courthouse. Though county officers ensure that few manage to register, the "Freedom Day" action is regarded a victory by civil rights activists.

"You know," muses Walker, "everyone has seen those pictures, those videotapes of Dr. King leading all of those marches. Right. But then you see all these people walking in back of Dr. King. Those are people who got beaten, some of them got put in jail. Now, when you walk through the museum, you're seeing footprints on the wall, right? We collect footprints from people who were at Bloody Sunday, the people beaten and tear-gassed and forced to end their march, or the five-day march from Selma to Montgomery. We make a cast of their foot, we have a caption that has their names, about what they would do when they participated in those marches.

What's the significance of museums and monuments like this?

"The Voting Rights Museum represents a victory," explains Walker. "You got a new law out of that struggle. And so, people can be reminded every time they walk through those doors that you can go out there and achieve another victory.

"Here in Alabama, there were three major movements that changed three different laws. The first one was the Montgomery Bus Boycott – that changed interstate travel. And then the Civil Rights Act came out of Birmingham, (access to) public accommodations, hotels, restaurants. And the Voting Rights Act came out of here in Selma. And out of those three movements, President Lyndon Johnson said it best, the right to vote is the most important right that we have; without the right to vote, all your other rights are meaningless. It didn't just happen overnight. That had been a journey to get to where we are."

During January 1965, Martin Luther King, Jr., and other civil rights leaders organize demonstrations that lead to violent responses by police, covered in national media.

On February 1, King and other demonstrators are arrested for violating an anti-parade ordinance; hundreds more are arrested in similar protests in the days following. On February 4, civil rights leader Malcolm X gives a Selma address claiming many African-Americans did not support King's strategy of nonviolent civil disobedience. The next day, King is released from jail and his "Letter from a Selma Jail" is printed in *The New York Times*. On February 6, President Johnson announces he will send a voting rights proposal to Congress.

A few weeks after his Selma visit, Malcolm X is assassinated while addressing his Organization of Afro-American Unity at the Audubon Ballroom in Harlem.

In nearby Marion, Alabama, on February 18, state troopers violently break up a nighttime march; later, one of the troopers shoots unarmed young African-American protester Jimmie Lee Jackson. The Army veteran and church deacon is protecting his mother as she and his grandfather are beaten by police at Mack's Café.

Although Alabama Governor George Wallace promises to stop it, the Selma to Montgomery March begins on Sunday, March 7. Southern Christian Leadership Conference (SCLC) leader Hosea Williams and Student

Non-Violent Coordinating Committee (SNCC) leader John Lewis assemble some 600 demonstrators for the 54-mile march east to the state capital to present Wallace their voting registration grievances. The marchers are stopped by state and county police on horseback at the Edmund Pettus Bridge. The police shoot tear gas into the crowd and attack protesters with billy clubs when orders to disperse are ignored. Televised footage of the "Bloody Sunday" scene, with 16 hospitalized and more than 50 others injured, generates national outrage.

THEY LOST THEIR FEAR

You were a little boy when Bloody Sunday happened. And you were there for the last leg of the march to Montgomery. What are your most vivid memories from that experience?

"The sense of pride of actually reaching the Capitol and watching Dr. King give his speech on the Capitol steps," says Walker. "It was a tremendous feeling of elation, satisfaction, the fact that this actually had happened, we have accomplished this."

After these years of talking with thousands of visitors who come to learn and to relive the history of the voting rights struggle, what do you tell young people about how to engage effectively in politics or social movements?

"Well, I saw a quote, several years ago from my friend's father, Mr. Reverend Thomas Threadgill. And it said that no generation can expect to see the end of struggle. But each generation has a responsibility to advance the struggle. So, when young people come through here, I just tell them: do your part to advance the struggle, that's all that's required of you. I'm free as long as I continue to struggle to be free. Once I stop trying to be free, then I may lose that freedom."

And who or what are they struggling against?

"Struggling, trying to make things right for the world, so wherever you find yourself, whatever condition you find yourself in, you will advance that condition to be better than what you found it, make the world better for the next generation.

"It's been 400 years of struggles for equality, since slavery began in this country. I talked with an elderly lady back after we opened the museum in 1994," recalls Walker. "She was living in Montgomery, Alabama; she told me she came over in the last leg of the march, same as me. She was working for a white woman who had a friend over to the house, and as the marchers approached Montgomery, she said, 'I'm gonna go join them.' And the two white women tried to discourage her. They said, 'Why you want to get involved with that, miss? You don't understand what it's all about.' And she answered, 'You know what, you're right. I really don't understand what it's all about. But as hard as you all are trying to keep us from having it, it must be something good.'"

There were numerous moments when civil rights leaders could have thrown in the towel. What are the qualities that drove them to continue taking risks?

"Number one," says Walker, "people felt that they were as low as they could go. So, they were going to improve their conditions, whatever way they could. But, number two, over the last 25 years of working here at the museum, I recognize that all the people that participated in that movement were linked by a common thread, which is, at some point, all these people had lost their fear.

"They didn't lose it all at the same time. But once they were no longer paralyzed, once they had realized they could get up and do anything; there was no stopping them. They would determine and go out there and achieve whatever it was they were trying to achieve. It was still dangerous. But once they lost their fear, they weren't afraid of that danger, they were willing to make those sacrifices. If I lose my life today, I'm going to do what I believe is right, to try to change my condition. And that's one thing that the other side never really adjusted to. They couldn't understand how people could be beaten and abused, and come right back the next day."

In response to Bloody Sunday, King calls for volunteers from across America to come to Selma for another march two days later. He leads a group of 2,000 – more than half white, with hundreds of clergy – to the Edmund Pettus Bridge where he gathers the marchers in prayer. Then King disperses the crowd, as he has followed a short route agreed upon with authorities to minimize potential violence. The plan has only been shared with SCLC leaders and thus confuses many demonstrators who had traveled long distances to join. Yet King maintains the peace and the day is later labeled by the movement as "Turnaround Tuesday."

That night, James Reeb, a Unitarian Universalist minister from Boston, is beaten to death by Ku Klux Klan members.

What do you think is the attitude of most white Alabamans towards the history of civil rights in this state?

"White people in the South really have to accept the fact

that they lost the Civil War. The masses still desire to rewrite that history. People start from that perspective, yet we shall go beyond that and let people know that is not going to happen."

What perspective are they trying to maintain?

"It's this simple," insists Walker, "that white people are better than black people. And if you really talk to white folks, and get them to be honest, a lot of them will admit that, because that is a master that they've had pretty much all their lives. On the other side of that coin, you got people of goodwill, people that showed up without any call for them to come stand with black folks in Selma. White people came down here, and some of them had their lives taken. You have to remember that you can't just settle on that side where the "Friends of Forrest" congregated, you also got to remember that there are some people that have genuine hearts and goodwill that are going to do whatever they feel is right."

FRIENDS OF FORREST

To get to Live Oak Cemetery, home of the memorial to Confederate Lieutenant General Nathan Bedford Forrest, first grand wizard of the Ku Klux Klan, you need only take a one-mile stroll from the Edmund Pettus Bridge. Walk a few blocks down Broad Street, turn left on Selma Avenue. You'll pass St. Paul's Episcopal Church, founded in 1838; in April of 1865, following the Battle of Selma, Union General James H. Wilson burned much of the city, including the church.

Live Oak, founded in 1829, contains the remains of numerous Selma notables. Edmund Winston Pettus himself, Brigadier General of the Confederate States of America, Grand Duke of the Ku Klux Klan, and United

States Senator, lie here. Senator William Rufus King serves as Vice-President of the United States for a brief six weeks before his untimely death. There is Benjamin S. Turner, a former slave and the first African-American to represent Alabama in Congress. There are a lot of Confederate soldier graves, providing a respectful memorial to those fallen for the cause. You can sit in the carved stone Jefferson Davis Memorial Chair. And, featured prominently, a monument to General Forrest, *Defender of Selma, Wizard of the Saddle, Untutored Genius, The First with the Most. One of the South's Finest Heroes.*

A blog post titled "Friends of Forrest" from *Cold Southern Steel: Defending Southern Heritage* states:

> We hope you ALL will make plans to attend this historic & monumental event!
>
> We Won! We have the deed to Confederate Memorial Circle! It's time to Celebrate, Commemorate & Re-Dedicate!
>
> The Friends of Forrest and Selma Chapter 53, UDC Cordially Invite You to Attend & Share the Celebration of our Historical & Monumental Victory!!! Saturday, May 23, 2015 1:00 PM. Confederate Memorial Circle, Historic Live Oak Cemetery, Selma, Alabama

It's a serene, beautiful old cemetery, enlivened with Spanish moss, with majestic oak and magnolia trees. Both simple and ornate headstones commemorate Selma's mayors, senators, soldiers, community leaders, and ordinary citizens. The cemetery, commemorating the battles that took so many lives, becomes its own battlefield when local "Friends of Forrest," defenders of southern (Confederate) heritage, insist on honoring the former Klan leader.

"Three years after it disappeared, Nathan Bedford
Forrest's bust is back atop a monument erected in his
honor at Old Live Oak Cemetery," reports the *Selma
Times-Journal* in a May 23, 2015 article by Daniel Evans.
"Over a decade since the unveiling of the original
Forrest bust, a second ceremony was held Saturday
by the United Daughters of the Confederacy and the
Friends of Forrest to honor the Civil War general.
When the red curtain covering the new monument was
removed, cannons were fired and cheers erupted from
the crowd of 100 or more."[22]

The KKK originates in the 1860s during post-Civil
War Reconstruction, donning white robes, conical
hats and masks, terrifying newly-freed African
Americans, especially leaders and activists. Through
their history, they have advocated white nationalism
and white supremacism, and anti-immigration policies,
with frequent diatribes against Jews and Catholics,
deemed not real Americans due to their loyalties to
their religious identities (Israel, the Pope, etc.). Cross
burnings and parades are common methods of
intimidation.

Forrest is a war hero (the Battle of Selma among others)
or a war criminal (his forces massacred unarmed black
Union troops after their surrender in the 1864 Battle
of Fort Pillow, Tennessee) depending on your attitude
toward the Confederacy.

Selma attorney and Forrest critic Faya Rose Touré calls the
general a domestic terrorist. Comparing the glorification
of Forrest in Selma with the ban of Nazi memorials in
Germany, Touré complains, "Jews would not tolerate a
statue of Hitler in their neighborhood and what they
put up in our neighborhood back then was pretty much
the same thing. Descendants of those who enslaved us
insist on honoring someone with Klan connections."[23]

A SEMINAL MOMENT IN AMERICAN HISTORY

Bill Tomey works in sales and marketing for the *Selma Times-Journal* on historic Water Street, a short walk from the Edmund Pettus Bridge; he's also the paper's historian. He and his partner, Dave Hurlbut, have restored a downtown building formerly housing the Jewish "Harmony Club." A thoughtful, gregarious man, he gathers Dave, young staff writer Brannon Cahela, and local hardware store owner Alden Holley for beers and a conversation about Selma's place in Alabama history.

Holding court behind the bar, Hurlbut shares stories of Selma's social clubs over the years before the conversation turns to the Selma to Montgomery March.

"A seminal moment in American history, period," declares Hurlbut, then remarks "about the whole slavery thing. Let me just tell you something. The Egyptians enslaved the Jews. Is anybody going to talk about reparations for that? What about feudalism, white people enslaving other white people in Europe and making them build castles in goddamn freezing weather?"

"Segregation was an awful institution," says Tomey. "It was and you hear this term: 'It's just the way it was.' But the fact that it was that way when you grew up doesn't mean everybody is evil."

"They come here and they use it like a goddamn photo op," protests Hurlbut, "and then Selma is left holding the bag. We carry the mantle of the nation's civil rights woes when I can take you right now to places in Boston, where they say nigger this and nigger that, and after eight o'clock at night if you and I are in the wrong neighborhood as white people, we're fucking doomed."

There was a voting rights issue in Selma in 1965, wasn't there?

(*Loud crossfire of voices.*) "Everyone be quiet," shouts Hurlbut, "I want to explain this. You cannot have a constitutional republic with entire classes relegated to second class citizenship. It is a recipe for disaster. What happened here had to happen one way or the other. It had to happen but what I'm saying is, it wasn't just Selma, it was fucking everywhere."

Hurlbut presents a history lesson for context. "From 1540 to 1699 this was Spanish, as (explorer Hernando) de Soto claimed it. When he got here, there was an Indian nation of about 50,000 strong. There's your four major tribes: Creek, Cherokee, Choctaw, Chickasaw. Up under the Creek, there's a lesser tribe called the Alibamu, hence the name of the state, Alabama. From 1699 to 1763, the French. There's a monument across the street to Jean-Baptiste Le Moyne Sieur de Bienville. And he meets with the Alibamu Indians. (Dave attempts to quell the heated crosstalk). *HOLD ON!* From 1763 to 1779, British, then from 1779 to 1801 reverts back to the Spanish. They're just trading it back and forth. 1801 an American territory, 1819 a state, and I think you can go from there.

"So, my point is, when you see words like Alabama, Cahaba, they're Indian words. And I can tell you something. They can bitch about slavery in the Confederacy. De Soto was a goddamn bastard. What he did to the Indians was worse than slavery. Much, much worse."

"Everyone time we're in the national media," argues Holley, "it will be absolutely purely negative. I mean, we are backwoods redneck Alabama, hate black people. I mean, you're not gonna hear anything good about Selma."

"Raping us of our identity," complains Tomey. "Tourists come here thinking they're gonna get the Racist Disney World. The City of Selma was compassionate towards the protesters."

Huh. Really?

Hurlbut adds, "Those guys that beat them up when they got across the bridge were state troopers."

"Mayor Smitherman said no police officers go across that bridge. Do you know about the flood posse?" asks Tomey. "Around '60, Sheriff Clark deputized a lot of guys to get people out with boats. People are on top of homes, black and white. And they went out to help people."

Dave says there were coffins floating down the Alabama River.

"The flood posse stayed together," states Tomey. "It should have been disbanded. And really, it was a good old boy thing. That's who was on the other side of the bridge was Sheriff (Jim) Clark and his flood posse and then (Governor George) Wallace's state troopers."

Holley says, "I really believe it was the state troopers and then, when things got out of control, the posse came in. That's my personal belief. I talked to the sheriff about this."

"But hundreds were not beat up," clarifies Tomey. Then, he adds, "The whole lynching thing is getting way, way mythologized. There wasn't that much lynching going on here. If we lynch as much as – though everybody's worshipping it with that museum over in Montgomery – we wouldn't have any black people. Come on. It's absurd."

"What about hanging in the Old West?" asks Hurlbut.

"I'm the only one in here who was born and raised in Selma," says Holley. "The people I've talked to, the people I have known, the racism that everybody views being in Selma was not there in the 60s. I mean, it just wasn't. It's all bullshit."

On March 15, 1965, President Johnson addresses a televised joint session of Congress, calling for expansive voting rights legislation. He concludes his speech with the civil rights anthem, *We Shall Overcome*. The Voting Rights Act of 1965 is introduced two days later as 25,000, protected by a federalized Alabama National Guard, march from Selma to Montgomery.

An estimated 8,000 people gather at Brown Chapel AME Church on March 21 and begin the five-day march to Montgomery. More than 20,000 join the marchers when they reach Montgomery on the 25th for the rally at the State Capitol, where Dr. King delivers his now-famous "How Long, Not Long" speech. That night, Viola Liuzzo, a white mother of five from Detroit, is murdered by Klansmen as she drives toward Montgomery to pick up marchers.

THE VILLAGE PLACE IN MONTGOMERY

The Village Place playlist runs a heavy rotation of sixties and seventies-era R&B. James Harrell co-manages the Montgomery tavern and a small group meets in the lounge on many an afternoon for a few beers and some top-shelf storytelling. Retired state junior college president Doug Chambers is there tonight, along with retired union organizer Gus

Towns, and, during the chat, next door neighbor Randall Williams drops in. James, a member of the Montgomery Industrial Development Board worked for George Wallace after the Governor renounced his segregationist past. The subject tonight is civil rights, the attitudes of modern Alabamans on race, and the fruits and torments of community activism.

"There was no problem. Until they tried to cross that bridge. But you know, when you think about it, most white Americans didn't think it was a problem. It took years. 'What's wrong? *We've been nice.'*"

That was the point of a local Selma resident interviewed. Why pick on Selma when there was racism in Boston?

"Selma was chosen for a reason. Those images of state troopers attacking protesters was seen around the world."

"The German people now despise the Nazis. But you ask an interesting question. Once a racist, can you stop being a racist?"

"It's a learned trait. It's passed on from generation to generation."

"You're not born a racist."

"YEAH, but you're born into it."

"I had a white female coworker, I was her boss, she made a comment that she just felt like black and white people should not mix."

How long ago was that?

"Ten years. I have been retired nine. I asked why do you feel that way? She played piano in her church. I asked, what if your son, in the Army now, brought a black person home, introduced her as the woman he was in love with? She said, 'I would do everything in my power to make sure they don't get married.' I asked, 'How long you been feeling that way?' She said, 'All my life.' Key phrase there, all my life. I met her family, nothing like her, wonderful people. I said, 'You know, this is a new day.' And she said, 'I know, I just don't think they ought to mix.' And she was just sincere."

"Does that make her a bad person though?"

"No, I didn't say she was bad."

Not a bad person. But the implications are, you can't come in my bar, and you can't sit at my lunch counter. That means, what, we shouldn't have the same schools. She said it in a sweet, non-intimidating way. But the implications are brutal.

"But it's good to go back to the question, can people stop being that way? The way they learned, it will be more complicated to get out. It is easy to get on drugs, it's harder to get off. You have to want to. You still have a generation in the South with their kids telling mom and dad, 'This is a new day and age,' and they are told 'You are going to the University of Alabama, you do what I say or I'm gonna cut you loose from the will.'"

"I think racism now has manifested itself into economics."

"But hasn't it always been?"

"Racism seems to be getting more global than it ever has in our lifetime. I think part of that is Trump has given people carte blanche to do whatever they want. Look at New Zealand. Says he killed those people because of Trump."

"America, we're still experimenting, we are not a monolithic people, we're not Germans, we're not Brits, you know, we are a hodgepodge."

We used to be proud, when I was growing up, of calling America a melting pot.

"We never quite got in that pot. And I think getting in the pot now, there are some growing pains."

"Hate is going to destroy the world, it's not going to be fire this time, it's not going to be water this time, it's going to be pure hate."

If we could document what's in your neighbors' brains about race, what do they think?

"They love me as a person. But they don't like colored folk. I have keys to their houses. They get to know me, but they don't want to get too many of *me's* because that means they're changing out of their comfort zone. Montgomery is like that a lot."

When you walk around Montgomery and Selma, there are a lot of civil rights monuments and signs.

"Don't mean shit."

"We didn't give whites enough credit, and particularly Jews and Catholics that were out there, and the union leaders. We should have been embracing everybody (mentions white ministers and activists whose homes were bombed or who were beaten or killed)."

What do you think the movement leaders did right?

"When they first started making efforts to go across the (Edmund Pettus) Bridge, they never lost focus, regardless of what they might encounter. They never anticipated being beaten down. If it had not been for a Martin Luther King type of thinking of nonviolence, this never would have been successful. The young people, Stokely Carmichael said, 'Hell, let's fight.'"

"The young people were tired of the shit that was going on."

"Selma didn't just happen. It was chosen. King and the Southern Christian Leadership (SCLC). Only had 14 black people that could vote."

That was like one percent?

"One percent. It was chosen."

"But the key thing though, is that they had a referee in that King said, when they tried to stray, do this or that, he said *nonviolence*. Stay focused on our goals."

"I'm 69 years old, and even at 69, I feel sad for America. From a personal perspective, I have had a successful career – James introduced us and all that we did – but you still have to fight from feeling a second-class citizen."

"HOW LONG? NOT LONG."

Pastor Leon Ross is a native of Philadelphia, Pennsylvania, but is esteemed around town as the longtime pastor of the Weeping Willow Baptist Church and member of the Montgomery Improvement

Association. A black King James Bible on his desk, his church office offers no hint of retirement, and he retains the fire and conviction held as a frontline participant and observer of Alabama's great civil rights struggles. He preached his "initial message" the first Sunday in June 1966.

"The Montgomery Improvement Association is an organization that Dr. King had founded," apprises Pastor Ross. "He was on that board for many years." He explains why it was pivotal in the civil rights movement.

"Because, on December 1, 1955, a black woman named Rosa Parks, a seamstress at a department store named Montgomery Fair, sat on a bus. She had worked all day and she was tired. She didn't sit in the white section; she sat in the colored section, but the driver asked her to get up and give her seat to a white man. She told him she wouldn't, and that started the movement.

"On December 5, at the Holt Street Baptist Church, there was a mass meeting of about 2,000 folk inside the church; the church seated about 1,000. Another 2,000 were in the street."

On the night of Ms. Parks' arrest, Alabama State professor Jo Ann Robinson of the Women's Political Council, a group of African-American women professionals, mimeographed 52,500 flyers, distributing them throughout Montgomery's black community.[24]

> Another woman has been arrested and thrown in jail because she refused to get up out of her seat on the bus for a white person to sit down. It is the second time since the Claudette Colvin case that a Negro woman has been arrested for the same thing. This has to be stopped. Negroes have rights too, for if Negroes did not ride the buses, they could

not operate... You can afford to stay out of school for one day if you have no other way to go except by bus. You can also afford to stay out of town for one day. If you work, take a cab, or walk. But please, children and grown-ups, don't ride the bus at all on Monday. Please stay off all buses Monday.

Key to the boycott is a citywide carpool system, with vehicle owners providing rides for boycotters. Many white housewives pick up their black domestic workers. Black taxi drivers reduce their fares to ten cents, same as a bus fare. The city responds by pressuring local insurance companies to stop insuring drivers in the carpool system, so boycott leaders take their business to Lloyd's of London. Other protesters use bicycles, walk, or hitchhike. Black churches around the country collect new or near new shoes for those walking to work. Four local black churches as well as the houses of King and Abernathy are firebombed.

Eventually almost 100 boycotters are charged by the city with conspiring to interfere with a business. King is given a choice to pay a $500 fee or spend more than a year in jail. The sentence backfires and leads to national pressure; he is freed after two weeks. Ultimately, the Supreme Court's December 1956 Browder v. Gayle ruling earns the civil rights movement its first victory.

Ms. Parks was active, of course, with the NAACP (National Association for the Advancement of Colored People). That's politics. But what was it, speaking as a pastor, that drove her to take that kind of risk for justice?

"Have you ever heard of being sick and tired of being sick and tired?" asks Pastor Ross.

"That's basically what happened. Said no to a white bus driver who had said, 'If you don't give up that seat, we're going to arrest you.' Now, this was a soft-spoken seamstress. Why did she do it? It was time. She had got sick and tired of segregation, of blacks being treated as second-class citizens. So, she didn't (move)."

There was a very nice fellow I met while in Selma, claims wonderful relationships with African-American customers. When asked if there was a problem in Selma in 1965, he answered, the racism that people attribute to that community was just not there. "It's all bullshit."

"I lived in Selma," responds Pastor Ross. "I know what you're talking about. You know that's a blatant lie that the civil rights movement was not needed. We had to ride at the back of the bus. We couldn't vote. We were treated like second-class citizens. Our women were raped. Then the Ku Klux Klan will get together, burning crosses in your yard.

"And you tell me there was no need for a movement?"

One fellow said, "Well, there were some lynchings, but it was very rare."

"That's a lie. We were lynched wholesale, to tell you what I know. If a black man looked at a white woman, they would kill him and lynch him. They'd kill him because they'd say he whistled at a white woman.

"Now, Dr. King taught nonviolence, I walked with him. I talked with him. I think I missed one mass meeting. I lived around the street from Dr. King in the Alabama State University area. They bombed Dr. King's house. He had blacks that were willing to use shotguns, pistols, and brass knuckles, and Dr. King told everyone to go back home. If somebody had come to defend you right now and you were kicking him out, you would sound like you were crazy. He said, 'Man, I don't need you.'"

Why do you think nonviolence was important to the movement? Was there something about that message that touched people, that helped to drive public perceptions of the civil rights movement?

"He based his philosophy on Mahatma Gandhi who did not believe in violence. Dr. King was following Jesus. Scripture in the Bible, we don't interpret it right. It said, if you slapped me on one cheek – you know what it said – I turned the other. He believed that violence was not the answer. He knew it was going to get him into trouble, and even when they were on a plane in Atlanta, coming to Memphis where he was assassinated, they had the plane guarded all night to make sure it wasn't sabotaged.

"I believe he endorsed nonviolence, not only as a Christian and a man of God, but he endorsed it because there was another word in the scripture that said, 'Don't be overcome by evil, but overcome evil with good (*Romans 12:21*).' I hate you; you hate me. This circular hate keeps going. You have to break it in order to break the cycle. If you hate me, I've got to love you, even if I don't want to, if I want to make a difference. That's what I believed he taught, passive resistance and nonviolence, starting with the Freedom Rides. They were huge. You know the Freedom Rides."

From the Greyhound Station here in town.

"That bus station and a whole lot of others, too," adds Ross. "They were going to arrest him then, right before the protest started; Baton Rouge, Louisiana, they had just had a similar protest, but our movement here in Montgomery not only triggered the United States, but around the world. Hearing the word of Dr. King, people decided to straighten up their backs and stand for what they believed. So, if anybody tells you that there was no reason for the movement, they are crazy and out of touch with reality."

What unique character or vision do you think he brought to the movement as a leader?

"Back to the scripture, 'Where there is no vision, the people perish (*Proverbs 29:18*).' He was a visionary leader way ahead of his time, and it goes back to his history. His dad and his granddad, both of them were vocal about mistreatment, not only of blacks, but of any race, whether they were Jewish, gentile or whatever. I believe he embraced nonviolence because he felt, and I still feel to date, that that's the only answer.

"Violence is not the answer, and Dr. King decided to give his life and paid the ultimate price for what he believed. One thing he said was, if a man hasn't found something worth dying for, he isn't fit to live, and I believe that. I believe that."

King's legacy continues past his death. The Fair Housing Act of 1968, for many the last great legislative achievement of the civil rights era, prohibits discrimination in the sale, rental, and financing of housing based on race, religion, national origin, or sex. Mired in debate in the Senate, it is passed by the House of Representatives just days after King's assassination by a white supremacist on the balcony of the Lorraine Motel in Memphis, Tennessee on April 4, 1968.

You met white pastors that opposed the civil rights movement, tell me about their theology and their reading of the scriptures.

"They said that Dr. King was a rabble-rouser and a troublemaker. At the Birmingham movement, when they bombed the Sixth Avenue Baptist Church and killed four little girls, that made the news. They went to Sunday school on a Sunday morning. You would think that they were safe in church.

"Have you ever heard of the *Letter from a Birmingham Jail?* He wrote it on scraps of paper. They told him to get the 'h' out of Birmingham. He was talking about how they were supposedly Christians, men and women of God, and they embraced the violence that was going on in Birmingham."

But they had an understanding of theology, an understanding of Christianity, that said, 'What we're doing is godly.'

"I can't understand it either," exclaims Ross. "I didn't understand it as a youngster, and now, more than 80 years later, I still don't understand it. How could you talk all that bullshit out of your mouth? You're getting in your pulpit on Sunday morning and preaching love for your neighbor, then get out there wanting to kill somebody all because they want their rights and want to be treated as citizens. We say that it's 'the land of the free and the home of the brave.' How are you going to get in your pulpit and say one thing and then Monday through Saturday leave somebody out? There's something wrong with that."

Tell me about your personal time with King. What kind of a man was he?

"He was mild-mannered," recalls Ross. "I've seen him in different (venues), most times in church. He was a sincere man, and he had a demeanor that was almost like magic. Everybody wanted to be around him. He wasn't flamboyant. He was soft-spoken. The last time I heard him speak, it was at a church on Holt Street called Metropolitan Methodist Church.

"But, since you asked, there was something unusual about Dr. King. To me, he didn't flaunt who he was. He would go in the pool rooms. He would go into night clubs. He went where people were. That's my perception of him.

"I don't have to tell you," concludes Ross, "that he was one of the best orators that I've ever heard. I have Dr. King's books and all this stuff, but you have to have been around him. It was an unusual experience. I ain't met nobody else like Dr. King. You would kind of say that he was just unusual."

These are closing words of Dr. Martin Luther King, Jr., on the steps of the Alabama State Capitol after the march from Selma.[25]

> Last Sunday, more than eight thousand of us started on a mighty walk from Selma, Alabama. I come to say to you this afternoon, however difficult the moment, (*Audience: Yes, sir*) however frustrating the hour, it will not be long, (*No sir*) because "truth crushed to earth will rise again." (*Yes, sir*)
>
> How long? Not long, (*Yes, sir*) because "no lie can live forever." (*Yes, sir*)
>
> How long? Not long, (*All right. How long*) because "you shall reap what you sow." (*Yes, sir*)
>
> How long? (*How long?*) Not long: (*Not long*)
>
> Truth forever on the scaffold, (*Speak*)
> Wrong forever on the throne, (*Yes, sir*)
> Yet that scaffold sways the future, (*Yes, sir*)

And, behind the dim unknown,
Standeth God within the shadow,
Keeping watch above his own.

How long? Not long, because the arc of the moral
universe is long, but it bends toward justice. (*Yes,
sir*)

How long? Not long, (*Not long*) because:

Mine eyes have seen the glory of the coming of
the Lord; (*Yes, sir*)
He is trampling out the vintage where the grapes
of wrath are stored; (*Yes*)
He has loosed the fateful lightning of his terrible
swift sword; (*Yes, sir*)
His truth is marching on. (*Yes, sir*)
He has sounded forth the trumpet that shall
never call retreat; (*Speak, sir*)
He is sifting out the hearts of men before His
judgment seat. (*That's right*)
O, be swift, my soul, to answer Him! Be jubilant
my feet!
Our God is marching on. (*Yeah*)
Glory, hallelujah! (*Yes, sir*)
Glory, hallelujah! (*All right*)
Glory, hallelujah! Glory, hallelujah!
His truth is marching on. [*Applause*]

The crowd is awash in American flags. With each
'*Glory, hallelujah*,' King's right hand raises and
points higher.

5. VIETNAM: THE AMERICAN WAR RESISTER

Americans hold a conflicted attitude toward overseas military adventures.

Three decades after the end of the Cold War, used as the justification for massive military spending, the United States has approximately 800 military bases in 80 countries and spends, fully loaded, a trillion dollars on defense-related matters, very little of it to defend our shores.

The founding fathers have specific ideas on the matter, baked into the Constitution.

George Washington warns against foreign entanglements: "A large standing Army in time of Peace hath ever been considered dangerous to the liberties of a Country." He asks, "Why quit our own to stand upon foreign ground?"

James Madison, the architect of the Constitution and First Amendment, believes, "Of all the enemies to public liberty, war is, perhaps, the most to be dreaded, because it comprises and develops the germ of every other. War is the parent of armies; from these proceed debts and taxes; and armies, and debts, and taxes are the known instruments for bringing the many under the domination of the few."

Only Congress is given the power to declare war, via Article I, Section 8, Clause 11. And yet the country has been involved in military conflicts with or without congressional approval for 222 of its 239 years. It's never gone a decade without a war; the longest peacetime

America knows is 1935-40, during the isolationist period of the Great Depression.[26]

Anti-war movements are different than other social movements, argues Daniel Lieberfeld in the *International Journal of Peace Studies*, because they question citizens' support for a nation's most basic duty of security. "The fundamental claim in antiwar protest is that those who control the state have broken the social contract by asking citizens to bear the burden of an unnecessary and harmful war. Because this challenge concerns the state's legitimacy, state officials are more likely to repress antiwar protest than would be the case with other social movements."[27]

There is opposition in some form to every war in the country's history. But when American presidents offer a pretext, any pretext, for grand, expensive "conflicts," citizens generally go along. Even when the mission is obscure or self-evidently disingenuous or involves a location that is both remote and mystifying. They go along, until, in the case of Vietnam, they change their mind.

THE HUMAN COSTS OF THE VIETNAM WAR

The Vietnam War or, as Vietnamese call it, the American War, has its human costs.

- A conservative estimate of two million Vietnamese dead through violence, deprivation, starvation, and Agent Orange and napalm exposure. Vietnamese officials place the human cost between three and four million.

- Fifty-eight thousand U.S. dead, another 150,000 wounded in action.

- Unexploded ordnance and mines kill 40,000 Vietnamese since 1975 as farmers and kids encounter odd, shiny objects in the fields that won't be completely cleared for at least 200 years.

- American B-52's ravage Laos, dropping a bomb payload on a country roughly the size of Southern California every eight seconds for nine years in an attempt to limit Communist logistical support along the Ho Chi Minh Trail.

- Cambodia suffers between 50,000 to 150,000 dead in its eastern provinces from President Richard Nixon's Operation Freedom Deal covert bombing campaign. The devastation is a major recruiting vehicle for the Khmer Rouge who take over the country in 1975.

LOST OPPORTUNITIES

There are opportunities to stop the war before it starts.

Ho Chi Minh, a Vietnamese nationalist attends the post-WWI Versailles peace talks in January 1919 as Nguyen Ai Quoc. He is the founder of the Association for Annamite Patriots, an organization of Vietnamese nationals based in Paris that opposes the brutal decades-long French occupation of Indochina. He asks for a meeting with U.S. President Woodrow Wilson and other world leaders to press his country's case for independence. He is refused, a disappointment given that self-determination is one of Wilson's core tenets in his Fourteen Points.

When the Japan invades Vietnam in 1940, it reaches an agreement with the French colonial government allowing access and occupation. Ho's communist-led independence fighters, known as the Viet Minh, fight the Japanese, eventually joining forces with the U.S. Office of Strategic Services (OSS). In the early days of World War II, President Franklin Delano Roosevelt tells his son Elliott that Americans wouldn't "be dying in the Pacific tonight if it hadn't been for the short-sighted greed of the French and the British and the Dutch." Roosevelt believes that, unless the French pledge eventual independence for her colonies, the United States wouldn't be justified in returning them "at all, ever." He writes to his Secretary of State, Cordell Hull, in January 1944, "France has milked it for 100 years. The people of Indo-China are entitled to something better than that."

On September 2, 1945, the same day the Japanese sign the surrender agreement formally ending World War II in the Pacific, Ho proclaims Vietnam independent at a Hanoi rally attended by an estimated half million, and presents the Vietnamese Declaration of Independence, which begins with the preamble to the U.S. Declaration. While Vietnamese nationalists long for and expect U.S. support, the new Truman administration instead decides to support the French fight against the Viet Minh, eventually funding 80 percent of the war's costs.[28]

The Vietnamese continue their struggle for independence and gain the upper hand, resulting in a 1954 peace conference that splits the country into the Communist north and capitalist south. When the U.S. resists the promised national election two years later, South Vietnamese known as the Viet Cong challenge the authority of the government with the support of the North.

The United States views the conflict as a critical front in the fight against communism; the Vietnamese as a short though vicious chapter in a millennium-long fight for independence. The coming decade of direct military combat with the United States comes after more than a half-century of resistance against the French and a thousand years of struggle against a succession of Chinese imperial armies.

OPPOSITION GROWS AS THE WAR ESCALATES

There are numerous perspectives as to which anti-war efforts turn the tide against the American debacle in Southeast Asia, including the contrarian belief that they mattered not at all, that it was a matter of time, that while most every battle was won by the United States military, the war was doomed to failure.

On September 21, 1963, the War Resisters League (WRL) organizes a demonstration at the U.S. Mission to the United Nations in New York City, arguably the first formal protest against the Vietnam War in the country. Nineteen days later, the WRL joins other groups to protest a speech of Madame Ngo Dinh Nhu, sister-in-law of South Vietnamese President Ngo Dinh Diem and 'de facto First Lady,' at New York's Waldorf-Astoria Hotel. Diem would be assassinated in a CIA-supported coup d'état three weeks before President John F. Kennedy's assassination in Dallas.

JFK's successor, President Lyndon Baines Johnson quickly shifts the U.S. focus from an 'advisory' to an active military role with an increase in covert operations.

Twelve men publicly burn their draft cards in New York City on May 12, 1964, acknowledged as the first such act of resistance to the war. On December 19, the WRL and other groups stage the first nationwide demonstrations

in more than 10 cities, with over 1,000 turning out in
New York City and in San Francisco.

Johnson goes live on national television the evening
of August 4, 1964, to promote the Gulf of Tonkin
Resolution, a request for congressional authorization to
escalate spending and troops deployments in Vietnam.
It's a response to an alleged attack earlier in the day on
the USS Maddox by North Vietnamese patrol boats.
Years later, Secretary of Defense Robert McNamara
admits that the Gulf of Tonkin attack never happens,
but is a mistaken set of radar readings by ship crew and
officers.

One week into 1965, a civilian group led by Premier
Troung Van Huong overthrows South Vietnam's
military. General Nguyen Khanh overthrows that
government on January 27th. The Khanh government is
toppled three weeks later in a third coup with Dr. Phan
Huy Quat as president.

At the end of March, the Students for a Democratic
Society (SDS) organizes a "teach-in" at the University
of Michigan at Ann Arbor, attended by 3,000 students.
Over 120 similar events are staged around the country
before the school year ends.

The SDS leads a March Against the Vietnam War in
mid-March in Washington, D.C., setting a record for an
anti-war protest with participation estimated at up to
20,000. Senator Ernest Gruening (D-AK) and singer
Joan Baez are among the participants. SDS President
Paul Potter speaks to the crowd about the dangers of
America's foreign policy posture.

The march is a turning point for student protests, with anti-war priorities switching from nuclear weapon proliferation and the Cold War to ending the war in Vietnam.

THE EFFECTS OF ANTI-WAR PROTESTS

Todd Gitlin's office is a stone's throw from Columbia University's Low Library administration building and Hamilton Hall, both occupied by student protesters in 1968. He now serves as professor and as chairman of the Ph.D. program of Columbia's Graduate School of Journalism, considered one of the world's preeminent academies of the craft. Gitlin is a prolific author, having penned eighteen books, and is both a public thinker on the matter of protest and public assembly, and, from an early age, a front-line activist, having served as third president of Students for a Democratic Society in 1963-1964. He organizes the SDS march on Washington in March 1965.

Did protests significantly contribute to the end of the war in Vietnam?

"Protest retarded the worsening of the war in Vietnam in certain crucial instances," says Gitlin, "which were generally unknown to the demonstrators at the time, because the administrations in the White House were keeping secret how they were reacting. Both under Johnson, and probably even more impressively, under Nixon, major escalations were planned but were called off because of political apprehension on the part of the administration. The war was getting out of hand, and people were grumpy. People in Congress were grumpy and people in their own parties were grumpy.

"At crucial moments, the movement exercised a veto power. It was significant. It saved a lot of lives.

"Did it end the war? No.

"Did these moments intensify the momentum of the legislators who wanted to see an end to the war? Yes.

"Did that eventually lead, in the '70s, to cutting off aid and to a decision by Nixon, first of all, to so-called Vietnamize the war? It was a fraudulent withdrawal because the air war intensified as the ground war got the American troops out of harm's way, but the bombs were still raining down.

"Because the war had become so controversial, so damaging politically, eventually Congress passed some crucial legislation that unplugged the war from funding. That was crucial. It took way too long. If certain events had been different, if certain politicians had made wiser moves, that war could have stopped before it started.

"On balance, something was achieved. It wasn't everything, but it was highly significant. It had also the effect of what George H. W. Bush later called the 'Vietnam syndrome,' which he thought he kicked once and for all, meaning that it became much harder for the administration to move large numbers of troops into foreign territory."

Still, deployments in 80 countries and the country has found a way to continue to fund Cold War-era military budgets.

"But," responds Gitlin, "Reagan, certainly a more bombastic and military-minded orator than we'd had before, even more so than Nixon, was forced into covert activity. The whole foofaraw about Iran-Contra was an attempt to disguise intervention. If he wanted a war, it had to be a weekend war like Grenada, after the U.S. had been driven out of Lebanon by a terror attack. There was a whole lot of fraudulent framing of what was happening, but it still is true that, between 1973 or so and 1990, there was no large-scale American military troop deployment."

"THIS MADNESS MUST CEASE"

Operation "Rolling Thunder," a U.S. bombing campaign against North Vietnamese targets, is launched in March 1965 and continues for three years. Johnson authorizes the use of napalm in the operation. The first American combat forces arrive; roughly 200,000 U.S. troops will be in Vietnam by the end of the year.

On the second day of November 1965, Norman Morrison douses himself in gasoline and sets himself on fire below McNamara's office of in view of thousands of Pentagon employees.

> Norman Morrison was a Quaker. He was opposed to war, the violence of war, the killing. He came to the Pentagon, doused himself with gasoline. Burned himself to death below my office. He held a child in his arms, his daughter. Passers-by shouted, "Save the child!" He threw the child out of his arms, and the child lived and is alive today. His wife issued a very moving statement: "Human beings must stop killing other human beings." And that's a belief that I shared. I shared it then and I believe it even more strongly today.
> – U.S. Secretary of Defense Robert McNamara in the Errol Morris documentary, *Fog of War*

During the first two months of 1966, Senator William Fulbright (D-Ark.), the chairman of the Senate Foreign Relations Committee, holds televised hearings with Ambassador George Kennan – architect of the USSR containment policy – challenging government justifications for the war.

Johnson increases the ceiling on the number of troops to 525,000 in January 1967. In April, Reverend Martin Luther King, Jr., declares "this madness must cease" in his speech, "Beyond Vietnam: A Time to Break the Silence," at New York City's Riverside Church.[29]

> We must stop now. I speak as a child of God and brother to the suffering poor of Vietnam. I speak for those whose land is being laid waste, whose homes are being destroyed, whose culture is being subverted. I speak for the poor of America who are paying the double price of smashed hopes at home and death and corruption in Vietnam. I speak as a citizen of the world, for the world as it stands aghast at the path we have taken. I speak as an American to the leaders of my own nation. The great initiative in this war is ours. The initiative to stop it must be ours.

On April 28, heavyweight boxing champion Muhammad Ali refuses induction into the armed services on religious grounds as a conscientious objector. He is sentenced to five years in prison, later winning on appeal to the United States Supreme Court in June 1971. During his three-year exile from boxing, Ali speaks often to the press and on college campuses about his political motivations, connecting his experiences with racial prejudice with America's conduct overseas.[30]

> "My conscience won't let me go shoot my brother, or some darker people, or some poor hungry people in the mud for big powerful America. And shoot them for what? They never called me nigger, they never lynched me, they didn't put no dogs on me, they didn't rob me of my nationality, rape and kill my mother and father... Shoot them for what? How can I shoot them poor people? Just take me to jail."

The National Mobilization Committee to End the War in Vietnam – nicknamed "the Mobe" – organizes The March on the Pentagon to Confront the War Makers from October 21-23. One hundred thousand gather at the Lincoln Memorial and the National Mall, one-third and one-half of whom continue to the Pentagon.

Four days later, Catholic priest Philip Berrigan, a World War II veteran, leads a group to a Baltimore, MD, draft board and drenches draft records with their own and chicken blood.

PACIFISM AND AMERICAN WAR RESISTANCE

"The protests had enormous impact," insists Ed Hedemann, longtime activist and organizer with the War Resisters League from the kitchen of the Brooklyn home he shares with partner and fellow organizer Ruth Benn. "The draft was bitterly fought and was ended. That was one of the great successes. The enormous demonstrations that kept building, and peaked in 1971. In public opinion, the movement had tremendous value in ending the war. Vietnamese fighting, or the guys in the U.S. military refusing to participate, were important factors, but you cannot leave out how popular opinion was changed with the resistance of people in this country."

We're most aware of the highly visible marches, rallies, and public events; what do you think were the most important efforts that brought the war to an end?

"Things like burning draft cards irritated the hell out of the government," says Hedemann. "You had people like (heavyweight boxing champion) Muhammad Ali, a very public person making a statement on principle; he hurt his career enormously to do that. (Popular folk singer) Joan Baez holding a press conference, talking about how she'd refuse to pay 60 percent of her taxes because of how that was contributing to the Vietnam War. It helped to have public figures speaking out. Then you had these visuals on television of the horrors of war."

"You saw every day what it looked like," says Benn, who served as Coordinator of the National War Tax Resistance Coordinating Committee (NWTRCC). "I think the G.I. resistance was huge when former soldiers were throwing away their medals."

The War Resisters League is founded in 1923, not long after the First World War. While religious groups often express conscientious objections to war, the WRL is perhaps the first, and certainly most enduring, secular pacifist organization in the country. The founders believe that while women are often opposed to war, it is important to get men, who do the fighting and the political decision-making, to refuse to participate.

"There is the famous story of A.J. Muste out picketing in front of the White House (nightly with a candle)," recalls Hedemann. "He was one man with a sign. A reporter comes up and asks him, 'Do you think you can change the government by doing this?' His response is, 'No, I'm not trying to change the government. I'm just trying to make sure they don't change me.'

"There is a lot of that, the small-scale actions, the impact. You never know when you do something, the impact it's going to have on somebody, a key person or there's a key moment, and then you just have to keep trying to do that. Sometimes it works and sometimes it doesn't, but it's not going to work if you don't do anything."

1968

Anti-war protests reach a crescendo in 1968 – the year of the Democratic Party convention, of the killings of Martin Luther King, Jr. and Robert F. Kennedy, of the Summer of Love, the year that President Johnson in a shocking admission of the corrosive impact of the Vietnam War on the body politic declares that he will not run for re-election, the year of the election of Republican Richard Milhous Nixon, who promises peace with honor, the year of the French student protests at the Sorbonne and the year that the students of Columbia University take over the Low Library administration building and Hamilton Hall.

During a ceasefire imposed by the North Vietnamese for the Tet Holiday, the Viet Cong attack 44 South Vietnamese provincial capitals, 64 district capitals, and five major cities, as well as the U.S. embassy in Saigon on January 31.

While the offensive is a military disaster for the Communists in terms of casualties and captured territory, it's a turning point in American public opinion on the desirability of a continued military presence. More citizens doubt the administration's war policy than defend it for the first time.[31]

Walter Cronkite, CBS anchorman and the "most trusted man in America" according to one poll[32], reacts to the Tet Offensive much like many other Americans – with shock, disbelief, and bewilderment. "What the hell is going on," he asks when the news of the first attacks reach him. "I thought we were winning the war."[33]

He visits South Vietnam a second time since 1965 on a two-week fact-finding trip which changes his previous

pro-war position on Vietnam. His goal was to find out
how the enemy could launch attacks at more than 100
locations – including the U.S. embassy in Saigon and
the South Vietnamese presidential palace – when the
president and his top aides insist that the war was going
well. He presents his findings in a one-hour evening
broadcast on February 27, 1968.[34]

> "Tonight, back in the more familiar surroundings
> of New York, we'd like to sum up our findings in
> Vietnam, an analysis that must be speculative,
> personal, subjective ... We have been too often
> disappointed by the optimism of the American
> leaders, both in Vietnam and Washington,
> to have faith any longer in the silver linings
> they find in the darkest clouds ... For it seems
> now more certain than ever that the bloody
> experience of Vietnam is to end in a stalemate
> ... To say that we are closer to victory today
> is to believe, in the face of the evidence, the
> optimists who have been wrong in the past. To
> suggest we are on the edge of defeat is to yield
> to unreasonable pessimism. To say that we are
> mired in stalemate seems the only realistic, yet
> unsatisfactory, conclusion. On the off chance
> that military and political analysts are right, in
> the next few months we must test the enemy's
> intentions, in case this is indeed his last big gasp
> before negotiations. But it is increasingly clear
> to this reporter that the only rational way out
> then will be to negotiate, not as victors, but as an
> honorable people who lived up to their pledge to
> defend democracy, and did the best they could.
>
> "This is Walter Cronkite. Good night."

Thirty-three days later, Johnson announces he won't
seek re-election.

In August, the Democratic National Convention is witness to violent clashes between police and protesters as Chicago Mayor Daley refuses to issue demonstration permits. Vice President Hubert Humphrey secures the Democratic nomination amidst the turmoil.

Richard Nixon wins a three-way race for president against Democrat Humphrey and Independent George Wallace of Alabama by promising an honorable end to the war while secretly suggesting to the South Vietnamese government that they abandon peace talks prior to the election to bolster his chances.

TAX PROTESTS AND WAR RESISTANCE

To protest the Vietnam War, the WRL's Hedemann says there were over 20,000 people refusing some or all of their income tax, with an estimated 500,000 refusing to pay the telephone excise tax, designed as "a war tax."

"In that whole (war tax) movement, I would say, maybe 30 have been sent to jail and it isn't for refusal to pay, except in two instances. It's been falsifying forms, not answering questions and saying, 'First Amendment' and that's very rare."

"These days, the military is very glorified," adds Benn. "If you go to the movies, you see an ad for how wonderful it is to be in the military.

Or the movie itself is an ad for the military.

"It's so deep into the culture, yes. It really has intensified," says Benn.

Hedemann adds, "I would say, most people go into the military, not because they believe in war. It's because of the economic pressure. That's why the military is made up of a lot of poor people. It's not made of rich people."

What's the driving ideology of the War Resisters League, and how did you decide to get involved?

"The focus was to prevent another world war or another war," says Hedemann, "and just get enough men to refuse to participate, to get up to a critical level. Albert Einstein was touring the U.S. in the early- to mid-30s as honorary chairman, (saying) that if we could get two percent of the population to refuse to participate in war, that would bring down the government, and that will stop it.

"That was the sort of operating psychology in the early years. It was, just don't participate in the next war. Things changed, of course, with World War II, but being against war in the '30s was a very popular thing. There was the Oxford Pledge, big thing, started in Britain, where people renounced war and would not participate."

"The history of resistance is pretty much shoveled underground," says Lisa Miller, another longtime WRL supporter who joins the kitchen table conversation. "When I first went to work at the War Resisters office, there were these World War II resisters who had spent time in jail. These were not people who were trying to get out of it because they have a bone spur. These were people who went to jail for what they believed. For the most part, their story is a part of American history that's not talked about."

Is there a playbook or model for being effective as an activist?

"My view," concludes Hedemann, "is to contribute something to society to make it a better world and to oppose the evil things that go on in the world to the extent that I can do that. I think that's being successful, whether or not I actually achieve ending war. I have this vision of a world in the future, maybe 100 years from now, and it's probably optimistic, that people or young people will look back and say, 'What is war? Why did people go to war?' and it will be a mystery, like people looking back to the 1800s saying, 'Why did people have slaves?'"

THE BEGINNING OF THE END

The first withdrawal of 25,000 troops from Vietnam begins in June 1969, totaling 110,000 by the end of the year. In November, Nixon signs into law a bill changing the draft to a lottery system; two lotteries follow immediately. On November 15, between 500,000-600,000 people participate the second Moratorium to End the War in Vietnam march and in Washington, D.C., the largest U.S. demonstration to date in U.S. history.

Student protests erupt nationwide in April 1970 when Nixon announces plans to invade Cambodia. On May 4 students clash with local police at Kent State University in Ohio. An ROTC building is set on fire; students hinder firefighters by slicing their hoses. The governor sends in the National Guard, which fires into a crowd of students, killing four and injuring 13. Four million students go on strike at more than 450 universities and colleges. The song *Ohio*, written by Neil Young, becomes a national protest anthem.

As the war drags into 1971, Vietnam Veterans Against the War (VVAW), led by future Senator and Secretary of State John Kerry, testify before Congress from April 22-28. Kerry asks the question, "How do you ask a man to be the last man to die in Vietnam?"

On June 13, *The New York Times* begins publication of the Pentagon Papers, a damning set of internal documents on government conduct in Vietnam from 1945-1967 leaked by one of its authors, Daniel Ellsberg. The Nixon administration files an injunction against *The Times* to prevent continued publication, but is stymied when *The Washington Post* also runs the papers, soon followed by more than a dozen other newspapers. Senator Mike Gravel (D-AK) enters over 4,000 pages edited by Howard Zinn and Noam Chomsky into the Congressional record. The Supreme Court rules 6-3 in favor of *The New York Times'* right to publish the papers.

On August 22, Ron Kovic, a wheelchair-bound Vietnam veteran, leads fellow veterans into the 1972 Republican National Convention in Miami Beach shouting, "Stop the bombing! Stop the war!" as Richard Nixon begins his acceptance speech.

GRASSROOTS DEMOCRACY AND THE LEVERS OF POWER

"The approach of the anti-Vietnam War protests was to stop business as usual and to make it as uncomfortable as possible for the business community," says Norman Stockwell, publisher of The Progressive, "Through the G.I. resistance within the military and also through the resistance that was going on in the streets, through keeping various government officials from being able to speak in public without getting heckled and harassed, and blocking streets, traffic and so on. I think that it had a significant effect on moving the dial, both of public opinion and, ultimately, of the opinion of corporate power as well, when it became too costly in terms of time and effort, and actual dollars, to continue the conduct of that war. "

Norman Stockwell worked in community radio for 35 years before joining the Madison, Wisconsin-based national print and web publication. The Progressive runs numerous projects including the Public School

Shakedown, which addresses issues in public education, and the Progressive Media Project, which trains activists from diverse backgrounds in the skills of writing op-eds for daily newspapers. 'Progressive' to Stockwell means "grassroots democracy and working for positive social change." The magazine is founded in 1909 by Robert M. 'Fighting Bob' La Follette, a popular governor and senator who opposes President Woodrow Wilson's stance on entering World War I. He is an independent presidential candidate in 1924 and is selected one of the five greatest United States Senators of all time in 1957 by a Senate committee.

"The motto of the magazine from its very first edition was, 'Ye shall know the truth and the truth shall make you free' (*John* 8:32)," recounts Stockwell. "It's the idea of giving people information, so that they can make effective decisions. La Follette was very much in that tradition of progressive activism, speaking out against corporate power, corporate influence in our electoral system, speaking for the everyday working people, particularly farmers.

"He also was a big proponent of direct democracy, and it was his push for the direct election of senators and for political primaries in states that ended up influencing the national structure of our government.

To what degree did protests end the Vietnam War in your view?

"It was a significant factor," believes Stockwell. "I think that what you had were protests in the streets making a difference, both in terms of raising general public opposition to the war, and raising the consciousness of the everyday public. People were getting killed, and they were the friends and neighbors of everybody who was watching the news and voting.

"A classic example is Admiral Elmo Zumwalt, who was a big proponent of Agent Orange, until his son got an Agent Orange-related cancer, and then, suddenly, he changed his view on it. I think those kinds of things were an influence.

"Also, the dissolution in the army itself, the Vietnam Veterans Against the War and Veterans for Peace, the actual soldiers refusing to serve, and the G.I. coffeehouse movement, as well as incidents of violence like fragging.

"What you had was the military becoming less and less effective, being hollowed out, if you will, by protest within. You had the fact that the Vietnamese, who had sustained far more casualties than the U.S. side, were willing to keep fighting and were fighting effectively, partly because it was their territory and they knew the ground better.

"All of those factors together, but I think that the protest movement was a significant factor in ending the war."

You mentioned consciousness-raising. Is that part of what protests do?

"I think people standing up and protesting raises the issue for folks who didn't know anything about it before. There's a great Pete Seeger song, My Name Is Lisa Kalvelage, about a woman who was born in Nuremberg, Germany, and was questioned after the war about what she did during the war, what her parents did, and so on. Then she and a couple other women go out and make hand-lettered signs and protest the use of napalm in Vietnam. That kind of incident happened over and over again all across the country.

"Ramparts magazine printed a whole full-color spread of the pictures of children who were burned by napalm, and then protesters took those photos to speeches by administration officials and said, this was what napalm did to children. That kind of thing, that role of consciousness-raising, is critical."

What makes for successful activism?

"I think that a couple of things have to happen for a movement to be successful," explains Stockwell. "One is that it has to reach beyond the groups that are most narrowly affected. It has to become something that other people see as, 'That's happening to them and it could happen to me, too,' or, 'What's happening to them affects me as well,' so you have to widen that circle.

"The second thing is that the protest movement itself has to effectively identify what are the levers of power in the situation. What is it that we can do in order to effectively stimulate the decision-makers to make change? In the case of the Vietnam War, it was making the war undesirable to the people who were voting the money to support it.

"You have those moments, but you also have a lot of roll back, and so it's very important to continually adapt strategies and tactics, and to build that circle of solidarity and community of interest in the issue. The small group of women with their signs protesting the manufacturer of napalm in California didn't stop the manufacturer of napalm, but it was one piece of a larger circle of protests, which eventually had the effect of informing people, and now napalm is a banned weapon internationally."

THE WAR ENDS

Nixon is reelected in a landslide and, in December 1972,

more than 36,000 tons of ordnance are dropped on
Hanoi and Haiphong in the 12-day "Christmas bombing."
It is the most concentrated air campaign in history,
exceeding the entire tonnage dropped from 1969-1971.
Massive protests and allies like Australia criticize the
assault. As the year draws to a close, American and North
Vietnamese negotiators in Paris are close to a peace
agreement after four years of negotiations.

At Nixon's second inauguration on January 20, 1973,
20,000 people attend a "Plea for Peace" concert at
Washington Cathedral. The next day, VVAW members
march from Arlington National Cemetery to the Lincoln
Memorial; 85,000 attend the demonstration.

A ceasefire is declared as the Paris Peace Accords are
signed on January 27, 1973. After repeated violations
of the ceasefire by both sides, the North Vietnamese
capture Saigon on April 30, 1975, effectively reunifying
the Vietnamese government under Communist control.

ASSESSING IMPACT

*When asked for an assessment of impact of Columbia
University's highly publicized stretch of building takeovers,
student demands, and police intrusions in 1968, Professor
Gitlin changes the subject.*

"I'm going to dance to the side of your question. What
is a protest? What is it we're talking about? Is a protest
a picket line or a sit-in; or is a protest an element in
a long-running campaign whose scope outreaches
the immediate goal or the immediate professed goal,
or what some people who organize the event think
is the professed goal, but then enlarges and rolls into
something else? It all depends on the time-frame we're
asking about.

"So, was the Montgomery Bus Boycott a success? Rosa Parks got arrested on the day after. I don't know what she felt. But some people probably understood that this was a moment in a campaign, and others might have felt like, 'God, they just did it again. They threw the black lady off the bus,' and so on.

"It wasn't clear for more than a year that the bus boycott would succeed in costing the bus company so much money that they would end up caving in, and even when that was achieved, can we say that the campaign was a success? Yes, one bus line was integrated. Others had been quietly integrated without anybody really noticing around the South. But we think of that as a benchmark, because it takes its place within this whole sway of activity that we call the 'civil rights movement.'

"If you go around and you find people who were at this or that demonstration, and you ask them, 'What do you make of it after this time?' it's going to depend a lot on who you're asking. Are you asking somebody who was in it for the duration, or somebody who just came in, went to an event, came to a certain conclusion about it, and then went away? You're going to get very different takes on the experience. That's the first element. It's sort of elementary.

"Let's think about the movement against university investment and other investments in South Africa in the '80s, which I was involved in as a faculty member at Berkeley and as an alumnus at Harvard. There was a lot of clamor, a lot of activity for a year or two, depending; it was a national movement. Did it accomplish the goal of getting university and some other funds to divest from South Africa investments? Partially.

"Did it end apartheid? No. Did it contribute to a process, which did undermine apartheid and help end it? Yes.

"You can actually trace a trajectory, which starts on a modest scale on a campus like this one or Berkeley, and then it snowballs. That's a very typical kind of protest that you could say, yes, it does succeed, but not in the first instance. That is to say, it's rare that somebody protests something, and then the next day, a change is made.

"Part of what you will find is that your sense of the meaning of the event or events is contingent on your sense of the time span. Are you playing a long game? How impatient are you? So, most protests, in the short run, fail.

There were massive protests against the 2003 Iraq War. There was and is a widely held belief that money has so saturated American politics that elected officials pay more attention to their funders than to their constituents. Thus, Bush and Cheney went ahead and did what they were going to do. Why were those protests ineffective?

"I think that analysis is very shallow," argues Gitlin. "As you suggested in the second part of your question, Bush was going to go to war. Everything was riding on it. His balls were riding on it. His daddy was riding on it. His 'weak in the knees' after September 11 was riding on it. I can't imagine a scenario that would have truncated that war or even nipped it in the bud.

"All wars are political situations, and had a different administration been in power, had there been wiser judgments on the part of many politicians, then the war, which was unnecessary and stupid from the beginning, as well as sinful, would not have materialized, but there was no way that war was going to be blocked."

Gitlin has a handy answer when queried what he would say to a young activist – his full-length book on the subject, *Letters to a Young Activist*, perhaps a political homage to the Rainer Maria Rilke classic *Letters to a Young Poet*. Gitlin has loads of copies lining an upper shelf of his office and, in a dangerous act of generosity, stands on the verboten upper step of a small ladder to fetch one. Apparently, the professor had some choice words for former presidential candidate Ralph Nader, which were not well received. So, Nader, finding the book on remainder, buys a thousand copies and ships them to the author as a sort of spite purchase. Gitlin takes a moment to sign a copy with the inscription, *"In the ecstatic search for decency."*

The book's conclusion neatly tracks the author's reflections on the Vietnam War.[35]

> Each challenge is unique and each is identical – to do what's possible by finding out what's possible and, in the process, overcome what seemed possible.
>
> Some borrowed wisdom.
>
> From Samuel Beckett in *Worstward Ho*: "Try again. Fail again. Fail better."
>
> From a civil rights song: "Keep your eyes on the prize, hold on."

6. THE CONSERVATIVE MOVEMENT:
A CONVERSATION WITH DR. PAUL MATZKO

"There is no ahistorical thing called conservatism," posits Dr. Paul Matzko, who's spent years studying the intersection of politics and religion in 20th century America. His book – *The Radio Right: How a Band of Broadcasters Took on the Federal Government and Built the Modern Conservative Movement* – pegs 1960s right-wing radio preachers as the nexus of modern conservatism.[36]

"Conservatism is a political construct that looks different depending on place and time. Nineteenth-century Tory conservatism in Great Britain is vastly different than 20th century American conservatism. So different that you marvel at the use of the same terms to describe very discrete phenomena."

It can mean anything.

"Yes. There's this stage in the history of American conservatism that goes from about 1964 to about 2016. The term that we use in academic history would be fusionist conservatism, with William F. Buckley, *National Review* as the kind of intellectual masthead."

Matzko holds a B.A. from the conservative Christian Bob Jones University, an M.A. from Temple, and a Ph.D. in history from Pennsylvania State University. He is the Tech and Innovation Editor at Libertarianism.org, the Cato Institute's "treasury of resources about the theory and history of liberty." The conversation is held at the Institute's D.C. headquarters.

THE FATHER(S) OF MODERN CONSERVATISM

On November 19, 1955, William F. Buckley founds the *National Review*, a "conservative weekly journal of opinion," boldly declaring, in its first issue, "It stands athwart history, yelling stop, at a time when no one is inclined to do so."

Buckley, for decades, is the genteel, literate holy-warrior of what he calls the conservative movement, a reaction to post-WWII liberal governance and social mores. Movements often take visible forms such as marches, campus occupations, and civil disobedience, but media is revolution by keyboard and image and Buckley presses his case for a half century. In his first speech to the Conservative Political Action Conference in March 1981, President Ronald Reagan praises the *National Review* as a guiding light.

From 1966 to 1999, Buckley hosts *Firing Line*, the enduring heavyweight champion of public affairs television programs, more than 1,500 weekly episodes in the can. "There's nothing like watching old episodes of *Firing Line*," Matzko reminisces, "and then watching anything being produced today, especially in the right-wing media ecosystem. The level of intellectual discourse has fallen off dramatically."

Firing Line provides a forum of elevated, persuasive voices to turn the rising tide for conservative values under siege. "He's interested in engaging with the best arguments of his opponents versus, today, it's just about owning the opponents, owning the libs. That's not the life of the mind, intellectual engagement. It's not a good-faith conversation."

Buckley is erudite, usually respectful, open to persuasion or expert at feigning it, while debating leftist thinkers such as Noam Chomsky, Christopher Hitchens, and Norman Mailer. Beat poet Allen Ginsberg asks and receives permission to chant *Hare Krishna* on-air, with harmonium accompaniment. Buckley allows lengthy answers and believes debate rather than hectoring is a superior form of persuasion, though gleefully delivering a dose of patrician snark when annoyed.

"Back in the '60s," explains Matzko, "you have coming together these threads, these intellectual streams, one of which is a Catholic social conservatism, a Catholic traditionalism. Buckley is represented there, but so are other Catholic intellectuals like Russell Kirk who emphasizes the importance of traditional social institutions, church, family, faith, home, hearth, etc. That is wedded with Cold War anti-communism, this fear that communism is not just the U.S.'s enemy, but an existential threat to Western civilization as we know it. The Milton Friedmans and Chicago School economists, Hayek, the Austrian folks, that stream gets incorporated into the mix as well, the government should stay out of economic affairs.

"That tripod makes sense in that particular place in time, that particular cultural milieu. But the problem is, that milieu changes. After the end of the Cold War, the logic of having the economic laissez-faire people and the national security state/ military-industrial complex-type people working together in close harmony stops making nearly as much sense. So, as conditions change, that thing we call conservatism, those internal tensions between those streams start to heighten and they start to become divides.

"We're seeing since the end of the Cold War, but accelerating the last decade, the splintering apart of fusionist conservatism into its constituent subsets, and the rise of something new to replace it, one ideology to rule them all, which is ethno-nationalism, Trump-style economic populism combined with this nativist vision, of America, for America."

THE RISE AND REACH OF CHRISTIAN RIGHT RADIO

Matzko rejects the prevailing creation myths of modern conservative ideologies and allegiances. At its peak in the 1960s, the *National Review's* circulation was dwarfed by the audiences of right-wing evangelic preachers, and the audience profile does not fit the stereotype.

"It's a movement of the mind. It starts with the intellectual class, and then they find their champion. Clarence Manion, a Catholic lawyer (dean of the Notre Dame Law School and host of the radio show *Manion Forum* which later airs on television) and radio broadcaster recruits the ghost writer (L. Brent Bozell, Jr.) for *The Conscience of a Conservative*, (Arizona Senator) Barry Goldwater's campaign biography. No one writes their own campaign biographies. Essentially, they recruit Goldwater to be the political face of the conservative movement."

Bozell is Buckley's brother-in-law and comrade-in-arms on the Yale debate team. His son, L. Brent Bozell III, would years later become head of right-wing media watchdog, the Media Research Center, and go on to co-author *Whitewash: What the Media Won't Tell You About Hillary Clinton, but Conservatives Will* (2007).

"The standard narrative is, it starts with a bunch of intellectuals who recruit some politicians, who – even when Goldwater gets crushed in '64 – inspire the younger generation of conservative activists to get engaged in politics and in movement activism. Eventually, as they age and get careers, they're ready for the Reagan revolution.

"The problem with that narrative is it's not a social movement narrative. That's not a movement of grassroots people and activism. It's a movement of intellectuals and politicians. That's the top-down narrative of the rise of the New Right." And Matzko thinks it's wrong.

National Review's circulation of 60,000 by the mid-1960s is impressive for a magazine. "But it's not Buckley who's inspiring grassroots activists. Carl McIntire is the biggest broadcaster of right-wing radio by 1964, reaching 20 million people a week. That's as many as Rush Limbaugh in his peak in the early-2000s.

"McIntire is the largest," adds Matzko, "but Clarence Manion, Billy James Hargis… there's at least a dozen broadcasters on 100 or more radio stations nationwide with huge listening audiences and annual budgets in the millions. These are big outfits."

Christian fundamentalists such as Hargis take a strong stance on numerous political issues. They view government-enforced racial integration, particularly the desegregation of schools as required by the landmark 1954 *Brown v. Board of Education* Supreme Court ruling, as a liberal apostasy. Hargis and McIntire lead the attack, leveraging the growing outrage of white listeners. They argue that civil rights agitators are part of a plot to destroy Protestant churches and create a godless America.

A stocky man in suit and tie sits with a sheath of papers in a small radio studio. He looks concerned. No, he's angry. The coast-to-coast broadcast starts with its theme music, the soaring finale of *The Battle Hymn of the Republic* – "*His truth is marching on!*" An announcer introduces the program with an urgent tone: "And now speaking *for* Christ and *against* communism, Reverend Billy James Hargis." Hargis lifts his script and begins to read.[37]

> Developments in Red Cuba 90 miles off the shores of Florida hold more ominous warnings for a sleeping American public. While the deadly enemies of America close in for their final stages of encircling our nation, enemy agents intensify efforts to chip away at the foundations upon which American freedom rests. More and more strange voices call for surrendering of our national sovereignty to some type of world authority. There are increasing efforts to centralize authority in our federal government in Washington, D.C. under the guise of federal aid.

Hargis expresses weekly outrage at welfare programs, foreign aid, involvement in international organization such as the United Nations, insisting that they're all part of a communist conspiracy to bankrupt America. His successors would also rail against budget deficits and executive power, almost exclusively during Democratic Presidential administrations. There is support for anti-communist Muslim insurgencies and no concern of a global Islamic caliphate; until the Cold War ends, after which Muslims become a fresh existential threat to God's providential nation.

HOUSEWIFE POPULISM

"What they do," explains Matzko, "is take ideas from the intellectual class, the Buckley types, and repackage them and use them in their broadcasts. You're a housewife living in St. Augustine, Florida. You hear on the radio that President Kennedy is undermining American sovereignty

by encouraging the import of Eastern European goods
from behind the Iron Curtain – Polish hams, Yugoslavian
wicker baskets. You're told this is destroying American
sovereignty and power, and putting our boys in Vietnam
at risk because that money is being funneled by the
Soviets to Ho Chi Minh and the Vietcong.

"The next time you go to your department store, you see
one of those baskets on the shelf. You see a Polish ham
advertised in the display case. You start to think, I won't
have this. Because you're being fed this diet of outrage.

"Then, you're told on the radio that there are people
who are doing something about this and you should join
this grassroots committee formed to boycott retailers
who are selling these Eastern European goods. You
reach out and ask, is there a chapter in your area? No,
there isn't. 'I'm going to start one.' I have this obligation
to my community, to my family, to fight for America and
stop the import of these goods.

"Ultimately, the committee starts over 400 chapters
around the country. They get the biggest retailers in
the country to drop the boycotted goods. The Polish
and Yugoslavian embassies complain to the Kennedy
administration about how much that hurts their
trade with the U.S. Congress rebukes the Kennedy
administration because it's getting so much pressure
from constituents. That is effective grassroots
movement activism, fueled by right-wing radio."

Hargis has an unexpected pause in his ministry in 1974,
when forced to resign as American Christian College
president due to allegations he had seduced male and
female students.

"Later in his life, McIntire stops broadcasting entirely
due to a struggling ministry and taxes owed. The city of

Collingswood, New Jersey seizes his building and letters with it. So we have a unique view into his listeners.

"In his papers, there's stuff that normally wouldn't be kept, including several years' worth of donor envelopes," Matzko explains. "You can go through and see exactly who is sending in money across a several-years' span of time. I can tell you that the median donor to one of these right-wing radio stations is likely a middle-aged woman, a suburban housewife. The letters say, 'Mrs. Husband's Name.' If you look up the addresses, they're in the suburbs of Philadelphia, the suburbs of St. Louis, the suburbs of Miami. It's suburban dwellers and small-dollar donors, most giving $1, $2, $5 a month, not big-dollar donations.

"This also cuts against another theory that's popular in the historiography of the right-wing, which is to emphasize the corporate backing of modern conservatism, industrialists, corporate executives, people with money. It's not untrue; there are corporate backers of modern conservatism. But small-dollar donors are the ones who fuel right-wing radio. They are distributed all across the nation."

Not just the rural South.

"The letters written in donor envelopes tend to be from stay-at-home moms, married to white-collar employees, pharmacists, doctors, lawyers, engineers, small-business owners.

"That's the median listener, and it makes sense. You're home all day doing chores or whatever. You turn on the radio. They're the ones who are getting the heaviest dose of this new medium."

GRASSROOTS CONSERVATIVE POLITICS

What appealed to those women or to those listeners? Was it a fear that the world was changing? Was there some core economic or sociological driver?

"I looked at historians like Michelle Nickerson and others who described right-wing women who are engaged in conservative grassroots politics. They call it housewife populism.

"It's actually not just conservative," proposes Matzko. "See, there's a long tradition of housewife populism on both left and right, going all the way back through American history. And behind the idea of housewife populism is the idea that America, the nation, is our national home. And just as I have an obligation as a housewife to care for, protect and provide for my literal home, I am, in a sense, housewife to the nation. I have a moral obligation to protect, provide and care for the national home as well.

"You can see how that fits into the boycott. They decide what comes into the home, what is pure, clean and good. So, too, shouldn't the housewife populists have a say in what comes into the national home. Not these impure Polish hams, these communism-infected Yugoslavian baskets."

Yugoslavia was of course independent, but in the mind of many Americans, it was all part of the international communist conspiracy.

"To the American housewife, it doesn't matter. One of these donors sent a donation to Carl McIntire. 'Thank you for your good work in defending our country. Here's my little donation. I got this Christmas advertisement from Krakus (a Polish meat manufacturer).' There's a little note stapled to it. 'How long must I endure this? My son is in Vietnam.'

"I can criticize the policy understanding of what they were doing. I can't criticize their visceral feeling. They were feeling what they were feeling."

They're feeling what they were feeling because that sense was perpetuated by politicians and media.

"Yes, they're being taken advantage of in that sense," says Matzko. "She literally thought, when people buy Polish hams, they're putting bullets in the guns of the people shooting at my son over in Vietnam. As silly as that causal chain is, put yourself in her shoes for the moment. What would you feel like if you believe what she does? How angry that would make you and how much would that impel you towards movement activism? Women like this, those that Lisa McGirr writes about in *Suburban Warriors* really are the movement drivers."

> These "kitchen-table" activists have fundamentally shaped the course of American politics, and yet, until now, they have lived in obscurity. They have done so in part because their mobilization has been overshadowed by the more flamboyant Left and its movement culture... But at the same time, buffered and buffeted by these progressive gains, conservative intellectuals, politicians, and pastors - together with thousands of grassroots activists – set in place the ideas, strategies, and politics that would pave their road to national power. [38]

"By reorienting from looking at the intellectual and political leadership of conservatism as the source of the New Right to looking at the grassroots activists, it makes it a story that's less about a bunch of elite men, more a story about ordinary women. That's a helpful corrective.

"They're the ones who are forming coffee klatches to talk about conservative books – like *The Conscience of a Conservative* by Goldwater, *None Dare Call it Treason* (by anti-communist author and pastor John A. Stormer), or anything by Phyllis Schlafly – the ones who are out there forming conservative consciousness, knocking on doors for political candidates. It's women who drive the right."

The *AuH$_2$O* 'Goldwater Girls' in the 1964 election is a contingent of women supporters who dress up in the chemical symbols for gold (Au) and water (H$_2$O). They go to all his rallies. Contrary to perceptions, it's a woman-driven movement, according to Matzko.

"Political historians talk about a period of center-left, consensus liberalism after World War II, which unifies around a couple of things. First of all, general support for a broader welfare state. There are arguments with just how big the welfare state should be, but there's a kind of post-New Deal acceptance. The policy difference between Democratic President Truman and Republican President Eisenhower on issues relating to the welfare state are matters of quantity, not quality. They were relatively close."

Republicans in the '50s, '60s and '70s, were often at the forefront of social welfare (health care, education) and environmental issues.

"The distance between the two parties then is slight compared to today," points out Matzko. "What drives the rise of the new right is cheap, affordable and broad access to the radio airwaves and other media. Now radical voices, both from right and left, are able to reach a broad national constituency in a way that wasn't possible during the era of network radio control."

THE FAIRNESS DOCTRINE AND THE END OF EQUAL TIME

Until the late 1980s, radio and television station owners had to present controversial issues with multiple perspectives to fulfill a legal requirement for maintaining their broadcasting licenses.

Then, right-wing broadcasters rally their grassroots base with an audacious legal argument: regulations requiring the airing of opposing arguments infringe on their right of free speech. For six decades, the federal government seeks to promote free speech by allowing citizens of differing views to be heard, deeming broadcast frequencies a scarce public resource. President Ronald Reagan's FCC (Federal Communications Commission) chair rules in 1987 that the Fairness Doctrine will no longer be enforced; subsequent efforts to revitalize it fall flat.

As a result, describes Matzko, "Arguably, the combination of talk radio and Fox News, conservative cable broadcasting, has more influence in Republican politics than the Republican Party leadership these days."

Rupert Murdoch famously pays cable TV operators $11 per subscriber to help launch *Fox News* in 1996. Many scoff at the massive payout incentive at the time, but it turns out to be an excellent investment, one of the company's largest cash flow contributors.[39]

Liberal network Air America emerged for a brief moment (2004-2010), then died. There have been numerous liberal hosts over the years, with varying degrees of success, and the five-station Pacifica network has endured for more than a half century.

Why have conservatives uniquely harnessed the power of talk radio?

"Left-wing talk radio is flourishing in the late-80s, early-90s," says Matzko. "Historian Brian Rosenwald wrote a great dissertation about why talk radio takes this right-wing bent.[40] It wasn't immediately obvious. You had left-wing versions of Rush Limbaugh. His explanation is that right-wing radio didn't have competition in the same way that left-wing radio did in NPR (National Public Radio). Most of NPR's syndicated programming is respectable center-left. They're not radicals. If you're right-wing talk radio or if you're early-Rush Limbaugh, your listeners aren't the type of people who tend to listen to NPR. You've got everything right of center as wide open. That's your potential listener pool.

"If you're trying to start left-wing talk radio, a big chunk of your listeners will be listening to NPR."

In presidential election year 2016, 25% of Americans over the age of 18 cite radio as a frequent news source, according to a Pew Research Center survey, about 62 million listeners.[41] NPR estimates just under 15 million listeners each for *All Things Considered* and *Morning Edition*.[42] Popular shows at the time include Rush Limbaugh and Sean Hannity, both at 15 million, according to *Talkers Magazine*. Ten of the top 15 radio shows in America are conservative talk or financial in nature. Only the two aforementioned NPR programs and the BBC World Service are considered centrist or center-left.[43]

SOCIAL MOVEMENTS AND DISCONTENT

There is an element of protest to right-wing radio, a discomfort with certain trends in the culture, and these programs are articulating and empowering a listener's point of view.

"Sociologists like Talcott Parsons, Sidney Tarrow, and Charles Tilly defined a theory of where social movements come from, why do they sometimes work and sometimes not. For a successful social movement, you need a set of discontented people, some folks who are angry about some change. You have that in the 1960s. There are folks, potential conservatives, who are starting to be perturbed by the sexual revolution. Their kids go off to college and they come back with a prescription for the pill, or their primary school kid is in a Sex Ed class that's being mandated by the state."

And then there's the music.

"There was a sublimated racism there, too. Rock and roll and jazz are identified as black people's music, so there was opposition to this new music because it was white kids listening to black music, black music about sex. Sex, drugs, and rock and roll, right? I can't have my kids listening to that.

"In fact, early on, it was called race music before it was called rock and roll, because most of the early pioneers in rock and roll were black artists. Rock and roll's primary success comes from white groups 'covering' music written by and for black artists.

"Yes, they were angry about all the social transformations from incipient desegregation to the sexual revolution to just youth culture in general. There is a lot of cultural ferment, triggering discontent among proto-conservatives. But that's not enough. People can be angry about lots of things, but that doesn't lead to a social movement. You need what we call resource mobilization, someone to do the work of organization and you need someone to activate that discontent. How do they get to know that they share that discontent with other people? You have to build the movement to draw people together in the sense of a collective."

Matzko makes the argument that "independent radio, the rise of right-wing radio does that in the 1960s. It takes isolated discontented people and activates them, turns them, and gives them the sense of 'I'm part of a movement.' It's hard to imagine the Tea Party absent talk radio and cable, the famous soliloquy from CNBC. It goes national. Everyone sees. There's this guy who feels like I do. It makes them aware that there are (others), and then they're turning on the radio and hearing that there's this movement of tea parties being formed."

THE TEA PARTY AND THE RANT HEARD ROUND THE WORLD

On February 19, 2009, CNBC on-air editor Rick Santelli calls for a Chicago Tea Party in remarks that became known as the 'Rant Heard 'Round the World.' A $275 billion federal government mortgage bailout had just been signed by President Barack Obama, after a much larger bailout of the banking system.

Conservative activists begin organizing a series of 'tea party' events, mimicking the Revolutionary War-era Boston Tea Party, often focused on the growing federal debt and fiscal responsibility, though the Santelli rant made no mention of deficits. While cited as populist (a person or party representing the interests of ordinary citizens), Santelli's entertaining tirade, to the cheers of traders on the floor of the Chicago Board of Trade, attacks the government for helping "losers" avoid foreclosure caused by the subprime mortgage debacle.

> "The government was promoting bad behavior! How about this, president (Obama) and new administration? Why don't you put up a website to have people vote on the Internet as a

referendum to see if we really want to subsidize the losers' mortgages; or would we like to at least buy cars and buy houses in foreclosure and give 'em to people that might have a chance to actually prosper down the road, and reward people that could carry the water instead of drink the water?

"This was America! How many of you people want to pay for your neighbor's mortgage that has an extra bathroom and can't pay their bills? Raise their hand. (*Booing*) President Obama, are you listening?"

The homeowner package comes on the heels of the Emergency Economic Stabilization Act signed into law by President George W. Bush on October 3, 2008. It creates the $700 billion Troubled Asset Relief Program (TARP) for the purchase of toxic assets from banks. $441.7 billion is eventually recovered from $426.4 billion invested, producing a $15.3 billion profit.

"Without those media," says Matzko, "people would have been just as angry, but they wouldn't have been turned into a movement. You didn't have the resource mobilization and organization going on. That's the second component.

"The final component is a unique political opportunity. There has to be some kind of break in the structure, a sense of opportunity for that social movement to have a voice that they didn't have before. The break in the structure is that there's a sense of discontent with post-war consensus liberalism. People perceived that Republicans and Democrats weren't all that different from each other. Now they want a different alternative. All those things lined up in the '60s and that's where you get the origins of the New Right."

*Some conservatives and some people who might not even
self-identify as conservatives were excited by the Tea Party.
And though it was co-opted by certain organizations or
players. You don't hear much about the Tea Party just as
you don't hear much about Occupy these days.*

"When applying social movement theory to the
Tea Party," says Matzko, "we have discontent. The
discontent is a reaction to the bailouts, the financial
crisis, and then the government bails out a bunch of
wealthy, politically well-connected financiers, Goldman
Sachs and the like. Ordinary folks, we're not talking
about the proletariat workers, but about white-collar,
middle-class folks, they were angry, like, 'Where's our
bailout?' Or the government should let them fail. 'I'm
struggling. Why shouldn't they struggle?'"

BASIC INCHOATE ANGER

*Taking down the banks sounds a lot more Marxist than it
does Republican.*

"Yes, it doesn't seem inherently conservative. I think,
early on, it's inchoate. It's an expression of anger
and dissatisfaction that hasn't yet turned into a
movement, a concrete set of policy goals. It's up for
negotiation. It's like the gilets jaunes in France (the
'yellow vest' movement launched with charges of
unfair economic burdens on lower and middle classes
due to fuel taxes). Are they right-wing or are they
left-wing?

"But movements often start off inchoate. It's this kind
of broad discontent. You have the Tea Party and, yes,
it could go right or left; it's not clear. The resource
mobilization and organization that goes on ends up
being right-wing. Your talk radio host gets in on it and

starts saying, 'Hey, you should be angry about this kind of stuff,' and they start to give it ideological clothing. It starts to flesh out. It's not just inchoate anger; it's economic populism. It starts to take a little more of a conservative bent, in part because of who is mobilizing the resource, who runs the organization, and who the president is, and its opposition.

"In social movement theory, that's the political opportunity; it can be organized in opposition to the current administration. There are vested interests, whether you call it co-opting or not. I'm generally of the belief that this is a genuine expression of grassroots energy. Vested interests also want to see it succeed because it helps them attack the current administration. It's who takes advantage of the opportunity to mobilize and organize that dissent. That's a big takeaway for folks who are interested in social movement activism in the future; identify that anger and then try to capture as much of that energy for the cause or set of causes that you're trying to promote.

"Tea Party and Occupy are two sides of the same coin. There's the same kind of basic inchoate anger, the Tea Party a little bit earlier, but it moves towards the right. At first, folks don't know what to make of these things. The CNBC initial rant goes out live, but no one knows quite what to do with these folks. There's a moment of hopefulness, maybe we can turn this energy into supporting our tribe, our side.

"But, there's a reason the Tea Party really kicks off once the Obama administration takes office," says Matzko, "even though all the things that are identified as problems by the Tea Partiers are actually started by Bush during his administration. He starts the bailouts and the stimulus.

"It's no accident that, after 2016, it's a shadow of what it was during the Obama administration. The corollary would be, that's because of a political opportunity, that there is a useful target for that anger to be directed at, and there's a set of vested interests who are willing to incentivize the direction of the anger. They're willing to give these groups money and resources. But, as soon as the target changes, that interest changes as well.

"The same thing would be true for the anti-war movement," suggests Matzko. "It was huge during the Bush administration. The left-wing anti-war movement is all over the news. It's a real grassroots movement against the Iraq and Afghanistan war, the war on terror. Where does it go after 2008? It's a shell of its former self, as soon as Barack Obama – who, ironically, ran as the anti-war candidate promising to shut down Guantanamo and draw down the war on terror, etc. – removes the political opportunity. There's a utility to having an anti-war movement when the person in power is a pro-war Republican. It becomes awkward and inconvenient, that window closes, when you have the other side in charge.

"As far as the Tea Party, folks liked to discredit it as a legitimate social movement by saying it was 'astroturfed.' That's not a very useful conversation. All social movements are both. They're genuine expressions of grassroots anger. And there are constant attempts to subvert, co-opt and redirect their aims and missions. This is just a constant. Is it real or is it 'astroturfed?' They are fundamentally both."

ECONOMIC POPULISM AND THE DESTROYED HOST PARTY

Are Trump's economic policies consistent with those populist messages?

"It's more rhetoric. Of course, the interesting thing about the Trump administration is that it has always been kind of policy-bare. He'll say all kinds of (things). If you take any individual policy, you can find Trump saying multiple conflicting things about that policy. You take abortion and he, at various times during his campaign, said that he was for women's right to choose, was for a moderate abortion policy, and then ardently pro-life. Which version was it? Because it's all rhetoric.

"Is the Trump administration representing the interests of the person in the Tea Party? I don't know, that's a tough one. But you certainly made rhetorical gestures towards economic populism. What's interesting about this moment is, again, this is all in play. The future of economic populism in America seems quite strong, which is not in the interest of free traders and free marketers, but there is a dissatisfaction, this idea that the system is rigged in favor of big corporations that is gaining support from the broad swath of America and the American electorate, and both right and left are trying to make political hay off of that discontent.

"I think the Tea Party is a social movement. It ran its course. It's essentially over. But there is an energy that's somewhat reminiscent of 2008 around now that folks are trying to activate.

"The Tea Party plays a part in that broader story of the decline of the Republican Party as a modern party system. The Tea Party is another counterweight to party control of the process, because if you're a candidate trying to secure the nomination - and this doesn't just apply to presidential politics; it also applies to congressional politics - it used to be that you had to go to the party leaders as a supplicant and say, 'Hey, would you please give me access to the big-ticket donor list? Would you please give me access to the debate platform?' Or you go to *Fox News* and say, 'Hey, would you please get me on the good shows, so that I'll get eyeballs on my campaign, for potential donors?'

"But the Tea Party was another locus, a way in which candidates could go around the party-control of the process. You could go to Tea Parties and say, 'I'm the Tea Party candidate.' Won't this network of local Tea Parties send their donations and their support to me? I don't have to go to the party to ask for money, people or support anymore."

And that affected Republican primaries as well.

"Absolutely. In a sense, it used to be one organization that potential candidates had to curry favor with, and then you had two organizations, which, in a sense, was the right-wing media ecosystem, *Fox News*, talk radio - either make them (GOP) happy with me or make *them* (conservative media) happy with me, and I can have a shot.

"The Tea Party adds a third kind of loose institution - if I can have them on my side, I don't need to be *Fox News*' favorite candidate. I don't need to be the Republican Party leadership's favorite candidate. I've got the Tea Party. It's another agent in that matrix and, again, it loosens party control over the selection process.

"You can make an argument that the Tea Party, by hastening the unraveling of the Republican Party as a party, plays a role in the rise of Donald Trump, not because he was the Tea Party candidate per se, but because they contributed to that unraveling."

Were there social and political policies, starting with the economic policies and regulation of banks, that were affected by the Tea Party?

"That's a good, tough question. There's a political scientist who went through and looked at all the platforms of all these various local early Tea Parties and noted just how diverse these policy platforms were.

"Some of them were calling for stuff we identify as economic populism; some for more traditional conservative, limited government; they didn't want government breaking up the big banks, etc. There was no unifying platform in the early Tea Party movement. It's hard because it's like, which Tea Party are we talking about? It confused the question.

But let's just assume what it turns into by, say, 2012, by the second (election cycle) time around. It has solidified a little more. It has kind of identified with the ultra-conservative Republican in opposition to the RINOs (Republicans in Name Only, a slur against party members deemed not sufficiently conservative). It's Ted Cruz; he's not elected by the Tea Party, but at least he tries to rebrand himself. It becomes eventually identified with nativism and opposition to immigration reform, but that's not at all in the original matrix. In 2008–2009, they're not talking about immigration. But it becomes that.

"It becomes and identifies as ultra-conservatism. I'm not sure they get anything. I can't think of any meaningful policy accomplishments from the Tea Party. They helped shift the Republican Party to the right. There's a generation of Tea Party politicians who are more abrasively conservative. It did something meaningful in the sense that it (the parasite) helped destroy its host (the Republican Party), but I'm not sure it results in meaningful policy reform."

While winning the Supreme Court, the presidency, and, up until recently, the House, plus the Senate, and most State Houses.

"Fair," says Matzko, with a proviso. "In 2012, Mitt Romney's campaign did the after-election report that said if the GOP is going to survive as a party, we need to become more friendly to immigration; we need become a party that embraces diversity.

"It made sense and they had their shot at it. There's that striking campaign photo from the South Carolina Republican primaries in 2016, where you have Marco Rubio, Trey Gowdy, Nikki Haley, and Tim Scott hand-in-hand. All supporting Rubio's candidacy in the primary and holding hands in a victory salute. That's the Romney report in a picture. You have a black conservative, a Spanish-speaking conservative, a second-generation immigrant, Nikki Haley, and then you have white America, white spiritual conservatism in Trey Gowdy. The party loses that vision, so the Trump campaign plan works.

"For the destroyed host party, there's always a time lag between fundamental party realignments and the structure of politics changing, and when it actually shows up on the surface level. The Republican Party is like a revivified corpse. It's a zombie, shuffling along. It looks really impressive and scary, but it's rotting.

"What we see in 2018 is record-setting. The Blue Wave is one of the three biggest midterm upsets in modern political history. What's notable is that most of the Blue Wave that gets the attention are folks farther to the radical left. But they're not the big beneficiaries of the wave.

"The biggest beneficiaries were folks like the new congressman from the Charleston congressional district. It's districts that used to be safely red that turn purple and elect moderate Democrats like Conor Lamb in the Pittsburgh area. There's this whole new wave of districts that used to be safely Republican that are turning Democratic. That's what the Republican Party should be worried about.

"The party is winnowing out traditional conservatives. You're seeing this purifying process of folks who echo Trump more and more, winning influence in the Republican Party."

According to Matzko, 2018 is just the harbinger of what's going to come in American politics. "We have the potential for a generational level political shift in national politics on the level of the New Deal coalition in the 1930s. It took everyone by surprise then. This could be one of those moments going forward."

7. THE 27TH AMENDMENT: GREGORY WATSON'S SUPERHUMAN FEAT

Gregory Watson doesn't look like Clark Kent, but he speaks in confident, measured tones like Superman's alter ego, his superpower not immediately apparent, presenting his remarkable story with the attention to detail expected of a lifelong legislative policy analyst.

Beneath Watson's studious legislative analyst persona lies a superhuman feat, which he presents with both aw-shucks humility – "I just sent out letters for 10 years" – and the ultimate humble-brag – "I did this and no one will ever, ever do anything like it again."

A one-of-a-kind character, he single-handedly changes the United States Constitution by championing the ratification of the 27th Amendment. Proving your high school civics teacher's claim that any citizen can make a difference.

Specifically, the 27th Amendment provides that,

> "No law, varying the compensation for the services of the Senators and Representatives, shall take effect, until an election of Representatives shall have intervened."

And while it doesn't change the manner in which we go to war or balance the federal budget, it hits the brakes on congressional self-dealing abuses, such as the tax break Congress gave itself in December of 1981.

Congressional pay is an important enough matter to be proposed as the second of the 12 amendments to the Constitution sent by Congress to the states for ratification in September 1789. Amendments three through 12 were ratified in December 1791 and those 10 became the Bill of Rights.

While standing in line at Cooper's Old Time Pit Bar-B-Que, jostling in queue amongst Austin regulars and awe-struck out-of-town patrons, Watson bemoans the current state of arrogance with which state and federal legislators treat constituents. He describes one possible solution – having the equivalent ratio of members to constituents that we had at our founding, ensuring truer and more intimate representation. A rough back-of-the-envelope calculation of that ratio would raise the current 435 House members to something north of 7,000.

Unwrapping his meal, Watson describes how he came to launch his crusade. He has an unforgettable, stylized speaking style, presenting his ideas deliberately, in carefully crafted sentences, somehow managing to be both funny and dead serious.

"At the time that I stumbled onto the amendment, I had already been hired to work for a member of the Texas House of Representatives. I worked on it for 10 years, from 1982 to 1992."

What was the spark, where you said, I'm gonna do this damn thing?

"Well, when I wrote my paper (on the subject of unratified amendments) at the University of Texas, Austin, and got it back with a grade of C from the teaching assistant, I appealed the grade up to the professor. She told me she would take a look at it, and a few days later, when she saw me, she physically hurled it at me and said, 'No change.' That was when I decided I'm going to do this. I couldn't resist."

Surely there was a psychological barrier, no, I can't do this, I mean, come on, it's...

"That's what other people were telling me. I never told myself that. I did the research on the Equal Rights Amendment. And so, it was in the course of that research that I came across important things like the *Coleman v. Miller* decision in 1939 by the U.S. Supreme Court. That was pivotal. When I learned about that ruling, that's when I knew that any amendment prior to 1917 had no deadline on it. And 1789 was way before 1970."

Your mom is a strong advocate of the ERA, which gives you a first-hand look into the legislative hurdles to be overcome.

"Yes. Prior to moving to Austin, we resided in the Dallas area, and she, being a member of the National Organization for Women, received a lot of their mailings. It was fascinating to read those publications, because they would talk about, 'Well, we had a success in this state, we got ERA out of committee, we had success in that state because we got it to the floor even though it was voted down. Just the mere fact that we got it to a floor was a partial victory. Things went really bad in that other state over there.' And so, I was thinking to myself, the whole way the U.S. Constitution is amended, is so outdated. Was that intentional?

"I think Article V, along with the rest of the Constitution was written to make the process difficult. It's an imperfect document. And it was not in all cases well-written. There are things that the founding fathers could have articulated more clearly. So, while I agree that we should not replace it, I do not worship the document as being perfect and flawless. Because it is not perfect. And it is not flawless.

"But in those days, conducting a nationwide referendum on an issue probably wasn't thought of by the founding fathers. Today, we have initiatives and referenda. I am a strong supporter of such powers, because I don't trust legislators. Now, such powers can be abused, and they can be over-utilized. But as a fundamental principle, I believe it's important that the people should be able to vote on issues.

"Back in 1978, I was thinking, all of this could be made so much simpler if voters were allowed to vote in a national election, yes or no to the ERA. And we wouldn't be going through this victory over here and that horrible defeat over there."

Critical to Watson's success was his research. Once his vision for what he wants to do is clear, he finds a Supreme Court precedent in a landmark case establishing that, "Unless Congress establishes a time window for passing an amendment, it remains pending indefinitely and can be passed at any time. Congress has the sole power to determine whether it has been passed."[44] For Watson, that means his goal is achievable. Then he determines who he needed to convince.

When you go about your process, do you have a structured plan or does it unfold over the years, as you learn and deal with challenges as they come?

"Kind of a mixture. I knew exactly what needed to be done. And I knew exactly who to communicate with in order to get it done. Today, I don't believe that I would be able to get it done because state legislators, like members of Congress, ignore you. In fact, I think they even ignore people in their district; they would certainly ignore me being out of state. I got in on the tail end of the good old days, when elected officials in the state capitals were actually still responsive to citizen input."

Six states ratify the original amendment by 1791. Watson discovers that ratification by Kentucky, which becomes a state June 1, 1792, is on June 27,[45] information that's been lost in the state's archives since.[46] That makes seven.

The Ohio state legislature ratifies the 27th amendment in 1873 to protest passage by Congress of the Salary Grab Act. The act approves a 100% pay raise for the president and Supreme Court Justices, and a hidden 50% increase for Congress. Both raises are made retroactive to two years prior. The result is a Congressional salary increase from $5,000 to $7,500, a $5,000 windfall for each member. But public clamor forces Congress to repeal the act. Ohio's ratification of the proposed 1789 compensation amendment "was, in effect, a protest of the Salary Grab (that) outlawed" the type of legislation the Salary Grab represented.[47] That makes eight.

In 1977, Wyoming imitates Ohio and approves the amendment after Congress gives itself another pay increase. That makes nine.

In 1982 when Watson commits to the amendment's ratification, three-fourths of the 50 states or 38 states' legislatures or ratifying conventions are needed to approve ratification. That means he has to convince 29 other states to complete the ratification begun nearly 200 years before.

Are there certain milestones or bits of validation that gave you the momentum and energy to keep pushing?

"Every year, there was a minimum of one ratification," explains Watson. "So, I never experienced a situation of the movement stopping. I did it all through the postal service."

So, your cost for the entire campaign is a...

"Postage, envelopes, Xerox copies..."

And a few replacement IBM Selectric II typing elements?

"Well, I always had the same one. A lot of wear and tear on that typewriter."

His first task is to secure rosters of state legislators in target states.

"Once found, I would type letters to those state lawmakers asking them to file a resolution at their State Capitol to accomplish ratification. In some instances, as the movement progressed past its initial stages, I would go so far as to draft the resolution myself and send it as an enclosure with the letter. In a number of cases, I ended up sending a letter to every member of the Legislature in the quest for expedited sponsorship.

"Once officially filed of record at a given State Capitol," continues Watson, "I would monitor the resolution's progress. If stalled in a committee, I would contact the committee's chairperson to stress the need for conducting a public hearing on the resolution. There were also instances in which, if favorably discharged from the committee, I would contact the membership of the full body to urge them to support the resolution in the event that it arrived on the floor for an up-or-down vote."

Because Democrats are the party in power in the U.S. House of Representatives at the time, Watson concentrates his efforts on states in which both legislative chambers are majority Republican.

"Having eventually run out of them, I broadened the net to capture states in which there was split control (one chamber majority Republican and the other body majority Democrat). Then I worked on the states in which both legislative bodies were majority Democrat, but which wouldn't preclude a Republican from successfully passing legislation." The sponsorship effort ended up roughly 2/3 Republican, 1/3 Democrat, with a couple of Independents in the mix.

"Being pre-Internet, all of this was done by U.S. Postal Service – and I was not well-positioned to do any out-of-state travel. I am one of these people who keeps a great many things and have had to put them into more than just one personal storage unit. I did not create any electronic database; everything was very old-fashioned and primitive by today's standards.

"I would convince state lawmakers to file the resolution at the various State Capitols by pointing out to them the tremendous abuses which Congress was engaging in during the 1980s in order to boost Congressional salaries. Perhaps the worst example was the February 1987 trick that new-House Speaker Jim Wright employed to have an up-or-down vote on accepting or rejecting a pay raise that was automatically triggered by federal law. The vote was conducted one day too late to reject the increase. This allowed a majority of the members to go formally on record as 'rejecting' the pay raise but, because it was happening a day late, they got to keep the increase anyway.

"Examples such as that," Watson states, "almost handed to me on a silver platter by Congress itself, were just the ammunition that I needed to make the case to state lawmakers that they should ratify the amendment to place a modest restriction on such Congressional pay raises. My message was consistent: members of Congress should have at least some modest restriction on their unique ability to raise their own salaries."

Watson's near-encyclopedic knowledge of the arcana of ratification procedures allows him to emphasize this particular amendment has no deadline for ratification.

"Anything submitted to the states prior to 1917 had absolutely no time constraint in which the state legislatures had to act. Starting in 1917, Congress got into the habit of imposing ratification deadlines on proposed amendments to the Constitution."

Being a one-man show, he leverages his strengths and manages around his lack of technology tools and resources. A touch of stubborn persistence animates and drives him through the years of effort. Once officially filed as a matter of record in a legislature, Watson monitors the resolution's progress.

"Given the lack of the World Wide Web at the time, I had to periodically telephone the state legislative bill status hotlines to inquire as to where the resolutions in the various states stood at any given point in time."

How helpful is press coverage?

"Newspapers within Texas (his home state) periodically carried a story about the ratification's progress. Newspapers in other states wrote about it during and/ or after the states would turn down or pass ratification. There was also some nationwide coverage in *The New York Times, The Washington Post, Los Angeles Times, USA Today* and a few others."

Small successes give him the motivation to keep pushing.

Congress declares the ratification to be legal on May 20, 1992, and the 27th Amendment becomes part of the Constitution.[48]

It takes Watson a decade to achieve his objective.

Were you inspired by the idea that one person can change the world?

"I was. I would be far less convinced that in 2019 given that elected officials feel very, very comfortable just blowing off citizen input."

Why is that, do you think?

"Because they can ignore citizens and get away with it. The average voter is so stupid, he or she will rubber stamp his or her incumbent back into office, election cycle after election cycle after election cycle after election cycle."

Gregory, are you suggesting that we are becoming more stupid as a country?

"Yeah, and we're getting more and more calloused as a country. These huge callouses have formed around elected officials to where they think, and it is true, they're almost invincible. It is next to impossible to throw an incumbent out of office. The incumbent had to have done something really, really, really, really, really, really, really, really bad in order to lose the next election."

Do you have personal advice for people who might want to do the kind of thing that you did, if they want to take on a big challenge?

"Go for it, of course. But understand that in this world today, doing it all by your little old self is probably not going to result in much. They're going to have to do what groups like the Convention of the States Project has done. It has very astutely recognized that state lawmakers have become just as jaded as their counterparts in Washington, D.C. You have to build an army of people in order to get the attention of these impervious waterproof state legislators to do anything. And, there's a new forum called the Internet, which I did not have access to in the 1980s and early 1990s."

In March 2017, 35 years after Watson received his "C," his professor officially changes his grade to an "A."

8. TUNIS: *DÉGAGE!* DAWN OF THE ARAB SPRING

Fifteen people walk in a circle, another dozen milling about. Most carry photos or posters of Mohamed Brahmi, a beloved Tunisian opposition leader gunned down outside his home on July 25, 2013, unthinkable in a national culture that prides itself on nonviolence. Tasnim Kotti, mother of three, six years "wearing hijab" prior to the 2011 Jasmine Revolution, patrols the group, encouraging protesters, engaging in logistical conversations with her comrades. She comes to this spot in front of the Ministry of the Interior every Wednesday.

Avenue Habib Bourguiba is the heart of Tunis' city center, ficus trees lining both sides of its central median. Street musicians amuse small gatherings while bistro hawkers implore tourists with exotic claims of well-priced native cuisine.

Looming over the protesters are two nearby monuments. The first is an outlandish bit of Dear Leader tribute art, founding president Bourguiba on a massive stallion, joyfully lording it over the masses. The second is the Clock Tower, Zene El Abidine Ben Ali's ostentatious, 38 meter-high, gilt-topped monument to himself. Ben Ali seizes power from a doddering Bourguiba in 1987, then builds a repressive kleptocracy that loots the country for 23 years until he's brought down by events following the desperate public suicide of one very angry fruit vendor.

Physical protest, taking to the streets, is a political tactic with its detractors. A pervasive, cynical view is, "Who cares?"

Protest objectives seem obtuse. Passersby see them as they hurry to lunch, offering a sideways glance, if that. A few pause to talk; then the demonstration is forgotten. Or so it seems.

For the first of the Wednesday protests in 2013, there is a large weekly turnout, as there is on the anniversary of Tunisian independence from France, or the annual commemoration of the Chokri Belaid assassination; news coverage, social media posts, comradery and solidarity in remembrance of a political martyr. But it's been six years since the assassinations of Belaid and Brahmi, so, why come out week after week?

A FRUIT VENDOR LAUNCHES THE ARAB SPRING

The Jasmine Revolution starts with one person.

Mohamed Bouazizi, a 26-year-old produce vendor in the interior city of Sidi Bouzid, supports his extended family by earning ten dollars on a good day in the blazing inland heat. On December 17, 2010, a municipal officer shuts him down for having no license, though most all vendors are unlicensed, and confiscates his cart. The young Bouazizi is enraged, desperate, frustrated at the endless, humiliating bureaucracy that crushes his hope for a better life, and on this day, his desire to live. He stands in the middle of the road in front of the municipal government office and, with no hope of redress of his grievance, saturates himself with two cans of paint thinner, then sets himself on fire.

The country erupts in protest, first with hundreds in Sidi Bouzid, then thousands in cities across the country, and finally a hundred thousand in the capital, Tunis. Over 300 protesters are killed, which stokes more discontent. In less than one month, the all-powerful Ben Ali flees the country.

JAMAL DAJANI AND THE RIPPED POSTER

Palestinian journalist Jamal Dajani arrives in Tunisia January 1, 2011, and witnesses first-hand the events leading to the region-wide protests known as the Arab Spring. The nonprofit *Internews* is setting up shop in Tunis. It's just completed a development program, training journalists and working with local media outlets. And the newly hired Vice President MENA (Middle East North Africa) Dajani is touring offices in the region. Tunisians have been protesting across the country for two weeks, attacking government corruption, high unemployment, and police repression. Three demonstrators are shot and killed, many more injured by savage police beatings. Many are surprised to see the increasingly bold expressions of outrage and disaffection with the Ben Ali regime. Dajani isn't.

"There was unrest," says Dajani, "many young Tunisians were leaving the country. They were either working for friends, or in neighboring countries, because they just couldn't make it. Tunisia has a high number of educated young people with foreign education or national degrees. I could see the frustration."

State-controlled television station *Tunisie7*, and local newspapers and radio stations black out coverage of the uprising. But news and images spread via mobile phones, via Facebook and YouTube.

Dajani watches the demonstrations "just before all hell broke loose." He remembers a quiet, isolated moment, a symbol of what was to come. "If you went to Tunisia at this time, you encountered huge pictures of Ben Ali everywhere, 'the father of the nation.' Movie-size posters, shaking the hands of young people, with the workers, a man of the people; Soviet Union-type images."

Dajani leaves his hotel, the downtown Grand Tulip, for a stroll through town. "And then this young kid who must have been 13 or 14, went and ripped off a big poster of Ben Ali; onlookers are stunned. I realized that something big is brewing, because this would have been impossible for people to do before. He wasn't arrested, he just went on his merry way."

ABSOLUTE POWER, THEN A RAPID ESCAPE

Mohamed Bouazizi dies on January 5, 2011. Days before his demise, Ben Ali choreographs a visit to his hospital room. A widely-distributed macabre photo shows the president attempting an earnest bedside manner standing over the comatose, mummified fruit vendor. A camera crew records the presentation of a ten thousand-dinar check (about $14,000) to Mohamed's mother, Manoubya. It's a standard fare of autocrat showmanship but it backfires and enrages Tunisians. Ms. Bouazizi reveals the president's staff confiscate the check after the crew left the room.

On January 13, shortly after one of the largest demonstrations in Tunis, Ben Ali promises an investigation into the death of protesters, promises reforms and announces he will not run for reelection in 2014.

The next day, after imposing a state of emergency amid clashes between police and protesters, Ben Ali promises legislative elections within six months. He then flees the country to France, where his plane is denied landing rights. He ends up in permanent exile in Jeddah, Saudi Arabia. The following day, Speaker of Parliament Foued Mebazaa is designated temporary president.

"THEY FACE BULLETS WITH THEIR CHESTS"

Lamine Alibi begins his resistance to Tunisian autocracy while in high school; in the 1970s, his *Review* periodical is censored by the government. After a career as a French and history teacher in Tunisia's secondary schools, with a stint in prison as a member of a clandestine Marxist-Leninist cell, he serves on the central committee of the Patriotic Democratic Unity Party, part of the leftist Front Populaire coalition. As the Wednesday midday protest winds down, Alibi details the history of Tunisian protest, his comrade Tasnim Kotti acting as French/ English translator.

"The Tunisian revolution is an outcry of people with the courage and energy to say, '*That's enough.*'" Referring to the "Arab Spring" protests and revolutions that swept through North Africa and the Middle East in the years following Ben Ali's ouster, Alibi suggests, "Maybe this is what made the Tunisia revolution an inspirational example for other countries, to follow the energy of young people who are fed up with unemployment, with poverty, with low quality education, with the lack of opportunities, even to travel to go see the world.

"We've had a lot of young martyrs; as we say in our Arabic slogans, '*They face bullets with their chests.*'" A national commission counts more than 300 killed, over 2,000 injured during the demonstrations. "It's not strange for Tunisian people to rise against dictatorship.

"This is a psychological ingredient, it's something inherited," believes Alibi. "Who were the first people to rise against Ben Ali in 2011? It was the people of the inside of the country, the poor, the marginalized, the forgotten, have-nots, whatever you want to call them. They were the first to go into these streets and say '*Dégage*, go away Ben Ali.' Why? Because these are people with a history of resistance against the Ottoman Empire, against the French. And then, after that, the Bourguiba regime and, then, Ben Ali."

Alibi sees protesters as the 'heirs' of those who resisted colonization, who resisted dictatorship. "These people were there all the time, lurking, looking for the opportunity, and maybe the man who burned himself was just the suitable opportunity to get out.

"There is also this undeniable role played by the Tunisian General Labour Union, always involved in social and political demands and protests, which is a unique experience in Africa. Its founder Farhat Hached comes from our hometown and was killed by the French colonizer." Hached, one of the leaders of the independence movement, along with Bourguiba and Salah ben Youssef, was assassinated on December 5, 1952 by La Main Rouge (The Red Hand), an armed group operated by French intelligence.

Alibi relates a turning point in 2008 in the Ghafsa mining region, with Kotti sharing anecdotes and detail. The union launches a general strike and the government responds aggressively with detentions, torture, the slaying of three activists, and long prison sentences for protest leaders.

"Phosphate is a big natural resource," says Alibi, "the country's biggest source of wealth, and people there are not enjoying any of it. They are inheriting illnesses because of the gases and pollution. They are suffering joblessness, very low pay; they're getting killed in the mines. The family gets nothing, there is no development, no nice roads, no nice schools, no appropriate hospitals, no healthcare, even the water is polluted. People from this region have teeth that are all brown.

"Their great-great-grandparents said 'Stop' to the French colonizers, 'Stop' to the Ottoman sultans. The Ottoman Empire sold Tunisia to the French when they were bankrupt. But people of these regions stood against colonization; a lot of them were killed.

"There is this accumulation of political resistance, clandestine small groups of the left that were doing work, writing and distributing pamphlets. And this was done all through our history. After the independence (from France in 1956), it hasn't stopped."

THE FIRST LEGITIMATE NATIONAL ELECTION SINCE INDEPENDENCE

On January 17, Prime Minister Mohamed Ghannouchi announces a new government with Ben Ali loyalists in key posts. Thousands of protesters return to the streets the next day in Tunis and five other cities to demand Ghannouchi and Mebazaa resign from Ben Ali's Democratic Constitutional Rally (RCD) party. In 48 hours, all interim ministers quit the RCD but remain in their cabinet posts. The central committee of RCD is dissolved.

When thousands protest again on January 22 demanding the removal of all RCD members from the government, they're joined by two thousand police officers. The leader of banned Islamist party al-Nahda, Rachid Ghannouchi (no relation to the prime minister), returns to Tunisia at the end of January. After a month of protests, Mohamed Ghannouchi resigns and is replaced by Beji Caid-Essebsi. The RCD is dissolved on March 9, ending its decades-long stranglehold on Tunisian politics.

"I was in and out of the region during that period maybe half a dozen times," says *Internews*' Dajani. "One of the times was when they removed Ghannouchi, who took over after Ben Ali, and they had a whole campaign 'Ghannouchi *Dégage!*' meaning 'Ghannouchi, get out of here' or 'get lost.' They had a lot of euphoria and hope, for not only Tunisia, but the rest of the Arab world." There was a latent anger by the working class against the Ben Ali family, especially his wife's family, the Trabelsi family, and all the nepotism and control. This was really the spark that started the fire."

In June, the Tunis criminal court sentences Ben Ali and his wife, Leila, to 35 years in prison for "embezzlement and misusing public funds. The couple... is also fined $66m (£41m). The one-day trial in absentia focuses on $27m of cash and jewels reportedly found inside one of their palaces."[49]

Registration begins September 1 for political parties and independent lists to place candidates in the October 23 constituent assembly election; 81 parties, and hundreds of independents register.

"The fact of the matter, the progressives or the young people, they just were confused," explains Dajani. "Just do the math; you're not going to win. (All of these) parties fighting amongst each other is cannibalizing the votes and minds, so that was that big mistake. That's when the Islamists won; it was very obvious they were going to win."

Despite the challenges, the election is the first legitimate national election held since independence from France in March 1956. In November, roughly three weeks before the one-year anniversary of Bouazizi's self-immolation, Tunisia's three main political parties agree on a "power-sharing government." Hamadi Jebali of the Islamist Ennahda party is to be prime minister; Moncef Marzouki from the Congress for the Republic party is designated as president; and the Ettakol party's Mustafa Ben Jaafar is to be the new Constituent Assembly speaker.

PROFOUND, IMPERFECT OUTCOMES

"How do we assess the outcome?" asks Alibi during a break for lunch with Kotti at a nearby bistro. "We are proud of the overthrow of Ben Ali. But ever since the day he was overthrown, the same mechanisms of the old regime started working and, because our uprising was spontaneous, we were maybe unprepared to govern. Ben Ali's prime minister and his president of the parliament remained, until young people drove the Prime Minister and the president of the Parliament to resign, to start elections.

"Then, Islamists came by planes and private jets from foreign countries where they used to hide. They didn't participate in the revolution. They came back with the agendas and money they got and still get from the Gulf countries, Saudi Arabia, Qatar, the emirates. They won elections in 2011 and 2014 and they are preparing themselves for our next elections. So, maybe this is what we see as a failure. But it has nothing to do with us, the people who believe that it is a revolutionary process, and the fight must continue."

What is that process, what more needs to change?

"The Islamists and the old regime, they are working together because they have the same interests. They want the people to stay hungry, kept under due to higher prices, by terrorizing them and by propaganda.

"They killed two prominent political leaders in the country; Chokri Belaid on the sixth of February, 2013, and Mohamed Brahmi, the subjects of our Wednesday protests, a few months later on July the 25th, the date of our pseudo-independence. Instead of a celebration celebrating republican values, they assassinated Brahmi. He was a haj. He was the secretary general of the Popular Current, part of the Front Populaire. Pan-Arabic. This was horrible for the whole country. It was done to subjugate people."

A "haj" is a Muslim who has made the sacred pilgrimage to Mecca. Killing a Muslim, killing a haj as political assassination is an egregious violation of Islam.

"Media is keeping people unconscious through talk shows or small entertainment programs that will divert their attention."

During the conversation, there are short, direct responses translated by Kotti. Other times, there are very long answers, Kotti laughing as she tries to locate the original question. Most times, there is an energetic mix of French, Arabic, and English, the answers enhanced by Kotti's personal insights and experiences.

"We try to stay focused," adds Kotti. "People are not focused in this country. I'm not the kind of person that will blame the population. Poor people, they are poor, they are just thinking of feeding their children, so in order to get a little bit of entertainment in the evening, they will watch these distractions."

Across the Arab world, there were some unpleasant outcomes after the Jasmine Revolution. Is the movement that started in Tunisia ongoing?

"Anyway," considers Alibi, "we are proud of the liberty of expression that we have won. Today we can go into the street, protest."

Could you do that before? In 2010, if you did that...

"No. But even today it's not a given. We are trying to convince ourselves of that which is real, not just an illusion. We are not yet a democracy. The ballot box doesn't represent the real will of the people. One of the reasons why this happened, and will still happen, is that the winning parties are those who are financed by smugglers, by corrupt people, by those big oligarchies. It's true that we are disillusioned somewhat because we haven't achieved what we have dreamt of.

"This disillusionment can be understood or can be seen in the abstention of going to vote among young people," says Kotti. "People are no longer attracted with political discourse and maybe they no longer believe in their ability to change things through votes. We tried to organize campaigns to convince people to go and register to vote. And even if it's not possible for them because of remoteness, or because of some conditions, we go to them, register them ourselves or take them where they want to register. For me personally, I started to go a little bit extremist, no longer believing in the power of change through voting. For my kids, right, my son is still not at the eligible age of voting. First of all, I tried to get him off his gaming. Fortnite."

Maybe Fortnite replaces religion as the opium of the people. Don't worry about Islam, worry about Fortnite.

Kotti laughs. "Maybe there is still hope, because we the Front Populaire in the elections of 2014 won 15 seats in parliament. We are minority, and yet we are capable of bringing the most controversial questions, the hardest questions into the parliament. And we can stop the majority from adopting certain projects or bringing some laws against women etc. So, we are capable with these 15 seats, 15 of our comrades there fighting on the legislative level. But also, there is the fight of the streets, we are always in the street, wherever there is a protest, we are there."

If no one votes, you don't have the 15 seats. Every Wednesday, you go out there. Why do you go?

"So, it's for memory," Alibi says. "It's not to forget, to tell the people, the young people. Because they (Islamists) work on this, they're trying to rewrite history, even the present, they are trying to distort. They haven't participated in the revolution. And they're going to say, ah, we were there, we also went into the street, and there was one of us, and they get a picture of a veiled women that it is photoshopped. So, for us, it's very important to stand every Wednesday, to say that we will not forget. And we will not allow you to make people forget or to erase our memory.

"There is for example this Sudanese uprising where they have overthrown their president, and the army wanted to take charge and they said no. So, this is inspirational for us again. It's something natural, the outcome of all the hunger, all the oppression, all the inequalities, that has become a kind of natural demand for equality, for democracy, for liberty, so it cannot be stopped. It's a flow that you cannot can no longer control."

Kotti adds a final thought as Alibi excuses himself.

"As revolutionary people we are optimists, so we believe in a better world, and we believe in the human potential of aspiring for the best, for better conditions of life and for a place where people can live with dignity and happiness. That's it.

"And then we are driven with love, love, love for the man whose picture we held. We love him because he was a good orator, highly educated and very intelligent, but, also, simple. The whole country loved him, not only people of the left. Why? Because during this brief period between the date of the revolution and his assassination, he was talking about people's problems, because he really lived them, he witnessed them, experienced them and he had this way of attracting people through speech. And so, we loved him as our comrade, as our leader, and we feel grateful for what he did to assemble and bring people of the left together."

Toward the end of the Interior Ministry protest, a tall young man circulates through the crowd, conferring with Kotti and other demonstrators. He invites those present to the anti-imperialism protest he is organizing later today at the central bank.

"As a high school student, Marwen lived in the neighborhood of the martyr (Brahmi)," explains Kotti later that afternoon over tea at the International Hana Hotel. "They had a kind of club, a cultural house, with a library and a stage where people can do some theater, read, or do some painting. He was active there. And he could help these young people get better results at school, better their reading, improve their writing skills. He loved Brahmi very much. The assassination shocked him, it was like losing a father figure. Over the next few years, he had lots of battles with the Salafists and he got into jail, two or three times. The neighborhood was what we call a hot zone, full of those religious people who want to brainwash other young people in the mosque. So, you see, the mosque and the house of culture are two poles that were attracting young people differently."

Salafism is a Sunni Islam fundamentalist reform movement originating in late 19th-century Egypt, with roots in 18th-century Saudi Wahhabism, preaching a return to – their notion of – an earlier, more pure form of Islam.

The protest at the bank takes time to get started, mostly backpack-toting university students, many who have demonstrated together before. One young woman works part-time at a café but tries to get out to as many protests as possible. "I guess I'm addicted," she laughs. A red horizontal banner in Arabic with a half-dozen group logos is held by five men at the head of the 60-strong group and someone begins leading a chant. They move into the street after an opening rally in front of the bank, automatic weapon-toting police looking on casually. A police car obstructs the path but it is circumvented and no show of force is made to stop their onward movement. A few women wear head scarves, most do not. Kotti jumps out in front to lead a new chant. The atmosphere is serious but jovial, many of the protesters waving small red flags.

Kotti extends an invitation to another protest, "Progrès, Défis et Besoins pour l'avenir," hosted by Association Tunisienne des Femmes Démocrates. "It's about the feminist movement in the region," she explains, "accomplishments, challenges and needs for the future."

SIDI BOU SAID: AFTERTHOUGHTS ON THE REVOLUTION

Known for its gorgeous Mediterranean coastal towns, Tunisia stretches from the northern Atlas Mountains to the southern Sahara Desert, dwarfed in both size and oil reserves by its neighbors. To its west is Algeria, at 919,595 square miles, the largest state in Africa; to its east, Libya, 679,362 square miles against Tunisia's 63,170. Tunisia is ranked 48th in oil reserves, one percent that of its neighbor Libya. Its lack of large reserves could be a reason for lesser meddling by some western powers. The United States was publicly supportive of the country's democracy initiative. Tunisia is an MNNA, a 'major non-NATO ally,' a designation given to governments in strategic working relationships with U.S. armed forces.

A short drive north on the coastal road from Tunis is Carthage, home of the empire that dominated the western Mediterranean from the 7th through the 3rd century B.C., rivaling and almost destroying the Roman Empire before falling in the third Punic War. The greatest naval force of its time, with more than 300 colonies throughout the region, it was praised by Aristotle for its system of governance.

"Many of the Carthaginian institutions are excellent," surmised the Greek philosopher. "The superiority of their constitution is proved by the fact that the common people remain loyal to (it). The Carthaginians have never had any rebellion worth speaking of, and have never been under the rule of a tyrant."

Past Carthage lies Sidi Bou Said, a picturesque blue and white-toned seaside town. Walid al-Sadir, a student of economics in university, is these days part tour guide, part souvenir shop salesman, and business is down. He shares a common belief in this tourist town, named after a 13th century Sufi mystic, that economic life was better under Ben Ali. Incidents of Islamist terrorism, including the 2015 mass shootings at a tourist resort and the Bardo National Museum, have further depressed tourist appetites.

"Everything depends on our cultural legacy," proposes the former economics major. "It's not easy to pass from black to white quickly, you see. Revolution in France needs around 100 years to be good. Our revolution was so nice, so peaceful compared to around the world. So why we call a Jasmine Revolution because the jasmine is a flower of happiness, of joys of life. But is not easy to pass to democracy."

Was it time to change the system, to have a democratic government?

"Yeah, I think it was time," al-Sadir agrees. "Ben Ali was like dictator. In all processes, we have many steps we have to take. One step to be born, one step to grow, one step to go down. Ben Ali had his time, it was very good time. Tunisian money had value. But later he goes down, it's normal. People will continue in the process of taking care of our revolution."

Tasnim Kotti comes to Sidi Bou Said for a second interview and a stroll through the ancient town, stopping at the Museum Dar el-Annabi, home of the old mufti.

There is an extensive library in the 18th century family home given to the community as a public space revealing a love of knowledge, of world literature, including Parisian magazines and handwritten copies of the Quran.

"They were open to other civilizations, and they read everything, they're open to all types of music, because we are on the Mediterranean. So, we have been kind of on the road of many cultures, and produce this kind of openness and love of discovery."

What is a mufti?

"A mufti knows all about Sharia laws," Kotti explains, then emphasizes that "Tunisian people have moderate Sharia. You go to the mufti, he's the kind of judge" for government rulings and family disputes, a vital and respected community elder.

The mufti home, with memorabilia from successive generations, reminds her of her grandfather. "My name,

Tasnim, means *'a spring of water in heaven.'* It's taken from Quran. I was named by my grandfather, a scholar who was moderate and respectful of women, his wife, his daughters and in-laws, granddaughters. He encouraged us to study, to be active, saying jokes in French, as he participated in World War I with France in Indochine."

There is some nostalgia for exiled or dead autocrats, for the old order. The economy and tourism were in better shape, the currency was stronger, there was order, Islamist extremists were resisted if not repressed. Some autocrats in the Muslim world, like Ben Ali and Saddam Hussein, supported women's rights to education, to working, to freedom in dress.

"Ben Ali was not allowing much political freedom," says Kotti. "No opposition parties. Human rights organizations could not work freely. A lot of people were put into jail for writing an article, for distributing a flyer or newspaper where they criticize his economic and political policies."

Tell me why you protest, why is marching and gathering people important.

"First of all, we have to admit the role which social media is playing in making people gather, organizing into groups, launchings, calls, and events. Second, we believe in our advocacy of nonviolent activism. This is the front of the left. So, we are not armed or malicious. Third, if people are in the street, it will make pressure on governments, have the world in a condition to see us. There is more visibility.

"We organize concerts, music, meetings, conferences, seminars, we invite people to listen to other countries' experiences. We write flyers, we organize campaigns to distribute them. It can sensitize people.

"Then we wait. Maybe for the right time to do another revolution. People will be more aware. There are the younger ones, they go by night and create paintings on walls. This can also help; when you go into very, very poor neighborhoods and put things on the walls, even if they won't read the flyers or articles, they will read something with striking sentences like, '*Bread and Water, But Not Ali.*'"

What are the lessons you learned from the revolution and from your own political activism?

"Effective or not, never give up," insists Kotti. "Never stop, never go down this path and say, 'There is no outcome. Let's stop.' There will always be people who will wonder, 'Oh, what are you doing? What changed?'

"I have a lot of friends and colleagues on *Facebook*, women who tell me how I should settle. 'It will come,' I say. Even just to give the example to my children, it's enough for me. Perhaps now they're not old enough to be aware of what I'm doing. Sometimes they ask me where am I going. By going out, I am doing them a favor. They are safe at home or at their grandmother's home. I'm not neglecting them. On the contrary, I'm doing them good, since, one day, they will have an example to remember. Maybe things will be worse in their time. I act so they will get a story to tell and values to defend. I don't want them to go live like anybody else, just eat and consume.

"That is all: just don't give up, don't despair, live your life, and just do it. As when I do other activities, whether I prepare a lesson, couscous, go shopping or I go visit friends or family relatives, these are duties. For me, it's kind of a duty and a right, I enjoy both sides of it. I'm happy I enjoy it and that the revolution gave me this turning or starting point in my life. I went down into the street, especially when there were real threats of a backlash around women's rights. It was urgent to be there. When the constitution was rewritten they wanted to omit certain codes, we felt we had to go into the streets, thousands of women saying so many times, '*no, No, NO!!!*' Finally, after a few days, they surrendered."

HOW TO CREATE A DEMOCRACY

Years after his up-close encounters with the Jasmine Revolution, *Internews* journalist and media observer Dajani has relevant insight into the psychological, emotional and political transformations that occur when people submit to autocracy for decades, and then, suddenly, submit no longer.

"People were full of hope. Tunisians, especially the new generation, they're very intelligent. A lot of these people had graduate degrees and they finished college. They speak several languages, some of them have traveled outside the country. They had a whole different outlook, and they were determined that they were going to basically retake a country from the hands of a tyrant and move into a democracy. They had a very clear vision about what they wanted the future to look like.

"They were like, we can do a lot in Tunisia. We can set up something like a Silicon Valley hub, and get into high tech. They had a lot of hopes that there were engineers, doctors, lawyers who lived abroad and then came back.

"That was, I would say, the initial reaction, which later on kind of subsided because they faced attacks."

Were there certain unique tools, for Arab Spring protests in general, and for Tunisia, in particular?

"Remember, social media doesn't make revolution," Dajani says. "It's just a tool. I think the revolution was organic and instantaneous. It's pent-up anger. People (became) self-empowered. They just went from a hopeless state to a state where they felt like, okay, we can do something now. *This is not happening again.* This guy had just had enough, such that he had set himself on fire. This is a tyrannical regime.

"I think, once Ben Ali left, and they heard that he was on a plane, they thought that they had won. At that moment, they felt that their voice was being heard. The fact that, they went out in the streets en masse, they made this tyrant jump on a plane to Saudi Arabia. That's kind of kept them going, that they felt that they achieved something very quickly."

What was the concept of democracy that inspired or activated protesters in Tunisia?

"Remember, democracy was nonexistent in Tunisia. The mere fact of criticizing the ruling family or criticizing Ben Ali will send you to jail, so that's a simple kind of bare minimum requirement. Those young students, some of whom have said that they studied in France or other European countries, have experienced like, yes, I can be critical of the government and I'm not going to wake up the second day in a jail cell.

"I think it was the idea of democracy, to have freedom of choice for them to speak, freedom to protest, to assemble, all these things. They had a very clear idea about this."

In what ways were the original aspirations achieved?

"I would say, you have to look at it into it from two different lenses: one, the Tunisian lens; the other, under the whole so-called Arab Spring. For me, Tunisia, even though it has not achieved all its goals, in a way was the only successful revolution. Compared to what's going on in Libya, where now, you have a failed state and warring parties that have moved into power.

"Of course, if we compare it to what's going on in Egypt, the return of the military, a major (goal) was getting rid of Hosni Mubarak, and we have someone who is worse, with Sisi. Then, of course, what's going on in Syria, a total disaster. It's a catastrophe on a large level, and Yemen as well.

"Tunisia, which was the epicenter of the so-called Arab Spring has achieved some of its goals, transitioning peacefully into another system. They've kind of internally struggled. However, we haven't witnessed the violence.

"Some things happened and others tried to meddle," he continues, "and there were terror attacks, etc., but it hasn't transitioned into this crazy 'failed state' status, where people turn the guns against each other. There is a democratic process that is going on.

"The Tunisians asked, 'Now that we have gotten rid of Ben Ali, how can we create a democracy? How can we bring all these people together? You have people who want to take the country in one direction, and others who want to take it in another.

"I think they survived foreign intervention, which is very important. Every single country in the so-called Arab Spring suffered tremendously because of foreign intervention, all these warring parties, including the United States, NATO, Saudi Arabia, Qatar and so forth. And they tried, but they failed in Tunisia. The foreign intervention, I would just say 'conspiracy,' hasn't worked."

9. OCCUPY WALL STREET: WE ARE THE 99%

On March 31, 2011, a half year before the #OccupyWallStreet viral wildfire takes hold, Columbia University economics professor Joe Stiglitz declares that something is broken in America.

Twenty-five years prior, writes the Nobel Prize winner in *Vanity Fair*, the top one percent of Americans took in 12 percent of the nation's income. That figure doubled to 25 percent, with the top 1% controlling 40 percent of the nation's wealth. Men with only high-school diplomas experience a 12 percent income drop over the same period. This growing concentration of wealth is matched by few countries worldwide, Russia and Iran among them.

Wealth begets power, which begets more wealth, Stiglitz argues, who documents the dismantling of controls on campaign spending by companies and wealthy individuals. Ninety percent of campaigns for Congress are won by those spending the most, while the vast majority of members of Congress and nearly all senators are "members of the top 1 percent when they arrive, are kept in office by money from the top 1 percent, and know that if they serve the top 1 percent well they will be rewarded by the top 1 percent when they leave office." [50]

Stiglitz closes with a survey of citizens overthrowing governments in authoritarian strongholds such as Egypt and Tunisia, and laments, "As we gaze out at the popular fervor in the streets, one question to ask ourselves is this: When will it come to America? In important ways, our own country has become like one of these distant, troubled places."

There are myriad, conflicting opinions about Occupy Wall Street.

- It was a historic milestone on the road to global revolution.

- It was a failure, generously a constructive failure.

- It brought to the fore critical public issues, the idea of the United States tumbling into oligarchy, its democracy suffocated by the economic and political power of its wealthiest one percent, the saturation of money in politics, the abandonment of the middle class.

- It was a futile occupation of a tiny space that was cleaned up and permanently closed to protesters within a couple months, protesters whose active engagement soon dwindled to obscure irrelevance.

- It inspired hundreds, even thousands of #occupy events in solidarity, building a powerful national and international political movement.

- It publicized an issue that catapulted a Bernie Sanders candidacy to win 22 states, nearly defeating Hillary Clinton for the Democratic Party presidential nomination.

KALLE LASN'S PROVOCATION

Adbusters is housed on a quiet Vancouver street, easy to miss with its lack of garish signage. Stumble across the magazine on a news rack, and you may find the design and content unsettling – many pages just a single *in your face* image or a caption. "We are in kind of a visual era, aren't we," asks co-founder and publisher Kalle Lasn rhetorically. "All of a sudden, young people, I don't know how much they actually read."

The magazine delivers a relentless stream of provocations and has, over time, penetrated the collective consciousness with anti-consumerist memes such as "Buy Nothing Day" (inspired by Vancouver artist Ted Dave, popularized by the magazine) and "Digital Detox Week."

In the years before Occupy, Lasn concludes the world is heading in a bad direction – climate change, financial instability, in danger of spiraling into a long, dark age. He keeps asking, "What can be done? Can we really tinker with the DNA of the global systems?

"What if we on the left actually start asking, 'What are the big ideas without which a sane, sustainable future is unthinkable?'"

Occupy Wall Street is conceived as one such idea. "It was the time of the Arab Spring and we decided that the moment was right for something to happen in America as well," recalls Lasn. "A special moment after the 2008–2009 financial troubles. Young people were really disillusioned. They had their university degrees and were still getting nowhere. They felt the future doesn't compute for them. So, Occupy was a very special sort of one off-kind of an event. It was just something for people to get excited about."

On July 4, 2011, *Adbusters* editor Micah White launches the Twitter hashtag #OccupyWallStreet with the rallying cry, "Dream of insurrection against corporate rule," promoting the campaign on Reddit, in political forums and on activist websites.

One week later, *Adbusters* publishes a "tactical briefing," entitled, "A Shift in Revolutionary Tactics." It urges thousands to converge on Manhattan's financial district to "... set up tents, kitchens, peaceful barricades and occupy Wall Street for a few months. Once there, we shall incessantly repeat one simple demand in a plurality of voices."

WHAT IS OUR ONE DEMAND?

The post insists the event will have no leaders. And the "one demand" won't be determined until the "people's assembly" decides on one. One is suggested: "(We) demand that Barack Obama ordain a Presidential Commission tasked with ending the influence money has over our representatives in Washington." Then, for good measure, three more are tipped, including "the dismantling of half the 1,000 military bases America has around the world to the reinstatement of the Glass-Steagall Act or a 'three strikes and you're out' law for corporate criminals."

An enduring image of a ballerina balanced on Wall Street's iconic Charging Bull statue asks the question, "What is our one demand?" Obscured in the poster's background are militant protesters linking arms as they move toward the viewer, with this call to action: *#OccupyWallStreet. September 17th. Bring Tent.*

The briefing is signed "for the wild, Culture Jammers HQ."

An early tease of the project appears on the *Adbusters* site some months earlier. Staff writer Kono Matsu begins "A Million Man March on Wall Street" by emphasizing the need for leadership, organization, and one unequivocal demand. "Revolutions are not unplanned and leaderless events," writes Matsu. "Nor do they happen like 'spontaneous combustion.' The mass protests that have erupted in Cairo's Midan Tahrir square, and are close to toppling Mubarak's regime, were orchestrated by a handful of Internet savvy organizers known as the April 6 Youth Movement. For two years they planned, strategized, thought things through."

On Saturday, September 17, between one and five thousand activists (official vs. activist claims) show up at Lower Manhattan's Zuccotti Park at midday, with several hundred staying through the first night, vowing to camp until their to-be-determined demands were met.

DAVID GRAEBER AND THE 99%

David Graeber, professor of anthropology at the London School of Economics, appears on Amy Goodman's *Democracy Now!* newscast two days after the occupation begins.

In *TIME* magazine's 2011 "Person of the Year" feature on *The Protester*, Kurt Andersen writes that Graeber "nudged the group to a fresh vision: a long-term encampment in a public space, an improvised democratic protest village without pre-appointed leaders, committed to a general critique – the U.S. economy is broken, politics is corrupted by big money – but with no immediate call for specific legislative or executive action. It was also Graeber who (with help from four protestors) coined the movement's ingenious slogan, 'We are the 99%.'"

Graeber tells Goodman he attended an August 2nd general assembly meeting after receiving an *Adbusters* communique. Modeled on "horizontal direct democracy," specifically the *acampadas* (protest camp) process practiced by Madrid's 50,000 anti-austerity protesters in May, the intention, he tells her, is to reinvent democracy. Political parties "corrupted, bought and sold by the financial elite" will never deliver solutions. "People need to be going into the public square, meet each other, start brainstorming ideas. The system is not going to save us." He talks about the need to "recreate a society worth living in, creating it ourselves."

On September 24, a week after the protest begins, NYPD officers arrest more than 80 protesters as they march to Union Square. A video documenting an officer spraying mace on young women, seemingly without provocation, goes viral, attracting widespread sympathy for the protesters.

THE INFECTIOUS SPIRIT OF IT

Todd Gitlin is skeptical. The former president of sixties-era Students for a Democratic Society and author of numerous books on activism, including *Occupy Nation*, doesn't like the idea of "manifestations without demands." Then he starts visiting the park and "felt the infectious spirit of it."

"It feels to me in so many ways, that the advance of plutocracy in this country has been met with, basically, a combination of a huge yawn and a deeply reactionary Tea Party response," laments the Columbia University professor. "And now (at the Occupy site), I see life, I see signs of life. It's like the first week of spring, the flowers are out. A kind of visceral feeling that, these people are not dead. People had good and sufficient reason to be deeply disappointed and or enraged by the official response to the housing crisis, to the financial bubble. Obama had disappointed many people. And it took two plus years to get people out. But they were out, and, you know what? It's always good when they're out in an experimental mood. 'Okay, let's be pragmatic. Let's try this. Try that.' I mean, it didn't pan out the way I would have had it pan out. But at least signs of life are better than signs of death."

Within two weeks, more than three dozen organizations including labor unions and MoveOn.org have announced support for Occupy, many joining an October 5th march estimated at up to 20,000 participants.

New York City police in riot gear arrive in the early morning of November 15 to remove hundreds of demonstrators, making more than 200 arrests, effectively ending the occupation 60 days after it begins.

MONUMENTAL IDEAS

"The biggest lesson that we learned from Occupy Wall Street," says Lasn, "is that sometimes the near impossible actually is possible, that you can actually sit around a table like this and you can say, well, what's the one big thing that we can do that could really disrupt America right now? And then somebody stands up and says, 'Well, why don't we go to the iconic heart of global capitalism, which is Wall Street, and why don't we just fuck the place up for a while and see what happens?' And then somebody will say, 'Oh, no, that's too big, it's too idealistic. And, we can't do that.'

"And then somebody says, 'Fuck it, let's do it.'

"And then you come six months before the event, you have a poster, and you come up with the hashtag and a website. You start putting out tactical briefings and you talk to some of the people in New York who are actually on the ground and able to organize, people like David Graeber. And suddenly, something happens and then you have a few lucky breaks along the way. Like some police stupidly attacking young girls and suddenly creating headlines, which we didn't actually create ourselves, and basically knock this whole Occupy Wall Street thing into the national limelight. I think the biggest thing we learned is that it's okay to dream big, and think big, and not to be afraid of monumental ideas. And even if a meta-meme feels like a sort of idealistic pipe dream, you can still go for it. As the global situation gets worse and worse, then somewhere along the line, there's going to be a meeting of your idealism with the severity of the situation. And suddenly an idea, a meta-meme that felt impossible even a year ago, can take off all of a sudden and start transforming the culture in the deepest way that you can imagine."

THE NOTION OF SUCCESS

"Part of what was stirring about Occupy Wall Street was that it actually made the assemblies real," recounts Gitlin. He believes most Americans have no idea of the importance of freedom of assembly in the James Madison-drafted First Amendment to the United States Constitution.

"And the number was vast. I ran into a sociologist whose UC Riverside group had studied occupying encampments throughout the state of California, and there were hundreds of them, hundreds, this amazing phenomenon. It was short-lived. I am not trying to say it was a social movement. But it was an honoring of this core value of people coming together, not simply to stand up on soap boxes and yell at each other, but to actually deliberate. The language that didn't make its way into the First Amendment, but did make its way to most of the state constitutions, starting in Pennsylvania, with this: *The right of the people peaceably to assemble, to consult for the common good.*

"What they had in mind was a process that later political theorists called deliberative. It wasn't just, 'You have a right to spout off, to be talking heads yelling at each other on TV.' it's actually talking about the sanctity, the political sanctity of the creation of a public, right before your eyes and ears. It's a tradition that is not honored in this country. I'd say that the French, the Italians – Europeans – are actually more cognizant of it. They've had more revolutions, also more counter revolutions."

This idea of horizontal organization, LaDonna Brave Bull Allard at Standing Rock emphasizes there were no leaders. Without her and a half-dozen others, that thing wouldn't have happened, much less happen on her land, but she emphasized that and some Adbusters organizers emphasize that as well. Are you a fan of the idea?

"Not at all," scoffs Gitlin. "It's a nonsensical overreaction to various abuses of leadership – demagogic, violent, excessively hierarchical – in the '60s. But it's nonsense to say that there are no leaders. People don't act in unison unless somebody takes initiative. It's not necessarily that the leadership announces itself at a press conference or on a letterhead. But the leadership takes the form of clusters of people who take initiative.

"And so obviously, it happened in Zuccotti Park. I mean, somebody had to make decisions when they got together with some pizza in September 2011. Some people had to decide when they were blocked from demonstrating down at Bowling Green, 'Okay, let's go over to Zuccotti Park.' That was not spontaneous. That's leadership."

CULTURE JAMMING AND META-MEMES

Lasn first uses the term "meta-meme" two decades back in *Culture Jam*. He claims that just about everybody is operating on a surface level. His prime example is the fight to stop pipelines. "They get all these people together. And they march against pipelines. And they do something in front of the White House, and they get arrested. Sometimes they're successful, most often they're not, but now they are in the business of stopping pipelines. And yet, it's quite obvious that you're not going to, that it's a mug's game. Because you can stop all the pipelines you want, but ultimately, you have to stop the system that creates the pipelines. That is one level deeper that environmentalists have to think: what do you need do to really disrupt the culture, to somehow dig as deep as you can into what I call meta-memes, without which a future is unthinkable, without certain changes to the very DNA of our culture? We've identified a bunch of those."

What's your definition of a meta-meme?

"Just a really big idea, an idea that is so big that, without it, we probably won't have a future."

Was there an element of the Occupy Wall Street project that had to do with your "Culture Jam" idea of a "suicidal consumerist binge?"

"I grew up watching TV," admits Lasn, "and every few minutes you get a few pro-consumption messages thrown at you. When you grow up in a mental environment when even important political events and presidential speeches are interrupted by ads, when you're living in that kind of wrap-around advertising environment, then that warps everything, right across the board it warps everything. I think that's one of the reasons why we can't really get to the heart of what we need to do to solve climate change. There are big ideas which have the potential to fix climate change, but we human beings who grew up in the so-called first world have been mind-fucked. And when you've been mind-fucked as far as we have been, I think there's very little hope for you. If you're lucky enough, like I did, you go traveling and spend a few years having epiphanies about what life is really like on the planet. Then maybe you can break out of that media/ consumer trance, but most of us can't, most of us are just stuck there. And it's probably going to take a generation or two to snap out of it. And that well may be too late."

In Silicon Valley, venture capitalists and tech startups talk a lot about disruption, how to disrupt certain business trends or categories. What was Adbusters, what was Occupy Wall Street trying to disrupt?

"A leading question. I guess our culture needs various disruptions. When I wrote my first book, the *Culture Jam*, the game we were playing was to disrupt culture in various ways with ideas like 'Buy Nothing Days' and then 'Digital Detox Weeks.' They give people epiphanies, and they're also able to give structure, and launch a bit of a wave of activity, then launch a movement if your disruption is potent enough, like Occupy Wall Street.

"If you want to change political culture, then you can keep on voting for the right people, playing this tweedledum, tweedledee game of who's gonna win the next election. But if you really want to change political culture, then one has to go deeper. And one way to go deeper is to start asking questions, like, 'Why do we need all this secrecy?' Democracy just can't work if there's just these all these secrets everywhere. If you were to muck around with the DNA of political culture, and over a generation, have the people demanding like, We the People need to know everything. If we don't know everything, then how can we have really a democracy? It's not a new idea. Radical transparency has been part of the discussion on the left for a long, long time. But I think one can go even deeper than this talk about transparency, or we need a bit more oxygen, this idea that making secrecy taboo is a meta-meme. I mean that to me feels like a monumental step in the right direction for how we do politics."

How does your learning from Occupy inform new projects as you were obviously so close to it?

"I must admit that the big slogan we put on top of our poster – *what is our one idea* – that never really happened."

There was that a suggestion in an early tactical briefing for Barack Obama to ordain a presidential commission, tasked with ending the influence of money on the electoral process.

"In the very early days," Lasn recounts, "I remember trying to make the Robin Hood tax one of the simple demands, because (it) had already made headway in a lot of countries. And it's one of those ideas, of slowing down fast money, and then figuring out how to use that incredible amount of money that you can collect by having even a 0.1% tax on all financial transactions and currency trades.

"But, again, that didn't quite stick. I don't know exactly why. I understand the criticism that, somehow, we were never able to do what the Tea Party people did, get people elected and come up with some ideas that really change the culture. And yet, I never thought of Occupy Wall Street being something along the Tea Party track. I saw it as being something similar to 1968, the phenomenon that politicized me, when a tiny protest in Paris somehow exploded into this global phenomenon where the young generation suddenly realized that they don't like the way things were being run by the old generation. And they came up with what I saw at the time as the beginning of the first global revolution.

"And I always saw Occupy Wall Street just being one more step along the way. And all these people's, 'Oh, you guys did a bunch of shit together. You never did this. Never did that.' (They) just don't get it. You know, we politicized the whole generation. So, if you think about it that way, if you think about 1968 as the first little test, then Occupy Wall Street, other little bangs as well, like #MeToo, all kinds of other skirmishes. There's gonna be a third moment, and Occupy Wall Street will be remembered as one of the milestones along the way."

In the civil rights movement, activists reached a certain point in Albany, Georgia, where their voting rights protest just didn't work. And they learned from that, and pushed forward. There was a phrase, from a recent issue of Adbusters, that failure can be a springboard. Do you think that trial and error and being willing to embrace failure is an important part of social movements?

"My way of thinking is different from the way you phrase the question, like, I don't like the word failure. I never saw Occupy Wall Street as being..."

(Former Adbusters editor and Occupy Wall Street co-creator) Micah White called it a constructive failure.

"Yeah, whatever. But I don't think it's a failure. I don't think it's even a constructive failure. I think it was one step along the way. And now we are more ready than ever to take it to the next level. The factors that gave birth to it are still there, they've only intensified. And somewhere along the line, there's going to be more Big Bang moments like Occupy Wall Street and 1968. Somewhere along the line, I think there will be a global revolution. And then I don't think people will look back on Occupy Wall Street and talk about it as a failure."

How does a young person who has grown up in the mental environment you've described engage in the world effectively?

"For most people, I just feel like saying to them, you're all fucked up, go back and start from zero. That's really my advice. I think that if we can somehow replace all those surface kind of lefty books that have been coming out for the last 30-40 years, and God knows I've read many of them, if we can identify the memes and meta-memes and come up with books with big ideas, a new set of first principles, this is something I still believe in. Trying to talk some guy in San Francisco into living a more benign life, I don't have time for that.

"Let's face it, I think we have one more crack at the whip, it may already be too late. And the only way to do it is to change the system in the most fundamental ways, go all the way down to the very bottom of the swamp if you like, and pull out the bad roots and hopefully grow a few new ones. To me, that's the only thing that can now save this human experiment of ours on planet Earth."

In the Culture Jam book, you made some provocative statements; one of them is, a free, authentic life is no longer possible in America today.

"No, I don't think so. The Internet hadn't kicked in when I wrote that book. It was motivated by the reality of what a constant barrage of two or three thousand marketing messages actually does to your brain. I mean, once your brain has been pickled with emotionally coercive advertising like that, from the moment that you're a little kid, you're running around the living room, you're looking at the TV set, then you're a cooked goose."

Do you think you have a unique perspective coming from Estonia, living in Canada, in a number of places, the ability to look in a unique way at what's happening in American culture?

"I think that I'm a strange kind of guy. I left Estonia when I was two, was in refugee camps in Germany and other places until I was 13, then growing up in this totally alien culture of Australia, and finally finishing up in Japan, five years in the advertising industry, and then with the money I made, traveling for three or four years around the world, experiencing as much as I could, eventually settling down here in Vancouver. I have no allegiances to anybody, I've seen good or bad in a lot of places. And I think my brain is suited to look at the world in a fresher way."

For many people, the experience of travel is a kind of revolutionary personal act.

"I'm still running on that juice," reminisces Lasn. "I have never forgotten many of the lessons and epiphanies I had during those three years. And actually, there is an answer to that young guy in San Francisco, the answer is go traveling. Go traveling, go and find yourself. Find your true self. Go traveling, go to Thailand, go to magic mushroom village in Mexico. Look at the people in the streets of Calcutta (Kolkata) dropping off like flies and then come back and figure out what has to happen."

FINDING ITS PLACE IN HISTORY

"I'm not going to say you always win what you want," concludes Gitlin. "And when you win, it often turns out to be different from what you thought you were angling for. Did it succeed or fail? Well, if you're looking for concrete effects on political economic policy, you'd have to say it failed."

Assuming there was a specific agenda or goal when the hashtag campaign started.

"Well, to speak of goal is misleading. Wasn't the goal to simply exist, to make a demonstration, to show? And the show did turn the center of American opinion toward the left; it coined, it took from Joe Stiglitz, the 1%, 99% and put economic inequality more frontally on the political agenda. What they wanted was a manifestation of a sentiment. They got that. That uprising fed the Bernie Sanders campaigns and helped move the Democratic Party to the left. With consequences that we await."

10. SOPA/PIPA:
THE GREAT INTERNET BLACKOUT OF 2012

Rainey Reitman can't trace the precise origin of the largest Internet protest in history, the day over 100,000 websites voluntarily went black. Advocacy organizations fighting the SOPA and PIPA copyright bills didn't call for a blackout. She recalls an early suggestion from *reddit*, otherwise characterizing the effort as decentralized, with no one organization controlling messaging or campaigning. Internet 'hacktivist' Aaron Swartz claims, "They did whatever they could think of to do. They didn't stop to ask anyone for permission."[51]

But the measurable outcome of the January 28, 2012 protest is astounding. Wikipedia, among the highest profile participants, generates eight million calls to Congress through its member look-up tool. Over 10 million petition signatures are gathered along with four million emails, sent via vanguard organizations such as the Electronic Frontier Foundation (EFF) and Fight for the Future. On the day before the protest, 80 members of Congress are in favor of the Stop Online Piracy Act (SOPA); on the day after, 63 are in favor, 122 opposed, and the bill's author withdraws the bill.

"My background is in privacy," says Reitman, Chief Program Officer of the EFF and co-founder of the Freedom of the Press Foundation. A consumer privacy advocate running a three-person activism team, Reitman is thrust into the battle when the EFF staffer handling copyright quits around the time the Senate's

PROTECT IP Act (PIPA) companion bill is introduced. It requires a rapid ramp up on the history of copyright.

"The SOPA proposal," she explains, "was to ratchet up copyright enforcement so that if you were accused of having copyrighted data on your website, maybe snippets of a song or a video, your whole site could get taken down. The domain name server would actually de-list you. You'd be put on a blacklist; when people entered the URL for your website, it wouldn't return your site, it would just go to this black hole."

A MYTHIC VISION

The EFF is founded in 1990 by Internet visionaries and "digerati" John Perry Barlow, John Gilmore and Mitch Kapor. It's the era of bulletin boards, the early stages of what would eventually blossom into the World Wide Web. "The idea that you could connect with people all over the world continuously," says Reitman, "was something that came across as utopian, almost mythic." The organization is formed in reaction to government attempts to intrude on privacy and on user autonomy in these emerging spaces, taking traditional civil liberties battles into the digital world.

"To our minds," maintains Reitman, "this was a disastrous proposal. There's so many reasons that copyrighted works might end up being utilized, having these draconian reactions could make people nervous about engaging in social critique or utilizing fair use of copyrighted works. We were also worried from a security standpoint, the idea that you could basically mess with or even break the Domain Name System, and tons of security engineers and creators for the World Wide Web were deeply concerned."

COICA BEGETS SOPA BEGETS PIPA

Mike Masnick writes the respected Silicon Valley blog *Techdirt*, which he founds in 1997, with a focus on legal and business matters such as intellectual property, privacy and copyright reform. The blog becomes an early leading voice in the fight against SOPA/ PIPA.

What got you interested in copyright in general and SOPA/ PIPA specifically?

"There are a number of issues that I focus on constantly," explains Masnick, "because I think they're important to the future of innovation and free speech. Early on, I recognized, for better or worse - mostly worse - copyright policy for many years has been Internet policy. So, we're talking about how the Internet works, and what is enabled and what is allowed and what is not allowed."

The day the SOPA/ PIPA legislation crossed your desk, it hit you in a certain way. Why did you feel it was important historically and politically, why you were so passionate about it?

"There are actually three pieces of legislation," reveals Masnick. "The first was a piece of legislation called COICA (Combating Online Infringement and Counterfeits Act). And then the next year, Senator (Patrick) Leahy introduced the PROTECT IP Act.

"And it was bad. A few years earlier, there had been another piece of legislation which I thought problematic. In the three decades prior, there had been 15 new copyright laws passed having to do with piracy in some form or another; on average, every two years a new law was passed. So, there's just this constant parade of 'we have to keep expanding it,' and nobody taking a step back and saying, 'maybe piracy law is not the issue, maybe there's something else going on.'

"PROTECT IP was a very big step forward in what it initially enabled, but the original version of PROTECT IP would open up a private right of action to block entire websites. That was the thing that really caught my attention, because there's a good argument for a piece of content that is found to be infringing to be taken down. It's breaking the law."

A lot of people thought that's what the law was proposing.

"PIPA went much further," responds Masnick. "It said, you could demand to have entire websites taken down because they had some amount of infringing content. And that would mean that you would be using the law to censor entire websites that would have plenty of non-infringing material. Which raises all sorts of First Amendment questions."

TIVO, BETAMAX, AND THE PLAYER PIANO

Which might, by coincidence, be a commercial competitor. Or someone with a contrary political point of view.

"If you look back at every new technological innovation that had to do with content and content consumption, every single time the legacy industry would freak out and say, it was infringing; the history of radio, oh my gosh, actually I'll go back even further, the player piano. The reason we had a new copyright law in 1909, the 1909 Copyright Act was almost entirely a response to the player piano. You had a piano that had a roll of paper, and it would play the music for you automatically. And musicians said this was going to destroy musicians, and the business of music, which at the time was selling sheet music. And therefore, we need an entirely new copyright law to deal with the player piano or nobody would ever write music again.

"More recently, when cable TV came about, that was infringing. When the VCR came about, when the MP3 audio player came out, that was infringing. When TiVo came out, every single time, people would realize this is a technology that provides better service.

"But if we allow copyright law to ban those new technologies," believes Masnick, "we would never get those innovations and oftentimes the content industries themselves will never get the benefit. My favorite example of this is the VCR where Hollywood sued and lost, thankfully. It was actually fairly close – the Sony Betamax case (Sony Corp. of America v. Universal City Studios, Inc.). The most incredible thing is that Jack Valenti, who was the head of the MPAA (Motion Picture Association of America) for decades, gave this congressional testimony in 1982, with the famous line '... the VCR is to the American film producer and the American public as the Boston Strangler is to the woman home alone.'

"A few years later, home video made more money for Hollywood than the box office, right? The thing that he insisted was going to kill Hollywood saved Hollywood. The RIAA (Recording Industry Association of America) just put out their latest numbers, and the music industry, the record labels are making more money than ever. And most of this is coming from streaming, the exact service that they spent years trying to kill. A big part of my fear with the original SOPA/ PIPA approach was you would take down entire websites, you wouldn't give them a chance to find those new business models to enable this stuff."

THE FOUNDERS' VISION FOR COPYRIGHT

EFF's Reitman believes copyright is a "wildly misunderstood concept" because we think of it in terms of property rights, like a house or a car, a physical object. "Copyright is different. It's a property with limited rights designed according to the U.S. Constitution to prompt art and science in the world. That would become part of the public domain or become a thing that we could all eventually enjoy. Today, one of the most powerful censorship tools for online speech is copyright."

What was the original intent of copyright and how did the framers of those regulations in the Constitution intend to balance the rights of artists to make a living and the public good?

"The copyright clause of the Constitution is very simple," says Masnick, "to promote the progress of science and useful arts, we will provide this exclusive right for a limited period of time."

> Article I Section 8, Clause 8, Patent and Copyright Clause of the Constitution:
>
> [The Congress shall have power] "To promote the progress of science and useful arts, by securing for limited times to authors and inventors the exclusive right to their respective writings and discoveries."

"That preamble part of the clause is what I think is the most important," believes Masnick, "they're explaining the nature of this law, which is to promote the progress of science and useful arts. Which everyone mixes up, by the way, because if you look back at the language of the time, science meant learning and education and useful arts meant tools.

"If you go back and look at the letters written between the founding fathers, there was this tradeoff, which was, well, yes, we want to incentivize people to create and invent, and then at the end of that limited period of time, it becomes public domain. So, there's this element of balance there that was built in from the very beginning. And what's happened over time is that the law has changed again and again. The first copyright law was the Copyright Act of 1790, which had a fairly reasonable limited time of 14 years. It only applied to maps, books, pamphlets, and charts. And you can renew it for 14 years.

"Over time, more categories got added, and then the time frame kept changing. And the really big change is the 1976 Copyright Act. If you want to get a copyright the first 200 years of this country, you had to register and send off a copy, you would get a registered copyright. In 1976, we switched to any new creative work considered covered by copyright."

The term was then extended to lifetime plus seventy years.

"Soon after that major change in copyright law," Masnick points out, "we have the rise of computers and the Internet, and, suddenly, everyone and anyone can create content and put it out there. And yet, we're living in this world where any content that you create is covered by copyright. But the way the Internet and computers work is they're constantly copying stuff. Hence, you have this massive clash, and the Internet is a sort of – I hate the name – 'wild west' area where there's no regulation of anything; the only regulation that comes to be used on the Internet is copyright law.

"So, people just use that for anything they don't like, using copyright claims to try and silence people. And so, it became this really important policy in terms of innovation and online speech. There was a lawsuit that what search engines do is infringing on copyright. Because they are going out and scraping and making a copy of the entire Internet, of all this work that is covered by copyright. I think the world would be a much worse place if we weren't able to search."

Has there been a shift from the founders' focus on the public good to the milking of commercial outcomes?

"Yeah, well, what's happened is we flipped the purpose in the means, right? The original purpose was to benefit the public, promote the progress of all these things. And the means was a limited temporary monopoly on this right. Now, the purpose is to give special rights to the copyright holder. We've completely flipped that equation. And the whole process was hijacked by often large corporate interests, who saw the ability to take this law and change its nature to be something that was a right special to them."

"IT'S GONNA BE GREAT"

When you look back, what was most effective in defeating the bill?

"There were a few interesting things that I observed," Masnick muses. "One was, this weird, useful coalition that came together early on and said, 'This is a real problem.' A very broad coalition involving people who don't normally agree on a lot of things, who all said, 'This is bad. We need to speak up about this, and we need to do something about it.'

"The other thing that was useful was that you had this mix of old-timers who had gone through a number of battles, who were very savvy about the process, about how it all worked. But who, I would say, were also somewhat jaded, maybe a little cynical. I would probably put myself in that category, if I'm being honest. I thought that the process was going to work as follows: we will make a lot of noise, we will complain, people will get really angry, and we'll get some press, and then we will lose. Because that is the way copyright law has worked for the previous 20 years. You fight, you fight, you fight, and then you lose, because copyright is this unstoppable train: Congress always passes the next worst copyright bill.

"But then you had people in the coalition who – this is a broad generalization – were younger, were naive or hadn't gone through these battles. And they were like, 'Well, *this is wrong*, we have to stop it and we will stop it. Of course, we can stop it, because it's bad.' And it was that combination of people that made the difference. Because you had the people who understood the process and knew who to present to, how to get a message out. And you have these youngsters who didn't know the process and believed we're going to win. The young, naive people came up with censorship day and 'shut down the internet.' That was all their idea," he acknowledges.

"My initial reaction was like, oh, man, you know, if that flops, that looks really bad, and then we lose all the momentum. But they were like, 'everyone's gonna buy into it, it's gonna be great.' They were right.

"The real lesson is that you can make a difference, right? I mean, that was the amazing thing. I came into that process extraordinarily cynical and I came out of it the opposite. If you're cynical about these things, then nothing will change. You won't always win, right? We've lost lots of other fights, we've won some; that's always going to happen. But being cynical means you will always lose. Stepping up, speaking out and speaking your mind, giving your opinion on these things, at least gives you a chance.

"And we saw that when enough people speak up and when policies that are presented are really bad, it doesn't matter how much money there is behind the other side. It doesn't matter how many lobbyists are involved. If enough people speak out, the thing that matters most in the end to the politicians is the voters. Most of the time, the reason why lobbying beats out public interest is because there isn't public interest. In those cases, the lobbyists will always win because they're the only voices in the room and the only voices that are being heard. When you get to a point where the voices of the voters massively outweigh the money of the lobbyists, then the voters will win. You're not always going to win, but you have the ability to take a chance and speak out and do what's right."

DRY RUNS, THEN 100,000 WEBSITES

Reitman describes the day of the blackouts.

"Over 100,000 websites either put up a black banner or shut down completely, or redirected, many of them to our EFF website. We changed colors and put a black banner up, but we continued to allow people to come and send letters to and call Congress. I often think of activism as, you have to be on the surfboard and in the right spot to catch the wave."

There's the matter of persistence over time, but also the matter of allowing and recognizing external forces that you need to surf.

"Yeah, external forces," she agrees. "I think it was either our second or third or maybe even fourth big day of action, where we asked people to put up banners; we'd done it a few times, we had a few dry runs. And I remember being in the office at midnight, because, for whatever reason, we thought it started at midnight Pacific Time, and went through midnight the next day. And I think, even at 10 p.m., some people in the East Coast are starting to blackout their websites. And it wasn't really clear at midnight, when we're all sitting there refreshing different sites and looking at traffic to our site, whether or not it was actually going to be successful. And then, yeah, different websites started going down. And there was a cascading effect where once a couple of websites went black that were really huge, like Wikipedia, other websites jumped on. Large websites that would have been embarrassed to have not participated were starting to change their website banner by 10, 11 in the morning the next day, when we were all back in the office again, having slept very little that night."

EFF also had success in engaging the tech community. Eighty-three prominent Internet engineers opposed SOPA explaining its technical implications in an open letter to the U.S. Congress. Reitman recalls a series of real-time logistical challenges during the blackout, being ready with messaging, handling the growing wave of web traffic. "We couldn't actually know if anybody was going to come to the party. We had to be ready and prepared to go either way."

An article of faith at a certain point, do this thing, with no guarantee of the outcome.

"You not only have to do it with no guarantee of outcome, but every campaign I did after that, there was a certain amount of hope. You go into it and you do the best you can. And then you have to hope that you get that really big wave of interest and publicity."

And that the second or third blackout had to happen to have this success, those prior investments necessary preparation for this type of action.

"I think that's totally true that we needed a couple of really important things happening in the early activities," says Reitman. "One of them was, we got a bigger and bigger coalition together of what I think of as more of your 'grass-tops' organizations, able to activate a community of people to speak out, who are able to bring a message that will resonate with that community.

"EFF has people that really care about our issues and the way we speak to them, but our coalition partners might have really different communities that care about them. And if we could connect with them and explain how it would affect their communities, then they'd be able to be the messenger for those communities and get them involved. Every time we had an activity or a coalition letter, or had weekly phone calls, and a very large mailing list, it was another opportunity to bring a few more folks into the fold and get them excited and get them prepped, so that the next action would be even larger."

VERIZON, DISNEY, PORNHUB, AND FAIR-WEATHER FRIENDS

What conclusions did you draw as to the potential of leveraging the business community for social activism?

"I'd say that large corporations – and to be fair, all of my experiences were with tech companies – are fair-weather friends. They will come out for battles that they think might impact them, but you can't count on them when the chips are down. That's just the reality.

But when they're there, they're great. The things that you get when you bring in companies to an advocacy campaign include publicity, for example."

Reitman cites as an example working with Pornhub on a net neutrality issue. "Pornhub gets a lot of traffic; if you're going to Pornhub, and there's a link to take an action, that's a lot of people seeing that link. Also, a lot of people are googling Pornhub. If you have a news article, one of the most popular blog posts ever was about this, that is showing up in Google News. It's got the word Pornhub in the title, people will actually go to the news article, because they'll be headed to Pornhub, but don't mind stopping over – I hope that's the reason – at this article to see what they are up to.

"And three, because it will engage the news. Because you're going to hit a group of people that otherwise might not have found it, you're not just talking to your regular folks. So, there's a huge potential for involving companies. In my experience, I've not seen companies throw a lot of money at these campaigns. But if you can get them to do things, you can get all those other benefits.

"Two other things that I think are really important about the SOPA action, and this isn't something that everybody in activist community groups like. We were able to cross political lines and get people on two sides of the aisle to care about this for different reasons. And I think that was important for winning a battle over a bill in Congress. I don't know if you need it for other types of battles. But for a bill in Congress, we needed that.

"And we didn't try to control everything, something I find activist groups struggle with. It was not the case that EFF actually called for the blackout, there's a lot of different theories about where it came from. But once people caught on to it, there were people doing things in their community groups and writing blog posts. And it wasn't coming through a central hub, approving messaging and the like, making sure it was in line with our objectives and signing off on it.

"Instead, it was very much like the web itself, a very decentralized organism that had its own momentum. The role of the EFF was about framing and amplification, connecting groups to each other. When groups would have activities, we had the ability to talk about them within a larger frame and to help them be repositioned, then amplifying the most important things so that they would get up into the media instead of being lost."

UTOPIA/DYSTOPIA

Paint a picture of a dystopian view of the future, 10 years from now, if EFF fails in its key strategic initiatives, and if some of the darker online trends come to fruition; what does that look like?

Reitman believes "bits of dystopia" are starting to take root around the world. "We're seeing places like China adopting social credit systems. We're seeing proposals to create separate Internets where you would only be able to access content that the government in that country (allowed); the rest of the world wouldn't be available to you. Yeah, so dystopia is where the idea of the free and open Internet wouldn't exist, that various Internets would be disconnected from one another. And we would have extremely limited access to information; it would be a heck of a lot more like watching television than a participatory system like we have today.

"The dystopian world I am most afraid of is one where we've lost private spaces, where you can experiment with ideas, or explore the world or explore yourself, and are now having everything you do tracked and compiled and kept in a database that you never get to access. And some of that compilation happens from companies and some of it happens from the government. And the worst of it happens when the two are joining forces and sharing data about you.

"The technology for that already exists. You can look at maps of surveillance cameras just in San Francisco, and it will terrify you. We already know that it is trivial to track people's online activities. We're very much reliant on the rule of law to hold those forces in check. So, dystopia would be losing the legal limitations on the technology so that there were no safeguards against constant unblinking surveillance."

Harkening back to the original ideas of John Perry Barlow and other EFF pioneers, go out those same 10 years and imagine you've been very successful.

"One of the cornerstones of the ideals that helped spur the larger digital rights movements," explains Reitman, "was this idea that the Internet itself could be a force to equalize, that you could enter in regardless of your background, or your history, or your economic status, and that you could come into a digital world where we would all be treated as equals. I don't think we're there yet at all.

"But I think the utopian version of where we'd like to get to is a heck of a lot closer to that, a place where people could connect and operate freely in a way that lifted up and lessened some of the inequalities we see in the offline world. I think that's part of it. Honestly, it's really tricky to figure out a way to do this. I think freedom of thought is a huge part of it, the ability to experiment with new ideas and connect with others and have access to a wide wealth of knowledge.

"And then," Reitman ends, "I think the best utopia is one that has pretty strict limits on the ability of powerful forces, like the government or corporations, to dictate how you engage with technology. That technology should be something that is beholden to users. And that they're the be-all, end-all of the debate compared to now where users are turning into the product, the thing that is marketed or controlled, or put into weird situations."

KEEP THIS THING OPEN

Brewster Kahle thinks there are a few pieces of the Internet that need fixing. An Internet pioneer and legend, he is an active civil libertarian and "the content guy" on EFF's board. AOL bought the WAIS text search company he co-founded for $15 million; Amazon bought his Alexa Internet project for $250 million. Ever use the *Wayback Machine?* Type in a website URL and a date, and the archived version renders on your browser. It's a fascinating and essential part of archive.org, another ambitious project he founds, with the modest goal of providing 'universal access to all knowledge.'

What is your vision of "the Electronic Frontier?" It's a catchy phrase.

"A line that's been working for me," says Kahle, "coalesces activities (around) no centralized points of control. So, that means no central corporate control, no control over ourselves technologically. Government should not be in the way. A move towards decentralization. A game with lots of winners. And we're building a game that has ever fewer winners."

What did you learn from the SOPA/ PIPA protest about mobilizing people and being active in the modern age?

"I think the 'Eureka!', the broader realization, was that the Internet is so important to us, not just as a cable TV replacement, it is the way that we live our lives. And those trying to seek control over the Internet ran into a strongly held belief that we have to keep this thing open, rather than letting it be shut down or controlled by large corporations and the government that works for them. That it would massively impact our lives. And it's not just in what movies we see, it's not just a video game platform. It's a broader societal piece of infrastructure.

"And people were looking to mess with it. And we rose up."

11. KYIV: THE EUROMAIDAN

At 8 p.m. on November 21, 2013, Afghan-Ukrainian journalist Mustafa Nayyem posts a message on *Facebook*:

> Well, let's get serious. Who today is ready to come to Maidan before midnight? "Likes" don't count. Only comments under this post with the words, "I am ready." As soon as we get more than a thousand, we will organize ourselves.

President Viktor Yanukovych has long promised Ukraine's voters that he will sign an association agreement with the European Union. Suddenly, he reverses course with the intention of aligning with Russia's Eurasian Economic Union.

One hour and 600 comments later, Nayyem suggests, "Let's meet at 10:30 p.m. near the monument to independence in the middle of the Maidan." Readers are encouraged to dress warmly, to bring umbrellas, tea, coffee, attitude, and friends. "A repost would be appreciated."

At the appointed hour, a small group of Kyivites, mostly university students, arrive at Maidan Nezalehznosti (Independence Square), wondering where the protesters solicited by Mustafa are. Within an hour, 1,500 gather, more by some estimates, most emerging from the Metro underground or arriving by foot.

A #Euromaidan Twitter hashtag is created, the name becoming a convenient handle for international media.

"Euro" to declare Ukrainian preference for looking westward, for integration with Europe, for liberal democracy; and "maidan" to denote a square or open space, a word borrowed from the Ottoman Empire. The words "Euromaidan" and "Maidan" become shorthand for the protests, also called the "Revolution of Dignity."

The next day, more protesters arrive, joining the small group camped in the Square, months of winter ahead of them. It rains as politicians begin to arrive to voice public support. Former world heavyweight boxing champion Vitali Klitschko, a national hero, addresses the crowd, though protesters insist he remove his political party banner. One of many recurring chants, "Ukraine is part of Europe." One sign appeals to the president, "Sign, Yanukovych, or Burn in Hell."

THE PROTEST EXPANDS

Three days after Nayyem's post, on November 24, more than 100,000 protesters show up in response to the call from opposition leaders. Clashes between rally participants and Berkut special police forces occur outside the building housing the Cabinet of Ministers. Police attack protesters with night sticks and tear gas. Government-paid young people in track suits called 'Titushki' skirmish with protesters. The term is inspired by martial arts athlete Vadim Titushko, who assaulted reporter Olha Snytsarchuk and her photographer husband, Vlad Sodel, at a May 2013 political rally. During the months of protest, the Titushki are accused of inciting violence and various provocations, attacking protesters in a manner police could or would not. Subsequent government and media investigations charged that many were felons released from prison for the work.

A CLASH OF VALUES

"It was a people standing up and saying they wanted to join the West, a clash of values," says James Brooke, editor-in-chief of the *Ukraine Business News*, a 30-year foreign correspondent whose past stints include bureau chief for the *New York Times* and *Bloomberg* (Moscow).

"(Russian President Vladimir) Putin gave Ukrainian President Yanukovych a $2 billion loan to make sure that he would join Russia's economic union. The Eurasian Union, without Ukraine, doesn't make much sense. So, it was a very daring thing where people said, no, we want to join Europe. The difference between serfs and citizens; they said, we want to be citizens. Which the President had promised all along. When he flipped on them, Maidan started."

Sergii Kharchuk is best known as an event impresario, organizing Kyiv's biggest amateur cycling race and an international rock festival before Maidan, before successfully running for City Council. Trained as an applied mathematician, he recalls the moment when he chose to participate and resist.

"I got this feeling immediately after I saw young people, students beaten by local police on the Independence Square on Maidan. It is really just one very short emotional moment when you decide to join a protest movement. At such moments, you don't think about results, about the future, what may happen with you, that you can be taken to prison or you can be beaten by police. You just act, I don't know, on a biological level, to protect your freedom."

300 YEARS

Ukrainians have various views as to the earliest days of resistance to imperial rule. For Kharchuk, it was a specific 18th century battle.

"We lost the Ukrainian state in 1712 when Ukrainian Cossacks and the Swedish army lost against Peter the First at the famous Battle of Poltava. For almost 300 years, we were culturally and militarily occupied by Russia.

"Ukrainians tried many times to get back independence. The last was a hundred years ago, in 1918, after the First World War, (when the) Ukrainian state was announced at a peace conference in Brest.

"Russian troops came to Kyiv, and we were occupied. The (Russian communist) Bolsheviks were kicked out by joint Ukrainian and German troops. When Germany left Ukraine, we faced a huge army coming from Russia." Ukraine was absorbed into the Soviet Union in 1922 as the Ukrainian Soviet Socialist Republic. "After this, we had the Holodomor (1932-33)," says Kharchuk, "the artificial famine which Soviet leaders arranged, where millions of people died through hunger."

The Holodomor, a compound of the Ukrainian words holod (hunger) and mor (plague), is Stalin's punishment of Ukraine's farmers for resisting collectivization, the forced surrender of their land to work on government-controlled farms. Eighty percent of Ukrainians work the land. The famine is further intended to crush aspirations for independence.[52] By June 1933, 28,000 are dying of starvation each day.

Ukraine achieves independence peacefully in 1991 during the USSR collapse.

"Frankly speaking," Kharchuk continues, "part of the population with Russian roots, especially ex-military officers, were not mentally ready to build a new Ukrainian state. That's why we did not vote for progressive leaders like Lech Walesa in Poland or Vaclav Havel in the Czech Republic. They decided to vote for ex-communist Leonid Kravchuk instead of progressive prisoner of freedom Viacheslav Chornovil. But we have been changing for the last 30 years, becoming more patriotic and pro-western."

KYIVAN RUS

"Russia claims that Ukraine culture, language and religion came out of Kyivan Rus, about five miles from here," Brooke explains at a downtown Kyiv cafe. "There was a very funny incident where the Russian foreign ministry posted an image (on Twitter), falsifying its history, and Ukraine came back with a picture of (Kyiv's) Sofia Cathedral and said, 'this is what we were doing in 1051.' For Moscow, they had a picture of birch trees.

"So, for Slavic culture," states Brooke, "it did start here. Kyiv was on the river Dnipro, Christianity came up the river in 970. Lithuania was pagan until the 1350s. The Russian view is that they and Ukrainians are the same people. They refuse to teach people the Ukrainian language inside Russia, they shut down the Ukrainian library in central Moscow. They think it is the invention of the Poles and the Americans and westerners. They did their best to destroy the culture. Stalin murdered 30,000 leading intellectuals here. Putin will say that Ukraine isn't a real country. His view is that it's like Texas; okay, Texas was independent for a year and a half, so what? They are basically Russians with an accent. The people who run the Kremlin are basically Soviet-generation people. And that was the attitude through 1991, that nationalists were Western agents, they're neo-Nazis."

On the last day of November 2013, 2,000 Berkut special police arrive after the Ukraine government confirms it will not sign the EU agreement. The Maidan crowd starts chanting "Revolution." Women stand in front, men on the Maidan steps, as protesters start singing the national anthem. Police beat protesters with iron instead of plastic batons, injuring more than 300. The Square is cleared.

Protesters escaping the Maidan assault walk 500 meters to St. Michael's gold-domed monastery. The grounds are filled to capacity by 11 the following morning. The monks and staff establish a food center as well as a place to donate winter clothes. The monastery serves as a triage facility.

The Automaidan is formed, activists driving their cars around the city "like a cavalry," delivering hundreds of protesters to the monastery, delivering provisions, and honking horns in front of the homes of government officials, including that of Yanukovych. One of the organizers, Dmytro Bulatov is kidnapped, held for an extended period, tortured, then released.

What was the deal that Ukraine struck for independence?

"Russia was weak in the '90s," says Brooke. "And there was a lot of goodwill, you may have seen that friendship people's arch at the end of Maidan. It goes up about 10 stories, friendship among the Slavic brothers, Ukraine the younger brother, Russia, the third brother is Belarus. A few weeks ago, some wise guy actually climbed the arch and painted a crack in it, as they're trying to figure out how to rename it, because, obviously, Russians have 500 tanks on Ukrainian soil. You go back even five years, when the Maidan started, the people used Russian social media sites, radio and TV was heavily Russian, the attitude was very friendly, very relaxed. There wasn't much hostility."

And then, the unpleasantness.

"That's why people were sort of shocked. They were blindsided. In December of 2013, I had a weekly column called *Russia Watch*. And I said when Ukraine's president goes to the Kremlin, he should look carefully at the maps on the walls, because I've heard Crimea is marked 'temporary occupied territory.' I got hate mail for that. 'How could you ever think that the Russians would take Ukrainian Crimea?' Three months later (during the Maidan protests), it's gone. Now Putin's lost his surprise effect. Had he been more organized and more successful, he could have probably taken over the eastern third of the country."

The key protester demands were about leaning towards the west, integration with Europe, versus Russia, and a subsequent revolt against the leadership.

"Yanukovich had said as the president-elect in 2010, before being run out of town on a rail in 2014, 'We will forge a pact with the European Union,' an economic free trade pact. That was his public discourse right until October (2013).

"That's when Mustafa Nayyem called people out through social media. Then the riot police went nuts and that filmed act of beefy, overweight, and overpaid riot policemen clubbing university students really pissed people off. What was maybe 5,000 people on the Maidan camped around that big column became a mass march of about a million, in a city of maybe three

million – not bad – and then the camping started and
the riot police were never able to shut it down. They
attacked it, they didn't use firearms until the very end.
Once they did, that was the end of it."

GOT TO BE FREE

Volodymyr Lavrenchuk, a graduate of the Kyiv
Economic Institute has been Chairman of the Board of
Raiffeisen Bank Aval since 2005. He produces the rock
musical *Got to Be Free*, 12 stories based on real events
from the Maidan. He composes the production's music
and lyrics, motivated by a desire to "draw a picture of
modern Ukraine."

"We make musicals on Chicago, on Greece, Italy," says
Lavrenchuk. "I have a friend from Texas who asked,
'Why do you Ukrainians not write books or make shows
about Ukrainians?'"

Lavrenchuk has no simple explanation as to why he
chooses to participate in the Maidan protest. "There
was no one moment. It is not the first revolution in
my life, it is number three. The first one was 1990, in
Kyiv where I was already in the bank as an employee. I
wasn't much involved. And then there was the Orange
Revolution."

THE ORANGE REVOLUTION

It was just after 2 a.m. on November 22, 2004, when
the call went out: "The time has come to defend your
life and Ukraine. Your victory depends upon how many
people are ready to say 'No' to this government, 'No' to
a total falsification of the elections."

State-controlled media claims victory for Viktor Yanukovych, handpicked by the sitting president. But credible exit polls show the winner is opposition candidate Viktor Yushchenko.

Yushchenko is poisoned and nearly killed while on the campaign trail. When reports come in of voter intimidation and damaged ballots, Ukrainians are outraged.

In freezing temperatures, over one million citizens pour into the streets of Kyiv. They march in protest and form human barricades around government buildings, paralyzing state functions. Restaurants donate food, businesses send tents, and individuals bring blankets, clothing, and money.

ART AND PROTEST

In 2013, "Thousands of us came to Maidan and stayed," Lavrenchuk recalls, "presenting our willingness to disagree with unfair elections, and the emotions were so bright.

"I think it's more than the protest; it's the spirit of culture that we can respect each other in time of crisis or danger. We have the skills to come to Maidan, or give visitors from another city some of our food or tea, because we have the spirit, we are proud of this period."

There were many displays of art in and around Maidan. Do you think that art in general and music in particular is an essential aspect of political change and activism?

"Art, or let me say, folk music and songs for Ukrainians played a very important role in the protest. We were always singing. The Square was immediately filled with musicians, with new songs, protest songs, some folk songs, there were hundreds of musicians. There was a queue to play in Maidan, including my friends. I'm a singer and a dancer and I'm a banker. We were always surrounded by a wide range of musicians, from classical orchestras to folk bands."

What drove people to the streets?

"If I would arrange the next revolution," says Lavrenchuk, "I will say students or youth is the trigger. If something is (done) wrong to them, millions of their parents or relatives or even neighbors will come to protect young people. The Orange Revolution was driven by students. And the (2014 Euromaidan) Revolution of Dignity was triggered by students, who arranged a camp on the central square. The camp was destroyed by police brutally, a number of people were beaten. Next morning, I saw it on *Facebook*, let's come and protest as a result. I came and I faced one million people. Did I expect they will come? No. But now after years, I would say clearly, the trigger was not only the brutal destroying of the camp, not only not joining the EU, which we were promised, but children, the future of the country were brutally beaten."

At Standing Rock, in Selma, Alabama, and in the Maidan, police brutality seemed to move people to participate, people who previously chose not to come out and protest.

"Very true. There were times with only a few hundred people on the streets, every night, for months. I switched on *Facebook* and thought, how can you sleep? Increased numbers came just to protect the students. The atmosphere was based on respect and mutual protection, that if we are together, they are more protected."

"THEY GIVE US CORRUPTION, WE GIVE THEM REVOLUTION"

Enraged by the beating of peacefully assembled protesters the previous day, an estimated one million Ukrainians fill the streets of Kyiv on December 1. The Trade Union and Kyiv City State Administration buildings are occupied to create an opposition-led Headquarters of National Resistance. An attempt is made to storm the Executive Office of the President, resulting in an assault by the Berkut, brutally beating anyone in their path. Opposition leaders and government authorities later assess the storming of the office as a planned provocation.

A week later, a second "People's Assembly" or "March of a Million" is staged with estimates ranging from tens of thousands to several hundred thousand participants. A monument to founding Soviet leader Lenin is torn down, inspiring similar acts in other Ukrainian cities. Frequent refrains include "Yanukovych and his gang raised a hand against our children" and "They give us corruption; we give them revolution."

Ukrainian reserve military officers, recruited to assist, begin constructing barricades to protect the protesters.

Two weeks before Christmas, 4,000 Berkut and military forces again attack Maidan, fighting for five hours to take control, then leave. More than 10,000 protesters resist, then fortify barricades. Maidan Defense Units, some named after the hometowns of participants, are trained by retired military in how to resist attacks. During the attack, Ivan Sydor of St. Michael's rings the bells in alarm, nonstop, from one to four a.m. They ring for the first time since 1240, when the Mongol Tatars invaded Kyiv and priests opened the doors of the original monastery to provide refuge. The monastery had been demolished on Stalin's orders in the 1930s, rebuilt in the 1990s after Ukraine wins independence.

THE WOMEN'S MAIDAN SELF-DEFENSE HUNDRED

Journalist Anna Kovalenko, deputy head of a Ukrainian magazine on antiques, begins a nightly radio show covering the Maidan protests, with updated reports every half hour. To deliver fresh details, she begins to report from the scene of the protests. "If you want new information," she decides, "you need to talk to people in the square to see what's going on."

Her first experiences in journalism affect her views on civil society and the right to assemble. "In 2008, I was in a meeting in St. Petersburg (Russia), in the center, close to a Metro, and civil society people were protesting. Police started to take away people in cars. I told them I am a Ukraine journalist, 'Hey, don't touch me.' I call to my radio station and said, 'Very strange, just because they protest, they are put in cars, but this is a peaceful protest.' My main editor said, 'Don't pay attention. This happens all the time there.' I was like 16, 17-years-old. 'How it could be?' No, I didn't want like this, never. And when I had this experience, when Ukraine police and Berkut hurt activists before Maidan, when they just protest and support EU, I decided I didn't want to be live in a police state."

During her time with the antiques magazine, she takes part in historical war reconstructions. During a radio report from the Square, she shares her knowledge of how 18th century Cossack units make barricades and protect people and buildings. Annoyed activists challenge, "If you're so smart, go to our commanders." She becomes the only female commander.

"Every night we get together at a table," explains Kovalenko, "and discuss what's going on. One night, some of the commanders start talking like, 'Oh, this woman in our unit is so awful, they are not disciplined. I don't know what to do with them.' And another commander says, 'Oh, we had the same problem.' So, hey, Anna, 'do you want to create something separate? Take all the woman with you.' I decided to do this and after two days, I had more than 150 women under my command. We did the same that the men did. We were on the barricade. We fought."

None in her squad is killed; one is wounded. A lot of the men die, however, including fellow commanders. One is a war veteran. Another goes inside a house and dies from a grenade. A third one dies of lung cancer, caused, she says, by chemical attacks against protesters.

"If I open my contacts list," says Kovalenko, "I can say, 'Oh, he died, she died. He died. She's died.' But I didn't take off their numbers. I like to think that I have an opportunity to call them."

THE FINAL DAYS

Ukrainian President Yanukovych visits Moscow on December 17th and receives a promise of $15 billion in credit plus lowered gas prices from President Putin. On New Year's Eve, between 500,000 and one million protesters gather, singing the national anthem every three hours. Cheers periodically erupt, "Glory to Ukraine, glory to the heroes." Two million people visit the scene of the protest on New Year's Day. In mid-January, Parliament deputies enact laws in a "show of hands" vote to limit protest activities. Thousands of protesters resist, ridiculing the laws with masks and intentional public acts of defiance.

A month later, frustrated that there isn't a specific set of political demands, the activists formulate one: the release of political prisoners, establishing equal power between the president and the parliament, and early presidential elections. A vote is taken at the Maidan and approved with a symbolic show of hands.

The next day President Yanukovych, working with opposition leaders, declares a truce. Within hours, each side accuses the other of betraying the agreement. At least 88 people are killed over two days with uniformed police snipers reportedly shooting at protesters from rooftops. Hundreds of injured are taken to medical facilities.

Two days later, boxer-turned-politico and future Kyiv mayor Vitaly Klitschko addresses a large crowd, announcing a deal has been made between opposition leaders and the Yanukovych government: there will be a return to the 2004 Constitution and elections by December, among other concessions. Open coffins with dead protesters are carried through the massive evening crowd. Klitschko embraces the agreement as an important step forward.

A member of a Maidan defense squad in battle fatigues leaps to the stage and commandeers the microphone. Speaking in measured but passionate tones, to the fierce roar of the crowd, he insists no such deal will be accepted. "My comrade was shot and our leaders shake the hand of a murderer. It's a disgrace," he shouts, tightly holding the microphone in his right hand and energetically gesturing with his left. He presents an alternative plan: either Yanukovych is gone by 10 a.m. the following morning or "I swear we will go on an armed offensive."

At dawn the next day, Yanukovych flees Ukraine, receiving asylum in Russia. Two days later, on the 24th, criminal charges are filed against him for the mass murder of Ukrainian citizens, and parliament votes to formally remove him from power. Legislators make clear their desire to integrate with Europe as the nation's top foreign policy priority – specifically, signing the association agreement with the European Union.

A new Cabinet of Ministers is formed on February 27.

"WE TOOK SOME LESSONS"

"I didn't think that Maidan was a separate revolution," reflects Kovalenko. "It was one of waves. In 1990, the Revolution on Granite – student protests which resulted in the resignation of the Ukrainian SSR Chairman. Then the 1991 Declaration of Independence. The huge campaign, 'Ukraine without (President Leonid) Kuchma,' in 2000, 2001. The Orange Revolution in 2004 (when orange clad protesters thwarted Putin's hand-picked presidential candidate's election). A lot of people who took part in those campaigns took part in Maidan. And all this time Russia tries to keep us in their zone of influence based on their anachronistic imperial ambitions. And then they went to Plan B, this military option, and they annex and occupy Crimea, and occupy Donbass."

The Orange Revolution lasts for two months. "And then," confirms former Kyiv city council member Kharchuk, "everybody came home and just thought that top national authorities will make changes. And it did not happen.

"We took some lessons from the Orange Revolution. We understood that if you just protest for short period of time, and then you go back home to normal life to watch football and drink your beer in the evenings, and you don't participate in social activity, it doesn't change your country. You have to be involved in activity on a daily basis. If you think that somebody else will do it for you, it will never happen. The involvement of people in social and political processes in the current Ukraine are much bigger after the Revolution of Dignity."

Putin's plan in 2013, says Kharchuk, is to penetrate Ukraine to make it part of the Russian empire again, with Yanukovych as his agent. The Russians began to publicly report that "Ukrainians are nationalists and fascists," says Kharchuk. "I think the Ukrainian police got a command from Kremlin to start shooting on the Independence Square protesters and the Heavenly Hundred were killed by instructions of Russian special service officers. Putin tried to put chaos and panic in the central part of Kyiv."

HALF OF THE ORIGINAL VISION

"Radio and TV now," estimates Brooke, "is, like, 92 percent Ukrainian language. In school, it's all Ukrainian. Russian is optional. Generations are now growing up with very good Ukrainian language skills. The Ukrainian church is no longer under the Moscow Patriarchate. And thanks to Putin, not only has NATO woken up, but you have a 250,000-man and woman standing army that is the second largest in Europe, second to Russia. That didn't exist when Putin did his Pearl Harbor attack, grabbing Crimea and the Donbass region (of Ukraine). The army was, like, 6,000 people. Volunteers, going back to civic action, helped save the country, literally."

About half of the original vision of Maidan is achieved, Brooke calculates. "People came with high expectations and demands, and a lot has been achieved. The new visa arrangement. They have a very open relationship with

Europe and numerous flights between. Progress has been made in reforming the government.

"The central bank's been totally cleaned up and just won awards as the best central bank of the year. And it's very open. They have regular press briefings; they post everything online. They shut down half the banks, corrupt pocket banks loaning to friends and family. ProZorro, an international electronic tendering system, was created that has won international awards. If you're buying anything for the government over $5,000, the tender goes up. It's often in English, accessible around the world. People can see what's up for sale. They claim it's saved $3 billion. But it's also cut out a lot of games, you cut out the man who was giving the ping-pong table contract to his cousin, that kind of thing. It's a much more rational free market solution where 10 ping-pong table contractors compete. And that's huge."

Brooke's change rollcall goes on. "All the Communist place names have been stripped off, without exception. It's like the de-Nazification which the Germans went through. Russia hasn't done this. You go into Donetsk or Luhansk (Russian-dominated Eastern Ukraine cities) and you see Lenin statues and, to piss off the Ukrainians, they put up Stalin posters. De-communization has happened in the Baltics, it's happened in Georgia. It's not happened in Russia or Belarus."

"We cannot get quick changes," notes Anna Kovalenko. "Which idea is Maidan? The idea to get Yanukovych out of the country? No, the idea was to organize the rule of law in the country. For some people, that's not understandable, but it is for me and for many other activists. I find people, maybe 20 years older, who have changed their thinking and they know that we're not part of the Soviet Union. They feel that this is an independent country and they can make changes."

"A TRIGGER SWITCHES INSIDE YOURSELF"

"There is a certain point when you just stop thinking about your personal safety," reminisces Kharchuk. "And don't recognize how brave you're becoming, because something, a trigger, just switches inside yourself, and you overcome the scariness or fear, and you're just getting on the street, together with your friends, just protecting or defending your freedom, and this is a unique moment. You're taking into consideration your career and peaceful life and family, but the major value is freedom. At a certain moment, you don't care about anything else."

There are people who say protests are a waste of time. People go home, they had fun, nothing is achieved.

"Sometimes we definitely feel so frustrated with the slow tempo of reforms. And some people pessimistically say it was a waste of time. We spend a lot of nights on the cold Maidan, didn't achieve results we were planning to achieve. But I don't share this pessimism. The long-term results will appear in a certain period of time. And things have changed substantially."

Kharchuk's son is too young to participate in the Orange Revolution. But he's a very active participant in the Euromaidan. As is Kharchuk's 14-year-old daughter. "She joined us for a couple of evenings bringing some hot tea or food to protesters. And now I see how socially active she is. If she sees some violence on the street, she calls the police immediately. Or she's protesting when somebody's parking on a pedestrian crossing way. It's a big experience, not only for short time of protest, it gives certain values for their whole lives."

PEA SOUP AND WINTER SHOES

"Hundreds of thousands of Kyivites from various social spheres united around one strategic goal: to protect freedom," recounts Kharchuk. "We were spending a lot of time every evening, every day, sharing food, supplying necessary things to military veterans of war, protecting civilians from Yanukovych's police trying to squeeze us out from Maidan.

"I'll never forget the feeling when older people, pensioners, professors, businessmen, students, getting together, were eating green-pea soup from the big pot on the Square, standing in the cold night singing the Ukrainian national hymn or popular Ukrainian songs.

"Many friends of mine who run restaurant businesses were just nonstop supplying soups and tea and sandwiches from their restaurant. And hosting people from other cities arriving to Kyiv to support us. A friend of mine is the owner of a shoe factory. He brought a lot of winter shoes to the Maidan because some students arrived from Western Ukraine in summer shoes. It became very chilly. People brought winter clothes or winter shoes – an outstanding level of solidarity. Kyivites were taking people from other cities to stay overnight in their apartments. I really will never forget; it was an emotional moment."

How did your participation in the protests, your observation of all three revolutions, change you personally?

"I'm not a politically defined person," insists Lavrenchuk. "There comes, after some period of time, a certain responsibility for your country. I talk to my colleagues in other countries because I'm a banker. I see these skills and these behaviors much more developed in the West. I've seen what happens in villages, in cities in Germany, in Austria, long traditions. In Ukraine, we have been living with monarchy or communists, let me say dictator regimes, with no responsibility for the country. You should report, but not take responsibility. Revolutions change mentality and I think I'm one of those people who got it during these three waves, got that this is my country, and I am responsible for good things and for bad things. And I should influence if this or that happens, show them two hands with actions, and if danger comes to the streets, to show, 'Look, please pay attention.'"

Is returning to the Maidan, an emotional experience for you?

"Yes and no," muses Kovalenko. "Yes, because I feel that I am part of this. But no, because my brain tries to protect itself. I don't remember, I feel this distance, I try to distance as protection I guess, as I cannot do anything about it. Yet, I remember a lot of people who died there, with whom I had friendship.

"Years have gone by, yet, I still have this pain. Lots of people in our country are stuck in the Soviet Union way of thinking. Lots of our journalists tell me, 'Maybe this is not the time for this. Let's just wait for a couple of years.' I say this is insane, because we are – and I am – the witness of historical events."

THE AFTERMATH

On the Maidan stands an exhibit honoring those who put their lives on the line, the National Memorial to the Heroes of the Heavenly Hundred and Revolution of Dignity Museum. Photos of the conflict and *Facebook* posts from participants are displayed.

Alongside is a narrow street enshrined as the Alley of Heavenly Hundred Heroes. Each dead protester is memorialized with a small shrine, a semi-circle of bricks with a photo, some with flowers, others with blue and white Ukrainian-colored ribbons or braids, many with religious icons. There are over 120 dead, 60 still missing; nearly 2,000 were treated for injuries.

The political portion of the Ukraine-European Union Association Agreement is signed on March 21, 2014 by the new Prime Minister, Arseniy Yatsenyuk. The economic section of the EU agreement is signed on June 27, 2014 by newly-elected President Petro Poroshenko.

Eighteen months later, on January 1, 2016, Ukraine joins the Deep and Comprehensive Free Trade Areas agreement with the European Union. Ukrainian citizens are granted visa-free travel to 26 EU member countries for up to 90 days during any 180-day period on June 11, 2017; the Association Agreement formally comes into effect on September 1, 2017.

The Berkut is permanently dismantled.

12. SEOUL: IMPEACHMENT BY CANDLELIGHT

Korean Shamanism has been long-repressed by the South Korean government, scorned as representative of the old ways. In a country that has fought hard for its place as a modern nation and economic power, institutional religions dismiss shamans as fraudulent, or worse, competitive.

But the old ways have a habit of resurfacing and many Korean politicians consult a *mudang*, a shaman priest or, more frequently, priestess, to seek answers that might ensure good fortune in an election. Shamanic characters have become popular in Korean television shows. South Korean President Park Gyun-hye often confides in her friend and shamanic advisor Choi Soon-sil, the details of which, in a remarkable sequence of events, brings down her presidency. Park is currently serving a 24-year prison term in the Seoul House of Detention.

A 'DEMONSTRATION-FREE ZONE' IN THE HEART OF SEOUL

Gwanghwamun Plaza, site of months of massive anti-Park candlelight protests, sits in the heart of Seoul, the impressive outcome of years of civic planning. Opened in August of 2009 on Sejongno Boulevard, it measures an impressive 34 meters wide, 557 meters in length, serving as a public space and road for centuries before it became a 16-lane highway; it downsized to 10 for a more "people-centric" home for monuments, museums, tourists, handholding couples, and commuters dashing across to their next destination.

Construction for the public plaza is delayed due to objections by the National Police agency, concerned that it might become a place for mass protests. Easily solved, announces the municipal government; it is declared a "demonstration-free zone."

It's a great place for a wander. Anchored by the magnificent Gyeongbokgung Palace, two grand monuments signify key moments and themes in Korean history. Sejong the Great, namesake of the Plaza's boulevard, is the fourth king of the Joseon dynasty. A subterranean museum below his statue provides an elegantly crafted exhibition of his contributions to Korean culture, from allowing a diverse range of social classes to serve as civil servants and a farmer's handbook to guaranteed extended maternity and paternity leave and public polling on a more equitable tax system for commoners. But his most enduring contribution is the creation in 1443 of the Korean Hangul alphabet, the native phonetic writing system, designed to promote cultural identity and literacy, the ability for any Korean to read and write.

Across from Sejong's royal perch is a monument to Admiral Yi Sun-Sin, who, in a series of 23 battles with the Japanese, is never defeated at sea and never loses a ship. As Korean naval commander, his epic victory is the 1597 Battle of Myeongnyang, where he destroys or cripples 31 Japanese warships while outnumbered 133 to 13.

A CULTURE OF PROTEST

"South Korea has a long history of popular protest," says Dr. Kim Sun-Chul, author of *Democratization and Social Movements in South Korea, 1984-2002*, among numerous other works on citizen engagement. A student activist in the late 1980s, he attended the first candlelight protests while on sabbatical from professorial duties in Korean Studies at Emory University.

How did the protests get started?

"There were social movement organizations that had been protesting the Park Gyun-hye government before the candlelight protests, and it was they who started the Saturday night protests. I went to the first protest, and there were less than 1,000. The second one was about 3,000."

Then, on October 18, 2016, TV channel JTBC finds presidential confidante Choi's discarded tablet computer. The tablet reveals Choi's involvement in policy decisions, in writing presidential speeches, and, ultimately, in a massive corruption scheme involving large Korean *chaebols* – family-owned conglomerates – such as Samsung. "That really angered the South Korean people. And from then on, it became a massive rally; every Saturday was a million plus."

Choi and President Park's staff allegedly use their influence to extort over $750 million from *chaebols* via two media and sports-related foundations, Mir and K-sports. Choi is accused of embezzling money during the process.

In his February 7, 2017 *East Asia Forum* feature on "South Korea's Candlelight Protests," Kim claims political protest has always spurred the country's drive to democratization. He traces the use of candlelight as a form of protest to 2002, when two fourteen-year-old middle-school girls were hit and killed by U.S. armored vehicles on training maneuvers. When the U.S. soldiers involved in the incident were acquitted, thousands gathered to protest and commemorate the deaths in

Gwanghwamun Square; the last mass vigil, on December 14, was attended by an estimated 100,000. "Ever since 2002," Kim writes, "mass demonstrations in South Korea have taken the form of candlelight protest."

PARK CHUNG-HEE AND THE MIRACLE OF THE HAN RIVER

Choi Soon-sil has known Gyun-hye Park since the 1970s. Park's father is Park Chung-hee, the South Korean president credited with engineering the economic "Miracle of the Han River." One of the poorest nations in the world after a decades-long Japanese occupation, followed by the devastating Korean War which took five million lives and flattened much of the country, Park institutes a series of economic measures to turn South Korea into the most impressive and visible of the new Asian "tiger" economies. He is also reviled as an authoritarian dictator that imprisons, tortures and murders leftists and political rivals, continuing the post-WWII practices of his forebear Rhee Syngman.

Choi's father, Choi Tae-min, leader of an arcane religious cult, comforts Gyun-hye as she grieves the assassination of her mother, first-lady Yuk Young-soo in 1974. A North Korean sympathizer aiming at her father kills Mrs. Park at a public event. Choi Tae-min claims he can channel messages to the deceased Mrs. Park. There are rumors about the nature of the comfort offered young Gyun-hye – and of wealth gathered through exploitation of his connections to the Park family.

THE ASCENT AND DESCENT OF PARK GEUN-HYE

Park Geun-hye makes history in December 2012 when she's elected South Korea's first female president in a country with the highest degree of gender inequality in the developed world.

A conservative, Park Geun-hye wins by a narrow 3.6 percent margin, with the support of many leftists eager for fresh engagement with North Korea and government spending to boost the slowing economy. "I will not forget your trust in me," she pledges in her victory speech. Public support for Park reaches 63 percent in July 2013, but plummets to 30 percent by January 2015, due in part to ongoing battles with South Korea's unions, disputes with North Korea, mishandling of the Sewol ferry disaster, and a national public outcry about administration corruption.

In the summer of 2016, a spark for the Candlelight Movement is lit by students at the prestigious Ewha Woman's University in Seoul. They protest a proposed two-year degree which could be earned through night classes that students feel will not live up to the school's standards. Sixteen hundred armed police officers meet a peaceful demonstration of only 200 students. The overwhelming show of force earns the public's sympathy and the plan is dropped, but students continue a sit-in calling for the university president's resignation. The injustice also causes students to scrutinize the administration further, feeling that such a draconian response from the university could indicate that officials may be hiding secrets. They soon discover that the school has shown favoritism in admitting an equestrian athlete, Chung Yoo-ra, the daughter of Park confidant Choi Soon-sil; striking a nerve in a country where young people work hard for merit-based admission to prestigious universities.[53]

South Korea's Parliament and a special prosecution team investigate the admission, and seven school officials, including its removed president and several professors, are indicted on criminal charges. Chung's admission is canceled.

The student action is considered an opening chapter in the national scandal that ends Park's presidency. And brings to the fore a new protest culture among those raised on K-pop and YouTube after the end of authoritarian rule in 1987.

October 25, 2016. President Park Gyun-hye acknowledges her close relationship with Choi Soon-sil.

November 28, 2016. 1.9 million people take to the streets in a nationwide anti-Park Gyun-hye rally.

COLLABORATION AND RESISTANCE: JAPANESE OCCUPATION

The National Museum of Korean Contemporary History sits adjacent to the Plaza not far from the Palace's Gwanghwamun Gate. It features a thematic exhibit called "Independence, When That Day Comes," a tribute to the anti-Japanese resistance during the decades of occupation (1905-1945), and the establishment of a provisional government in exile in China.

The 2019 exhibit artfully shows the daily life of Koreans in Shanghai, and the long-distance efforts to maintain active resistance, gain international support and prepare for the restoration of a sovereign Korea. With the unconditional surrender of Japan in August of 1945, their time has come or so they hope. The United States military occupies the south, and Stalin's USSR the north. The U.S., in accepting the Japanese surrender, announces it will retain existing Japanese collaborator government leadership instead of the long-suffering provisional government in exile.

Park Chung-hee's ideas about militaristic political control derive from his military education at Changchun Military Academy of the Manchukuo Imperial Army. Manchukuo is a puppet state installed after the 1932 Japanese invasion of the Chinese state of Manchuria. Park adopts the Japanese name Takagi Masao and graduates at the top of his class, for which he was gifted a gold watch from titular Emperor Puyi. Commissioned as a lieutenant, Park rises through the ranks of the South Korean military after the defeat of the Japanese, becoming a brigadier general by the end of the Korean War in 1953.

"There were different degrees of collaboration," explains Dr. Han Hong-koo, professor of Korean history at Seoul's Sungkonghoe University and author of the four-volume "History of South Korea." A prominent lecturer and scholar on Korean activism, he delivers the 2017 Kim Dae-Jung Memorial Lecture on Korean Studies at the University Cambridge, entitled, "Plazas of Candlelight: Understanding the History of Street Protests in South Korean Democracy."

"But, I can say that the right-wingers did not fight against the Japanese. Some collaborated deeply, some collaborated a little, and some did not collaborate, but they did not fight against them. The so-called socialists or leftists fought against them. So, even though (right-wingers) were called 'nationalist,' people did not give their 'mind' to so-called nationalists.

"Socialists had support during the colonial period. During the 1920s, Lenin was the only international leader who listened, and sincerely wanted to help them. Lenin defined imperialism as the highest stage of capitalism. So, national liberation or independence movements of oppressed countries were by nature anti-capitalistic, anti-imperialistic. It is true that those countries have to develop capitalism and pursue economic development, however, their language is anti-capitalist.

"Socialism was influential in South Korea, in East Asia, not because of communist theory, but because socialist countries advocated for national independence movements. The critical difference with the Eastern European socialist countries is they have a history of national revolution. In East Asia, nationalism empowered the socialist cause.

"The U.S. wanted to plug the expansion of communism, they wanted containment, but I think they made a serious mistake. They can choose another option. They chose the collaborators. They chose right-wing nationalists. The collaborators were more loyal."

Was it a question of civil administration, they are collaborators, but they know how to run the country?

"Think about the Korean Provisional Government in China. It was pro-Kuomintang. And in the last stage of the Second World War, the American OSS had a connection with the Korean Provisional Government, they have a special joint operation plan. But at the end of the war, the U.S. didn't want to join with the Kim Koo school, instead they choose the collaborators.

"Kim Koo was willing to join hands with the U.S. because the U.S. was anti-Japanese; he wants a Korea that is according to the Korean people's will. The Provisional Government has their own political platform, but Americans did not like it. It sounds somewhat socialist. The U.S. wants a system that is fully capitalist."

December 3, 2016. 2.3 million people participate in a nationwide anti-Park rally, the largest in South Korean history. More than 1.5 million gather from City Hall to Gwanghwamun Square and Gyeongbok Palace. Opposition parties introduce a joint impeachment motion which passes on December 9 with 234 out of 300 votes.

December 31, 2016. South Koreans celebrate New Year's Eve with a mass demonstration of more than one million people.

January 7, 2017. Hundreds of thousands of protesters demand Park Gyung-hye's immediate removal. Another demand: the salvaging of the sunken Sewol ferry, which left more than 300 dead, and an explanation of Park's seven-hour absence at the time of the sinking.

THE PROSTRATION MARCH: THE SINKING OF THE SEWOL FERRY

On the morning of April 16, 2014, the Sewol ferry sends a distress signal on its way from Inchon to Jeju. It carries 476 passengers and crew; 304 perish, including 250 high school students. Most of the survivors are rescued by fishing boats and other vessels that arrive at the scene more than a half hour after the South Korean Coast Guard. There is widespread criticism of the captain and crew, the ferry operator, and President Park Gyun-hye, who many charged with downplaying government responsibility. Four crew members are charged with murder, 11 others are indicted for abandoning the ship.

"In South Korea," explains Professor Kim, "there's a tactic called three-step, one-bow, a prostration march. Amazing. What people do is not in great numbers, but it happened when the Sewol ferry capsized.

"The parents of the victims marched from the southwestern corner of South Korea, where it capsized, to Seoul. Walking three steps and fully bowing, or just prostrating on the ground. You take three steps, and there's a guy who would bang a drum, or something, so, three steps, everyone together lies down on their belly on the ground, stands up again, three steps, lay on their stomach again. They did that for close to 200 miles. It's a show of resolve, but it's not just them acting; they're in connection with civic groups all over the country. When they enter a certain township, for example, people there would greet them, and join them in that march. Some people did it from start to end. But most people joined at a certain point. It's a remarkable statement of resolve, of commitment, of inflicting pain on themselves."

January 21, 2017. South Koreans take to the streets to demand the arrest of Samsung vice-chairman Lee Jae-Yong after a court rejects his arrest warrant, in the 13th candlelight protest. Hundreds of thousands also demand the Constitutional Court accelerate the impeachment review.

February 4, 2017. As the candlelight rallies reach their 100th day, 400,000 people gather at Gwanghwamun Plaza, insisting on an extension of the Special Prosecutor's investigation and for President Park to step down.

March 10, 2017. Park Gyun-hye is impeached, charged with leaking state secrets, bribery, and abuse of power. Eight companies admit to making payments in the scandal.

In August, Samsung's Lee Jae-yong is sentenced to five years in prison on bribery and embezzlement charges, including $36 million in payments to Choi's foundations to gain government support for a corporate restructuring.

"THE FIRST THING PEOPLE DO IS PROTEST"

"Corruption is a constant in South Korea," suggests Professor Kim. "People always have grievances. But mass uprisings, mass demonstrations occur infrequently. It's not necessarily the grievances that pushes people to protest, but the political environment, the conditions. Look up the political opportunity theory. There are certain aspects in the external environment that opens up the window of opportunity for people to act."

Political opportunity theory argues that the actions, and effects, of activists are dependent on the existence of a specific political opportunity.

"Whenever there was a big protest movement in South Korea," says Kim, "it was usually associated with openings in the political environment. In the candlelight movement case, it started from the civil society protest; at first, they (the protests) were very small. They became big when the National Assembly started to discuss it. The judiciary allowed citizens to get closer to the Blue House (the equivalent of the U.S. White House), and there was less police presence or, let's say, decreasing police repression. It all went hand in hand. It wasn't just the protesters that made this happen, other people in power positions also contributed (as did the) media."

In the United States, there's some disaffection with the two major political parties. South Koreans view civic organizations as a primary way to act politically, to change things, as opposed to depending on a political party.

"In South Korea, if there's something wrong, the first thing people do is protest. That's a culture, an outcome of decades of organizing, by a movement, by civic organizations, and they are tightly connected. Everyone knows everyone there. What that allows for is for the civic movement groups to develop very strong solidarity ties, and allow a degree of distance from political parties. They criticize the liberal parties, they criticize the conservative ones.

"In the U.S., even when large protests are organized, the Women's March, Never Again, they're all oriented towards election, it's part of a campaign to mobilize people to get woke and vote. In South Korea, the power of people protesting on the streets has held enormous significance, and it still continues. Right now, it's the conservatives, the right-wingers who are mobilizing, and they're calling for the overthrow of the government. Protest has become a major means, right next to political mechanisms, the National Assembly, parliamentary mechanisms, so it's dynamic, and the relationship between social movements and party politics are different."

THE IMPORTANCE OF DEMONSTRATIONS, LOGISTICS, AND CIVIC GROUPS

There's a cynical view among some activists in the U.S. that protests are relatively useless. Specifically, what does a protest do?

"A lot," Professor Kim answers. "If you look at the significant political changes that occurred in South Korean history, they were all sparked by protests. Sometimes, there's a massive uprising that generates relatively immediate outcomes. Sometimes it takes a longer time. But it's the basic idea of, if you don't act, there is going to be no change. So, people act up and fight, and when they gain in momentum, that's when lawmakers will align with them, or they might find representatives who can speak for them, and push for new legislation.

"In South Korea, the pace of change is very rapid, it's zigzag-y, rather than linear. But a lot of the changes have been triggered and pushed forward by protest. And the biggest difference, again, is who are the main activists; when I say the protest is the motor of change, I'm talking about an established institutionalized political actor in the civic organizations, and the tightly-knit network among the bigger organizations.

"There's a law that allows non-parliamentary members to petition for new legislation, and the civil organizations have been doing a lot of that. Sometimes in alignment with lawmakers, sometimes on their own. A lot of reform measures have been made that way. In the U.S., movement groups are aligned with the parties, let's say AFL-CIO, SEIU, women's organizations, gun control groups, they all look up to the party to do something. South Korean civic groups are more practical, they would align with anyone, but they know that they have to generate enough noise and disruption in order to get their issues looked at by establishment politicians."

A seemingly minor detail in your East Asia Forum article involved logistics, like setting up Lost and Found services. During the civil rights March on Washington in the 60s, we hear about King's "I Have a Dream" speech, but there were women who made 80,000 cheese sandwiches in order to make that march work. How important are mundane logistics for successful political action and protest?

"South Korean activists are experts in this," says Kim. "I was a student activist in the late '80s and I remember many, many times when just a random citizen, a lady brought food to us, brought water to us, when we're being chased, hit by the riot police. It's not just the people on the streets, you have to have people outside, it has to resonate with the people, and only then can a protest generate enough momentum for meaningful change.

"And during the candlelight protests, there are so many examples of that. Some of the corporate restaurants, coffee shops, were booming. Many like Starbucks just minded their business, but some local coffee shops, they opened their doors, or they set up like tables outside on the streets and offered coffee and hot tea. There was a lot of that. I don't think it's uniquely Korean. You can see this pretty much anywhere."

KOREAN UNIONS AS HISTORICAL VANGUARD

Labor unions have long played a pivotal role in South Korean politics. Limited in size and scope during the Japanese occupation, the General Council of Korea Trade Unions is founded in November of 1945, growing to a half-million members within two months. After the GCKTU holds more than 3,000 strikes, the United States military authorities restrict union activity, eventually resulting in the group's ban. The Federation of Korean Trade Unions (FKTU) is formed as an alternative to the left-leaning GCKTU, tightly controlled by the government.

In 1952, right-wing authoritarian President Rhee Syngman assumes control of the now-exclusive union. Under the military regime of Park Chung-hee from 1962-1979, the FKTU is further weakened and subordinated to family-owned chaebol conglomerates, which increasingly dominates South Korean industries. In July and August of 1987, millions of workers participate in nationwide strikes known as the Great Worker Struggle, demanding better wages, working conditions, and autonomous trade unions. Over the next 10 years, independent unions emerge, with hard-fought legal status.

Lee Keunwon, Political Strategic Committee Chair of the Korean Public Service and Transport Workers' Union (KPTU), suggests civil society organizations – led by unions – play a vital role in driving the protests.

"Long before the candlelight demonstrations began," Lee relates, "the labor movement campaigned for the resignation of the Park Gyun-hye government. There were many problems; the police raid of the KCTU's (Korean Confederation of Trade Unions) office on December 22, 2013 – the first ever – was particularly significant. Five thousand police gathered, then broke down the front door of the KCTU office on suspicion that leaders of the Korean Railway Workers' Union (KRWU, affiliated with KPTU), who were in the midst of a strike to stop railway privatization, would be inside the building. This was a violent invasion of KCTU, which represents Korea's democratic labor movement. From then on, the KCTU began the campaign for Park Gyun-hye to step down.

"In fact, it was unprecedented in the history of the world to throw out the regime and lawfully imprison the president through (nonviolent, peaceful) candlelight demonstrations. To understand this, you need to have a broad understanding of Korean society. There was a movement of anti-impeachment forces calling for the military to come out (to stop the protests), but this was not possible because of the 1980 Gwangju uprising. And the symbolic meaning represented by the candle, that is, public opinion, prevented conservative forces from taking action the way they wanted to."

The Gwangju Uprising is a seminal moment in the history of Korean protest. From May 18-27, 1980, citizens take up arms when local Chonnam University students demonstrating against martial law are shot, beaten, raped and (by some estimates, over six hundred) killed by government troops. The uprising is a symbol of military and police overreach, of defiance of authoritarian regimes, and of the fight for democratic institutions and liberties.

How did you keep your union members coming out to the protests every week?

"The labor movement had a policy of continuous outreach and organizing for the protests," says Lee. "But the fact that union members continued to come out each week was more a result of the continuous media reporting of the candlelight vigils. And the fact that the news kept reporting various misdeeds by the Park Gyun-hye regime, making participation natural. What forced the outcome that seemed almost impossible, was public opinion; the candlelight demonstrations were the place where that public opinion was expressed.

"The unions kept up the pressure and reinforced the protests though strikes. The candlelight struggle began on October 29, 2016. Immediately before, on September 27th, public sector unions affiliated to KPTU had begun a general strike. When the candlelight demonstrations began, more than 20,000 KRWU members were still on strike."

Lee claims labor union participation was crucial to keeping the candles lit on weekdays, sustaining and extending the Saturday. "With the Park administration rejecting resignation, the KCTU went on a general strike on November 30, 2016. Roughly 50,000 railway, education, and other KPTU members participated in this action."

What did your union do to support the protesters? Food? Organization? Transport? Communications?

"We did a whole bunch of activities," advises Lee. "We handed out candles and cold-resistant hot packs and mats to sit on. We also made cute buttons calling for Park Gyun-hye's resignation, made outreach materials, and performed other types of support so protesters could participate without difficulty. We mobilized all our broadcasting vehicles (vans topped with loudspeakers), and union members with protest experience participated with regular citizens to enable effective demonstrations.

"The KCTU is still the most influential of all civil society organizations working for the progressive reform of Korean society."

UNIVERSAL VALUES

Are there universal values or aspirations that motivate protesters across cultures? Or is it all national, cultural, or tribal?

"The activist in me is tempted to say there is a universal, something," posits Professor Kim. "The scholar in me would be more cautious. There are different values. When it comes to social movements, you have the social movement of the left, you also have the social movement of the right. And it's really hard to, let's say, attribute a common value to people who will rise up, who act.

"And I think it would be utterly unfair to just focus on one side, the side that you like, when talking about social movements. They're all seeking their values. In that sense, there is a universal sort of element, they all feel injustice. But what constitutes injustice?

"A trickier example would be pro-life, pro-choice. They're all seeking justice, they all are calling for what they perceive is right. So, in that sense, there is a universal, say, inner sense, emotion that drives them. It's hard to define what that is. It's going to vary.

I think that's different. In South Korea, it's so interesting, the heirs of the military dictatorship, now they're talking about overthrowing dictatorship. They're adopting the vocabulary, the idiom of the left right now.

"So, how do we talk about universal something? They're seeking their interest. They're seeking their values."

13. WEST VIRGINIA: THE WILDCAT TEACHERS' STRIKE

"Redneck" is a condescending insult for some, signifying a socially inferior position of working in the sun, laboring with one's hands. West Virginians insist on a different etymological origin: the red bandana, symbol of the largest labor uprising in the history of the United States, culminating in the Battle of Blair Mountain. Resurrected in living color a century later during the West Virginia Teachers Strike of 2018, a wildcat action that stretched to every school in every one of the state's 55 counties, inspiring similar strikes nationwide.

Jay O'Neal, one of two principal leaders of the strike, along with Emily Comer, ties the sea of red bandanas at teacher protests to the state's mythic mine wars. "There were battles that were fought between miners, union folks and mining company militias," instructs O'Neal. "There was a huge drive to unionize the West Virginian coal fields in the late-1910s and early-1920s. It reached its pinnacle when one of the miners' heroes (Matewan police chief Sid Hatfield) was assassinated by coal company thugs; people had just had enough, they decided on unionizing in this county and the southern part of the state. They decided to march. At one point, there were 10,000 miners squaring off on these mountain ridges against armed guards with machine guns. They called this the Battle of Blair Mountain. Finally, the U.S. Army stepped in."

"Black, white, and immigrant mine workers banded together (in 1921) for the basic right to organize, for basic dignity in work, and their punishment was eviction from their company-owned homes," says Stephen Smith, key organizer of the GoFundMe campaign to provide financial support to in-need teacher and school workers during the strike. "They were threatened. They were killed. They were met by corrupt politicians, by (Logan County Sheriff) Don Chafin, with the backing of the federal government. Defending themselves against the aggression of coal companies and the federal government, the miners were forced to take up arms.

"Because they came from not only all over West Virginia, but from all over the world, speaking different languages, coming from different cultures, they had to have a way of identifying each other in battle. The red bandana was a visible symbol that worked in the hills as they defended themselves against coal company mercenaries and, eventually, their own government. That symbol has been passed down over the last hundred years in West Virginia. The red bandana was chosen as a symbol in the teacher strike by a new generation of folks working across race and on behalf of working people."

CHECK YOUR MAILBOX

Why did thousands of teachers, previously daunted by decades of state government pressure against labor actions, rally for days, often in frigid rain?

The strike is a response to a February 21, 2018, bill signed by Governor Jim Justice delivering a two percent raise for 2019, one percent in 2020, and one percent more in 2021.

Teachers in the United States earn 20 to 30 percent less in compensation than professionals with similar educations, a much larger differential than in other industrialized countries. The salary for West Virginia teachers at the time of the strike starts at $32,435 a year, the average $44,701. Rising health insurance costs and stagnant wages – pay has been cut by eight percent since 1999 and there has been no across-the-board salary increase since 2014 – place WV teachers near the bottom of national teacher pay rates. The state spends 11 percent less on each student than it did before the 2008 recession.

Comer and O'Neal accelerate interest in a labor action several months before the walkout by creating a private *Facebook* group, which has the effect of getting teachers and public employees talking to each other, many for the first time. There are multiple West Virginia teacher unions, at times focused on competitive recruiting.

"That group allowed people to work together and look past the union label," asserts O'Neal, a history teacher at Stonewall Jackson Middle School in Charleston. "I think the difference was realizing other people were upset about the same issues, and when that started happening and messages started getting out, things just kind of quickly took off. People could see online, hey, I got this letter in the mail that my premium is getting doubled, so you might want to check your mailbox, your kitchen table and open it because it will tell you what is going to happen to you.

"Things just escalated really quickly. People started doing actions, protest and signs, and having local meetings. Finally, in a few counties, we'd do walkouts."

TROUBLEMAKERS, DISRUPTERS, AND WILDCATS

A month before the strike, leaders from three competitive key unions – the National Educational

Association (NEA), the American Federation of
Teachers (AFT) and West Virginia Service Personnel
Association (WVSPA) – hold an emergency meeting
across seven counties to debate a deal under negotiation
with the legislature. Details of the agreement begin
to emerge from a *Facebook* post intended for Mingo
County teachers that goes viral throughout the state.

At a January 23 Mingo County union meeting, attended
by more than 200 employees, State Senator Richard
Ojeda describes the escalating budget battle, which
leads teachers to suggest a one-day work stoppage to
demonstrate their discontent. Teacher Katie Endicott
insists that Mingo commit to a "Fed Up Friday" work
stoppage recommended by neighboring Wyoming
County teachers on February 2. The Mingo group
agrees to the commitment. Wyoming teachers approve
the action the following night.[54]

Mingo teacher and union activist Brandon Wolford
attends a Logan County meeting; he's later chastised
by union officials for working outside his county.
Logan union leadership advises against action because
only Mingo and Wyoming – of 55 counties – have
committed. Wolford reassures anxious participants
with a story from more than a decade prior where West
Virginia teachers in Monongalia County stage a similar
event and net a $2,000 raise from a single-day walkout.
The argument convinces Logan County teachers and
staff to join the action.[55]

The Mingo, Wyoming and Logan county teachers
and school personnel travel to Charleston on "Fed Up
Friday" to protest at the Capitol, joined in freezing
weather by educators from neighboring McDowell
County. With 87 percent of Mingo County school
employees away, classes are canceled.

State senators ignore the school employees' pleas. They expect no consequences because teachers haven't gone on strike in nearly 30 years.

However, the growing intrastate communication helps teachers realize they have a powerful if not depressing bargaining strength – many positions remain unfilled. It's difficult for the state to attract and retain teachers, much less find strike replacements because teachers in border counties often work in or move to other states where salaries can be $10-$20,000 higher.

When teachers return to work on Monday, they hear rumors that colleagues from around the state are planning another demonstration at the Capitol. Wolford is tipped off that the governor is traveling to Logan to meet secretly with the president of the county board of education, faculty senate president, and one representative each from teachers and service employee groups.

Wolford is skeptical about the outcome; the county board of education president is a lobbyist earning over $500,000 from the governor's businesses. Gov. Justice is the richest person in West Virginia, with a net worth of almost $2 billion. He runs and wins a four-year term as a moderate Democrat in 2016, but flips to the Republican Party less than eight months after taking office.

Wolford publicizes the meeting to three *Facebook* groups, but two of his posts are deleted by union leadership, and he is again warned not to interfere. But word has spread.

The West Virginia Education Association (NEA) and AFT leadership decide to put a statewide strike to a vote, and call a meeting for February 11 to present the results. Eighty-five percent of voting Mingo employees and numerous other counties across the state agreed to go ahead. Union leaders call for a statewide walkout on February 22, but many teachers remain apprehensive. Some families rely entirely on teacher salaries, representing an enormous risk.

Wolford reaches out to a friend at the Mingo County Federal Credit Union. She agrees to work overtime to help eligible employees get small loans that they could repay after the strike.[56]

These acts of resolve and foresight by teachers across the state result in an estimated 20,000 committing to participate. School workers such as bus drivers and cafeteria staff join, bringing the total to 33,000 strikers. Five thousand demonstrate at the West Virginia State Capitol; lines form around the building, and parents and teachers waiting as much as two hours to enter.

Teachers picket in front of their schools leading to canceled classes for 277,000 students. In an effort that materially contributes to parents' support – a quarter of West Virginia kids live in homes below the poverty line and half are eligible for the free lunch program – teachers and cafeteria workers prepare take-home student meals to minimize the strike's impact on families.

"Our real issue was our health insurance," explains strike leader O'Neal. "We have a state-sponsored Public Employees Insurance Agency (PEIA) plan that covers all public employees. And our premiums and deductibles were going up every year while we want living wages, so it's like an annual pay cut. The legislature was proposing a radical change, to take total family income into account, so many of our premiums were going to double. The main thing, at first, was to stop that and find a permanent fix, because we just watched this happen year after year."

On Tuesday, February 27, union leaders and the governor jointly announce a deal that features a five percent pay raise, and calls for a return to classrooms two days later on March 1, after a "cooling off" period. But distrusting the legislature's commitment to pass legislation reflecting the agreement, employees continue to strike closing schools in every county, moving the action into its "wildcat" (unauthorized by unions) phase.

On March 3, the West Virginia Senate, as suspected, rejects a bill passed by the state's House of Delegates approving the raise, proposing instead a four percent increase, as the strike extends into its eighth school day.

CROWDFUNDING SUPPORT FOR AT-RISK STRIKERS

Stephen Smith, executive director of the West Virginia Healthy Kids and Families Coalition during the action, recalls the moment he chose to get involved.

"I was lucky enough to be in on some of the initial conversations about whether or not a strike was possible, and so, fairly early on, it was animating to me as an opportunity to choose to not play by the normal set of rules; that we should all get together and go to the capitol, and make our case and, hopefully, these people will listen to us for once. Of course, those who were organizing did do many actions like that. But there was a sense from very early on that the folks leading strike had the ability to raise the stakes, saying, 'No, this is something for which we're willing to take risks.'

"The other moment for me was about a day into the strike, when it looked like it might last a while. A friend of mine and a couple of other advocates, parents and teachers, started talking about the real losses that people were taking by being on strike, both the costs of organizing, which are expensive, and also the costs of supporting kids who were in school. And then the very real cost if you were a long-term sub, an aide or a part-time person, as were many of the folks affected by the strike. You were losing pay.

"A bunch of us got together a day later to ask, 'How are we going to support folks who are taking real financial sacrifices?' Within about 24 hours of that, we put a strike fund, a GoFundMe page, and an online application process that ended up raising $332,000. We were able to distribute it, every single penny, no administrative costs, to nearly 1,000 teachers, school service personnel, and aides across the state."

In nine days, the page was shared more than 11,000 times on social media.

"I got to read these incredible applications for people who, in part because of the courage that they had shown during the strike, were on the cusp of being able to keep the electric bills on or pay for a medical procedure. Hearing those stories of people still supporting the strike, still supporting this thing that was taking away their own ability to provide for their families, was pretty damn powerful."

Is one reason why there's not as much labor organizing or citizen engagement here as in countries with more labor security, guaranteed healthcare, lesser student debt, that those who want to engage feel that they can't?

"Yes, and I think it cuts both ways," says Smith. "Sure, it's true that when there is more of a social safety net, people are able to fight harder because they have more resources to do so. I think the flip side that we're seeing in West Virginia and all across the country right now is that, as the government has failed to do right by people in a basic way, people are willing to stand up and say, 'Enough, we're going to do it on our own. It's time to take matters into our own hands.'"

THE TEACHERS WIN

On March 7, the state Senate and House finally agree to the five percent increase, and teachers and school employees end the strike. The teachers win other concessions, including the creation of a task force on health care with guaranteed seats for each of the three striking unions, the AFT-WV, the WVEA and the WVSSPA.

"West Virginia has the (48th) lowest-paid teachers in the country," says O'Neal. "They didn't make that big (insurance) change, which was a victory, and there will be no cost increases the next couple years. As the strike happened, (the issue) became a permanent funding solution, so this wouldn't continue to be an issue down the road."

"THEY DOMINATED THE SESSION"

Bill Kuhn comes from a multigenerational military family, a career path that seemed inevitable from an early age. He served tours in Iraq and Afghanistan and an internship at the elite Army War College, then used his G.I. Bill benefit to study political advocacy at George Washington University. His studies focused on West Virginia-related issues with the intention of launching a nonprofit. "The challenge of 41 people leaving the state every day just really spoke to me," says Kuhn. The teachers' actions inspired him to return to his home state to accept a program director position with Generation West Virginia.

"The teacher strike hit a chord about the state leadership's misalignment of values with what almost every West Virginian wants. It has been that way for a very long time. They are tired of the establishment, people with immense wealth and power, which has screwed them over every chance that they've got. I think that's where that bridge is between folks that are on the right and left.

"In border counties, teachers leave because they're going to get offered better pay, better benefits, and respect. I worked for an organization (Generation West Virginia) that was focused on attracting, retaining and advancing young talent; we'd get beaten by out-of-state competitors all the time.

"The tangible things rest with pay and benefits," says Kuhn, "but it's really about respect for education and for those who provide that education. The state doesn't care. It hasn't cared for decades about its education of its children. It baffles me. Economic growth takes place where the schools are strongest. That is where workers want to be, so that their kids end up having a better life. We've lost thinking about our generations in that way. You've got employers, entrepreneurs or startups that want to start something here, they don't have the tech to do it. Most college or high school students here don't know anything about coding, which the majority of your jobs are going to involve in some way. If we're not respecting our education system, not respecting teachers, their skill set, paying for the value of what they produce, then we're going to get a subprime product.

"In West Virginia, the tricky part is that Democrats controlled this place for 80 years and unions were a bit of a mixed bag for my family. I've watched the unions work really hard to do great things for my family, and I've watched them screw my family.

"The voters, on the surface, might seem like they're voting against their own interests, but their options are crap. The other problem is single-issue voters. We're not having more complex conversations with our neighbors around other issues. In a democracy, when you've got to compromise and you've got to lose some ground to gain some ground. That's hard because for some people that live up in the holler, there's one thing that they care about, and that might be agriculture, a Second Amendment issue, an abortion issue, or whether or not a certain tax rate's going to go down for them."

What do you think activists and teachers' unions from other states learned from West Virginia?

"Infrastructure. Folks thought that teachers were going to be quiet this (2019) session, that they were going to propose this bill and fly through. The teachers' union created enough infrastructure that they could mobilize quickly and could flex that muscle fast when it needed to, and it did so. They dominated the session. They dominated that conversation."

DEFUNDING OF PUBLIC SCHOOLS

Historically, education has been highly valued in American culture, funded from elementary school to world class universities. Are we seeing a loss of esteem or support for public school educators?

"There is still respect for educators," says history teacher O'Neal, "especially amongst families and regular folk; money has been diverted with the rise of charter schools and voucher programs in the last 10 or 20 years."

How has the rise of charter schools affected your work as a school teacher?

"Advocates will say that we can teach in different ways and try out new things. The real issue is the money, because even if they're considered a non-profit charter school – we actually do have some for-profit charter schools – the problem is twofold. One is that they will subcontract many of the services to a for-profit management company – anything from cafeteria workers and bus drivers to curriculum – so it's like they're finding ways to pull money out of the public system.

"Let's say, in your town, a charter school opens. That's a problem for the rest of the schools, because the money that would normally follow the students to your school is going to the charter school. You still have to keep the building, still have to drive school buses whether there are 50 kids or five. That's a really big issue as our public schools are underfunded."

What do you teach?

"Middle school, eighth-grade history."

What do eighth-grade history students in West Virginia understand about civics or the political system?

"The first thing that comes to mind is, look around, we live in the era of fake news. It's crucial to have children growing up to become critical thinkers, to analyze things for themselves and be good citizens. I think it's scary, what's going on right now. I've heard people call our schools the 'great equalizer,' they really are an opportunity place for kids.

"West Virginia is a very high-poverty state and, like it or not, this is the only place they're going to learn some skills. It's so important for the future to fund our schools well and make sure we're educating our kids. It's scary how we're underfunding them, and then have the money sucked out to private corporations and charter schools."

Can you achieve both things, have great consistent national public education and have a free-choice-based system in vouchers and charter schools?

"They're clever because they make it sound consumer-based, so it's your choice. It's all about parent choice and student choice, and you need to find what works best for you. When you hear it from that perspective, you think that sounds great, but, again, we know the reality is they are underfunding others. In school, we work hard to educate all kids.

"It's not like we teach the same way in every classroom for every kid. We know how to differentiate and work with different learners. Honestly, public schools have worked pretty well for America for a long time. They like to point out where they're failing, but almost always where they're failing is in high-poverty neighborhoods and high-poverty states because a lot of other things are failing. The schools are a symptom of a bigger problem, but they say, 'Okay, because of that we need school choice,' and that's just not how it works."

THE FOUNDATIONS OF AMERICAN PUBLIC EDUCATION

In the country's colonial years, education is limited to home learning, frequently administered by an itinerant teacher, or private charter schools called academies, for those could afford them. Perhaps some religious education at church. After the Revolutionary War, founders such as Thomas Jefferson insist the future of the republic depends upon an educated citizenry.

Jefferson founds the University of Virginia after being disappointed that his alma mater, the College of William Mary, has grown too religious and stifles science education. He lists UVA among his life's three greatest achievements, above the Louisiana Purchase and other milestones of his presidency.

Critical to Jefferson's vision is universally accessible quality education, for rich and poor, which requires funding of free local schools and restrictions on the growth of academies. Reformers believe wealthy families opting out would cripple this emerging social contract, undermining the egalitarian concept of public education as a social good benefiting all Americans.

As more families participate in public schools, Americans becomes committed to sustaining them. By the mid-18th century, most Northern states provide free, tax-supported schools. Chartered academies remained popular in the South, where education is often treated as a family, not public, responsibility.

Horace Mann is often called the father of the "common school." After serving as a member of the Massachusetts House of Representatives, Mann rises to become president of the state Senate in 1836, then gave up that powerful position to become the first Secretary of the Massachusetts Board of Education at its founding in 1837. Massachusetts' public schools go back as far as 1647. Mann believes social harmony and political stability depend on education, specifically, a basic level of literacy and the sharing of common public ideals. "A republican form of government, without intelligence in the people," says Mann, "must be, on a vast scale, what a mad-house, without superintendent or keepers, would be on a small one."

Horace Mann evangelizes six core ideas for American common education in his *Common School Journal*, which he founds in 1838. That citizens may not obtain both ignorance and freedom; that an interested public should pay for, control, and maintain such education; that this education will be best provided in schools that embrace children from a variety of backgrounds; that education should teach high moral and civic values but be nonsectarian; that education should be taught using tenets of a free society; and that it must be provided by well-trained professional teachers.

A SECOND STRIKE

How did the strike affect your attitude towards politics and organizing?

"It changed me a lot," says middle-school teacher O'Neal. "My political development sped up. I look at things a lot differently now in terms of people power versus the power of politicians. Before, I thought that if I got the right people in office, then we could fix these things and work it out. Of course, you'd like to have more favorable politicians in office, but you should get people involved, mobilized and organized. You've got a lot of power. We have a Republican-controlled governor in both houses of legislature and we're able to still make a big difference, because we've got all kinds of people organized. That has really made me rethink what's important and where I'm going to spend my time with politically."

There is a second strike one year later (in February 2019) with that issue in the forefront.

"Yes, that was a different issue. It was an election year, and so Senate Republicans and our governor basically came out of the blue saying, we're going to get all teachers and public employees another five percent raise, about three weeks before the election in mid-October (2018). We thought that was great. It was to buy votes, but whatever.

"Then the election happens, and January rolls around and we have our next legislative session when they kick back into gear, and, suddenly, out of the blue, they drop this huge bill with all kinds of anti-public education, anti-union stuff, paycheck protection – a union-busting measure – in it. We had to re-signup for our union every year. It had charter schools in it. In West Virginia, we don't have education savings accounts; all these things that we knew were just going to drain money out of public schools. They did really shady maneuvers to get it to pass because they didn't have the votes in the Senate and in committees, and they just went around them. Finally, we ended up walking out for two days to just shut that door to kill the bill because it seemed that there was no other option."

The walkout shuts down schools in all but one of the 55 counties, leading to the State House of Delegates voting to table the bill indefinitely. The shutdown is continued a second day to ensure Senate Republicans don't attempt to revive it.

When you think back to the teacher strike, what are you most proud of and what choices are transferable when you talk to teachers from other states?

"One is, we just did it. We listened to each other, we stood together and made a difference. One of the big moments of the strike was, after the fourth day, our union leadership met with the governor and came to an agreement.

"They announced it to us and said, 'Tomorrow is a cooling-off day and then on Thursday it will be business as usual, you'll be back in school.' All the teachers and school employees decided they weren't going to take that, and that we were not moving anywhere until we could get this deal signed in the law, so we stayed out five more days.

"They wanted it to be a four-day strike, but it went nine days. It was the right decision because everyone was listening to each other. They called it the wildcat moment, it was really nice to see. I hope it was a good example for other states, to listen to your fellow workers and fellow teachers, and make the decision together.

"It was a powerful moment."

NATIONWIDE TEACHER ACTIONS INSPIRED BY WEST VIRGINIA

Media stories proliferate about the influence of the West Virginia strike in the months following the action. A consistent theme is the wave of "teacher rebellions" that subsequently spread nationwide. *The New York Times* headlines its March 8, 2018, strike story, "West Virginia Walkouts a Lesson in the Power of a Crowd-Sourced Strike."[57]

By late May, there are statewide actions in Oklahoma, Arizona, Kentucky, Colorado and North Carolina.

The six-day Arizona "Red for Ed" walkout by some 75,000 teachers and educational support professionals in April 2018 is the result of two months of mobilization. The home of 1964 Republican Presidential candidate Barry Goldwater, canonized by many as a political father of modern American conservatism, Arizona lawmakers have been on a quarter century-long tax-cutting tear. There hasn't been a tax increase for 30 years. A *Vox* analysis of the state's recent tax history cites the realities Arizona schools have faced: a drop in funding per student by 14 percent from 2008 to 2018; decreases in annual corporate income tax revenues to rate cuts from $986 to $368 million in a similar period; teacher incomes falling from $54,396 to $45,700 since 2003.

Why do you think the strike caught the attention of the national press and teachers' unions in states such as Arizona?

"I think the whole country has been starved for major courageous labor action for decades," says West Virginia's Smith, "and it was a reminder of the power of strikes, the power of what happens when working people are willing to take the bold action of using their own labor as a tool in struggle." Smith believes mass labor action, "people taking power to their own hands," has become a rarity in modern American culture. Especially "every single school in every single county taking action together."

America has at times in its history been an inspiration to workers worldwide, for its labor freedoms and the First Amendment right to assembly. Why do you think unions and other forms of labor protections seen a reduction in popular support?

Smith believes there has been a sustained "unabashed" attack on labor unions for the last two generations. "As labor union membership declines, there are fewer people to stick up for labor unions, and the cycle continues. Thirty-nine percent of West Virginians were engaged two generations ago; it's right around 11 percent now."

There is a curious political spectacle that the same Americans and political leaders who bemoan jobs going overseas have been quite content with 50 years of unraveling of the labor protections that might have defended those jobs or retrained those workers.

"That's absolutely true in West Virginia," insists Smith. He believes there should be a party that "is always on the side of people who are working the hardest and hurting the most," and thinks the Democratic Party has not lived up to that mission "faithfully" over the last generation, nationally or in West Virginia.

THE FEELING OF POSSIBILITY

Despite the cynicism with which O'Neal, Comer, Kuhn, and others view the effectiveness of lobbying and party politics, Smith decides to run for governor after the strike. When asked why, he says he is tired of "the old way."

"I'm tired of doing the polite thing of going up to a Capitol building to convince people to do the right thing. I want to be a part of a movement that replaces them, not just in one race, but up and down the ballot.

"There are lots of tactical lessons from the strike," says Smith, "but the overwhelming cultural lesson, the most important thing that came out of the strikes for West Virginians is the powerful reminder that mass action works, that when we're courageous together, things get better.

"You saw it again this year (2019). The teachers went on strike again, as the conventional wisdom said, 'No, you can't do this. It isn't how things are done. People won't support you.' Of course, they did it and again it worked, on a much more complicated issue in some respects."

Smith shares a final thought. "I think, for most of us, it was just the fundamental pride of being a West Virginian. It was a good reminder that we can rewrite our own story and the story other people tell about us by acting courageously. The strike gave birth to the feeling of possibility, the feeling that, when we do these sorts of things bravely and together, we win.

"That's pretty powerful. We can't put that genie back in the bottle."

14. STANDING ROCK: MNI WICONI (WATER IS LIFE)

"You are coming to an Indian reservation in the middle of nowhere," says LaDonna Brave Bull Allard, Lakota Sioux historian and warrior in the fight against the Dakota Access Pipeline (DAPL). "We don't have taxis, we don't have buses, we don't have trains, there are no hotels." She promises to send Mayor Jarod, but swings by the Bismarck airport herself, car filled with shopping purchases along with some takeaway food for the family.

Allard doesn't want the donated car, a hybrid, but an activist insists. It's adorned with political stickers and, prominently, a Deadpool action figure on the passenger side dash, two swords sheathed on its back. Allard takes a group to see *Deadpool I* and *II* and loves it, her Standing Rock friends laughing uncontrollably. "Deadpool might a good symbol for the resistance," she laughs. "Two thumbs up and ready to defend at any moment with a necessarily sardonic sense of humor."

The DAPL oil route from North Dakota to Illinois has been fought by the Standing Rock Sioux tribe and other Native American and environmental groups since 2016. The pipeline is less than a mile from the reservation – which straddles the North and South Dakota borders, 100 miles east of Montana – and represents a direct threat to its Missouri River water supply.

Swept up in the Standing Rock reservation protests, Allard prefers her chosen passions, tribal historian and grandmama to 18 boys and one girl. Later in the evening, she brings her one-month-old great-granddaughter for an introduction, "Direct descendant of Sitting Bull." As with Occupy Wall Street, there are protestations that leadership was horizontal, distributed, often spontaneous, but each step of the way, people like Allard stepped up, pointed the way, made personal sacrifices, and set and implemented fluid strategies in an attempt to stop the pipeline's installation.

Allard once ran for the North Dakota state House of Representatives. "Got close," she says, but could not capture a key county. She never wanted to be an activist but says she had no choice.

"I'm not a frontline person. Before the camps, I was doing historic tours, lectures about the history of Sitting Bull, about all the chiefs, about our culture, our way of life. When the camp started, I contacted everybody I knew from all parts of the world that, "Hey, this is happening." That background I had with European people was helping me spread the word."

She was moved, overwhelmed as the world took notice. A literal gathering of the tribes – the largest of its kind in Native American history – was followed by the gathering of a diverse group of 10,000 environmentalists, military veterans, indigenous rights activists, and sympathetic supporters from around the country and the world, in the dead of the frigid North Dakota winter. Mongolians supplying yurts, New Zealanders performing haka. "Hindu, Sikh, Muslim, Christian, Buddhist, Native, every group standing together, one prayer and one circle," recalls Allard.

In December of 2014, Energy Transfer Partners (ETP) applies to the federal government to construct the

1,200-mile DAPL to carry more than a half million barrels of Bakken-formation shale oil each day through North and South Dakota, and Iowa to a terminal point in Illinois. The proposed route passes just outside the Standing Rock Sioux reservation and crosses under Lake Oahe, the tribe's drinking water source.

By the time they were building the pipeline here, they had already invested in construction from the Bakken oil fields.

"Even though they had no permit to start construction," points out Allard, "they already laid half the pipe before they got permission. Then the court said, 'Oh, they already spent all this money.'"

In April of 2016, the Sacred Stone camp is set up on Allard's property by tribe members. "This area was named Cannon Ball by Lewis and Clark," she says during a tour of the reservation, "because of the round sandstones. But we call this 'the place that makes sacred stones.'" She says she became involved, "the day Joye came and asked." Joye Braun of the Cheyenne River Sioux Tribe is a leader of the Indigenous Environmental Network, another of the essential women activists quick to deflect credit but pivotal in the business of planning, motivating, choreographing, and acting.

The Lakota phrase "Mni Wiconi," meaning "Water is Life," is an inspiration for protesters.[58]

Until then, what was your mode of engagement?

"We were going through policies and procedures," says Allard, "wanting them to do a complete environmental impact statement, wanting them to do complete archaeological surveys. Because that's what the law says, from the 1966 National Historic Preservation Act and the 1970 Environmental Protection Act. My assumption was, people follow the law. And what happened was, nobody was following the law.

"We hear back, 'I don't recall that. I will get back to you. I will form a committee. Let me do remote research on this issue.' It's the same with all of the agencies.

"At the beginning, there were no protests, all of it was training, in nonviolent direct action, de-escalation, security, and reconnaissance. We went out and took pictures of what was happening. The training curriculum came from the Indigenous Environmental Network, Honor the Earth, and Keep It in the Ground – all indigenous movements. We instructed what we were trying to do and why we were doing it. We wanted non-violent resistance."

At a certain point, it got much bigger. Did you ever think, 'Have I lost control of this?' or 'What's going on here?'

"No," says Allard, in a familiar self-deprecating refrain, "because I never thought I was in control. I was not a leader. I was not telling people what to do. But people were always walking up and putting a microphone in my face while I was busy running around, figuring out how or what needs to be done."

Because without all those logistical solutions, the political action is not effective. It doesn't happen.

"My job was making sure that kids went to school," she says, "taking care of a town. I wasn't involved in the frontline non-violent actions. I would drop off medical supplies. Is there enough propane for the cooking stove? At five o'clock in the morning, because we have no running water, I brought in water and breakfast food.

And I had to be in charge of monitoring the grants and putting in every receipt that had to be saved. We had Honor the Earth as our fiscal agent. It was a logistical nightmare. You have all these very compassionate people that want to help. This individual gives this person money, we don't know who that was. That happened a lot."

THE RUNNERS

The month the camp is set up, protest relays named "Run for Your Life" are organized.

"On April 20, the kids ran from the Cannon Ball community to Mobridge (South Dakota)," says Manape LaMere, a coordinator of the relays. "Somebody suggested, you guys should run down to that Army Corps office where they're making them decisions." Phone calls went out. People were asked if they could help, organize and protect these kids. In two days, we whipped up a flyer to share on social media, and those kids were already on their way by the 22nd of April.

"They came down (385 miles) to the Santee reservation. I had my buddy Sydney Tuttle (Vice Chairman, Santee Sioux Tribal Council) escort them to Sioux City (88 miles to the east), then I escorted them from Sioux City to Omaha (100 miles to the south). They started it with a prayer, made a commitment, and they followed through. I think that gave purpose and direction. What's the purpose? We want to elevate the discussion. Whether you're right or wrong, you need people discussing this at their dinner table." The runners arrive in Omaha on May 3rd, having covered roughly 550 miles.

Is there something symbolically important in the political act of running, walking, marching?

"Yeah, there's nothing more sovereign than a bird,"
explains LaMere. "As human beings, we can't fly.
But walking or running is a symbol of freedom. And,
then, the kids wanted to run from Cannon Ball to D.C.
Because they had a feeling of purpose.

"We were doing different styles of relay. We did what
we call a crow hop. Or, when everybody's running
together, various people would take the lead, and we
always had a female and a male running together for
equality and balance. It affected me to realize how much
hurt these kids have, yet they remained motivated, and
knew how important it was to stop this pipeline."

LaMere doesn't make his camp presence official until
the end of October. "Up until that point, I had just been
coordinating resources. I mean, we had phone calls with
Jane Fonda, Jason Momoa, Leonardo DiCaprio, and
people from the Black Eyed Peas."

Allard recalls the early days of the unprecedented
months-long protest, before thousands of
demonstrators arrived in support, impossible to
anticipate or fully control.

"When it first started," relates Allard, "there were 20.
That was manageable. Then, all of a sudden, you had
these people from all kinds of cultures, not everybody
following protocol."

Families came, so they worked to make sure children
were safe, "like old times of protecting the village. Food,
garbage, supplies. All the tribes coming in with their
ceremonies." It became, she admits, "really hard for
tribal government to manage."

Ten weeks after "Run for Your Life," on July 26, the Army Corps of Engineers grants pipeline permits for more than 200 water crossings. A coalition of Sioux tribes including the Standing Rock, Cheyenne River, Yankton, and Oglala file a lawsuit to block them.

On August 10, protesters block DAPL construction, resulting in numerous arrests, among them Standing Rock Tribal Chairman Dave Archambault II. Over 700 protesters are arrested during the months of subsequent protests.

A month later, on September 9, U.S. District Court Judge James Boasberg denies the attempt by the Standing Rock Sioux to halt pipeline construction. But three federal agencies announce that construction near or under Lake Oahe may not go forward pending further review. ETP chooses to resume construction.

In October, roadblocks are set up by law enforcement in black riot gear, flanked by two armored vehicles, to inhibit the movement of DAPL protesters. Casino and other tribe revenues are adversely affected. The roadblocks also affect access to health services such as the ambulance, dialysis and cancer treatments.

"Here, if you eliminate those services, people die," protests Allard. "We are so below property level that people are barely functioning on an estimated $12,000 yearly income. We have people who don't have furnaces and don't have heat in their homes and don't have electricity."

How long were the roadblocks set up and what effect did they have on travel?

"Eight months," says Allard. "A Bismarck hour ride becomes two hours. Stores might refuse to sell to tribe members and protesters, so they have to drive like five hours to Fargo to get supplies for all kinds of stuff."

THE MAYOR

How does a Northeastern architect become mayor of the Native American city of Fort Yates, North Dakota?

Jarod Galvin insists he prefers being behind the scenes, after choosing to stay on the reservation long after the protests ended.

"Since I came here, I've been trying to just do what I do until I am asked to do more. If the community feels that you're right for it – even if it is not your intention – that is what you should do for the betterment of the group. There were no architects in Standing Rock. LaDonna helped me get licensed in North Dakota. I was licensed in Vermont."

Galvin acquires his focus on delivering only what's needed during the protests. "By the time I arrived on October 10th, different native groups had formed sub-camps within Sacred Stone, while Oceti (Sakowin) and Rosebud tended to be self-sufficient. Sacred Stone itself was an amalgam of tons of different people – very similar to Burning Man, actually. You just walk around and you see if someone needs any help. Or someone drives up and says, 'I've got an entire van full of groceries. Where do I go?' Point and connect. So logistically, it was really fun to just be a hub and be like, 'Oh, you're here to help? What's your specialty? How about you go talk to that person over there?' There was a fair number of folks that were there for a very long time, but there was a high turnover. The pace was so fast. Many were focused on frontline actions."

He decides to run for city council when asked by a former mayor. "He stopped me on the street and asked me if I'd ever thought of it. I said I didn't even know if it would be appropriate and then asked LaDonna's opinion.

"I could drive up to Bismarck and get a relatively high paying job but I just wouldn't be doing what I feel needs to be done out here. It's one of the reasons (teacher) subbing is so perfect. If I don't have the time because of other projects, I just say no."

Galvin's architecture skills are useful as Fort Yates faces a need for long-term planning and reinvention, after being decimated by federal government actions.

"The damming (of the Missouri River by the Army Corps of Engineers to create the Lake Oahe reservoir) is in the early '60s. The city is pretty much cut in half with the (planned) flood. Most of the businesses left in the late '60s, '70s, and '80s.

"The most productive agricultural land got flooded (with livestock slaughtered en masse). Nearly all communities got shoved onto the most exposed hills with the shittiest housing, with no wood, forcing them to become dependent upon other sources of heating, electric and fossil fuel. It's exposed as hell and heat just expands out of it. (The government) didn't build (houses) well enough to withstand that kind of windy environment; previously they were down in the valley where you would have a town."

This yurt was contributed by a Mongolian contingent. How in the world did they get wind of this and decide to come out from Mongolia?

"The whole world knew," says Galvin. "We covered the yurts in tarps and insulated with a wood stove. There were whole months when I barely got out of the downtown part of Sacred Stone. It was just constantly working, installing things, and doing things. The whole world was there. It was really quite incredible. Seeing a group of New Zealanders doing intimidating dances like the haka."

And the reason why people came from all over the world for a domestic political issue?

"It was standing up," says Galvin. "And a lot of other native people came in order to show solidarity at a moment in time that it had the world's attention. It brought a lot of different native people together in the general struggle for native sovereignty and native self-determination. So even if it wasn't their fight, it was very similar to their fights."

"From the '60s on," says Allard, "we had no businesses redeveloped here. As a child growing up in Fort Yates, we had a bakery, a mercantile store, clothing store, restaurant, two bars, gas station, movie theater, bowling alley, barber shop – I remember all this stuff as a kid. After the dams were built, they were all gone.

"Then new laws made it almost impossible to develop new businesses. Right now, to get a loan, you need a semester of entrepreneur and accounting classes. Banks don't loan to reservations. The process is a nightmare. It can take 15 years to open a business.

"With no infrastructure, we drive to Bismarck for shopping. We gather supplies, we take a trailer, we never waste a trip."

Allard points to the Missouri River and the Oahe reservoir. "That is the community of Cannon Ball that they moved up the hill after the flooding. The whole community was down here in the valley when I was a child and the original waters were about a mile out.

"You can see the old remnants of the buildings that were here at one time, an old church, houses. We had a train depot with a roundabout. The pipeline is located right below that tower. That's where the drill station is."

So, it is really is right up against your land. How long have your ancestors lived in this area?

"Not very long, estimated maybe 900 years."

And before that, where did they migrate from?

"Right across the river. We've been in this area about 10,000 years. Before, this was all underwater. Every tribe has a different story of the great flood. My people, we went into the caves and lived under the Black Hills while the flood covered the earth.

"The summertime is beautiful. The water is so blue. I remember what life was like. And then the Army Corps came in and we were left to survive. I remember grandma saying there were hard times, there was no food.

"When I was a teenager, they said you know, you should fix your teeth. I said no, my teeth remind me that I come from starvation. And I want to live every day like who I am."

On November 20th and 21st, police and security agents use tear gas, rubber bullets and water sprays in an assault on protesters, 17 of whom are hospitalized; one officer is injured when hit in the head by a hurled rock.

THE MEDIC

"It was a city that came together," recalls Mitra, a retired military medic. Among the handful of activists who stay behind, she acquires the gear to launch a T-shirt business to support Standing Rock projects. When asked what brought her to the DAPL protests, she answers, without hesitation, "the dogs."

"I adopt retired military dogs and when I was watching the (law enforcement) dog attacks, I knew something was wrong. Those dogs were not trained. I know what a good protection dog does. So that's what started me watching. I've never seen the government attack its people like that before. Their behavior, the injustice, caused everyone to come."

You were in the military for four years; you went through certain training, had respect for the management of violence, ways in which weapons are used, in which tactical operations were carried out. As a medic, you saw the effects of violence on the human body. So, as you look at what some characterize as a highly militarized police force, how did you evaluate that professionally?

"They were violating every rule of engagement," answers Mitra. "You don't attack civilians; there were no weapons. They just did the wrong thing; they were not following any protocol. All the training, all the protocol that I learned – they were applying none of it. I think it was a purposeful instigation. Let's get them to fight us back. And then we can take the land."

"Most of these local people that have been here for a while are descendants of the Seventh Cavalry (famous for its skirmishes with the Sioux, including the Battle of Little Bighorn, in which Lieutenant Colonel George

A. Custer and his troops were routed). So just like the story is passed on from generation to generation in the native community, their stories pass from generation to generation. What values did they pass down? You know they hated the Sioux down here. They stayed here, reproduced, and told their stories to their children."

If what LaDonna shared is true, that the Sioux were proud and effective warriors; many of their ancestors were defeated here.

"So, imagine the resentment. 'How dare these natives stand up and bother us about the pipeline?' Because the pipeline is supposed to go to Bismarck. They're like, 'No, no, let's go down to the reds.' And then, 'Oh my God, how dare they stand up and complain?' The same attitude that they've always had."

What do you most remember from your experience in the camp?

"How, in the face of so much brutality, can they still be happy and cheerful and sing songs? In the face of such extreme tragedy, they still come together and honor their spirituality. How can you do that?"

"Everybody walked away with a different lesson," declares Mitra. "For me, I want my life to be completely independent from fossil fuels. That's why I went down to New Mexico and started working towards that. Because if there's no demand, there's no supply. I mean, I've been vegetarian for 35 years. I do my own gardens, food production. So, let me be also fossil fuel free. When the pipeline does break, I'm on solar power. I don't need the electric company. I got my wood, I can stay warm."

THE STUDENT

Barack Obama is the first president to visit the area, arriving by helicopter in April of 2014. A student, Kendrick Eagle, is selected to meet him, and a request is made to the president – a new school to replace the current one, built in the 19th century. Legislation to provide it is passed, though construction is yet to begin as of 2019.

On November 21, 2016, Eagle posts a video to YouTube, appealing for help.

"I put out a video to Barack Obama," says Eagle, "to see if he can come out and help us, because he came to Standing Rock and said that he had our backs. And then he denied the easement in December, though it didn't stop the pipeline."

Eagle is an active board member of the nonprofit agency Indigenized Energy, that has installed a solar farm in Standing Rock to fund reservation youth projects and reduce energy costs. "We're trying to teach younger people, what is a solar panel, how does it create energy? We're trying to educate people about renewable energy, which is the future."

Eagle hosts and narrates the video, which includes clips of Obama speaking at a Tribal Nations Conference just two months prior.

> You gave us a lot of hope, you flew us out to DC. We rode in a motorcade from the White House to We the Pizza with Michelle, went to an NBA game. I am here at Oceti Sakowin, asking you to come and help us stop this pipeline. Water is life. We need it to survive and live. Help us stop this pipeline. Stay true to your words.

THE VETERANS

After protesters are given an order to evacuate the camps by December 5th, a call for support goes out to Native American military veterans. Walk through the Standing Rock tribal center and you will find a large area dedicated to those who served. Native peoples serve in the U.S. military at a rate five times the national average, the highest per-capita participation rate of any ethnic group.

More than 2,000 veterans (4,000 by many estimates), including non-natives eager to support their former comrades, arrive at Standing Rock in the frigid cold to support tribal activists. Many are led by Wesley Clark Jr., screenwriter, former army lieutenant, and son of the retired general and former presidential candidate.

On December 4th, as veterans prepare for a likely confrontation, many promising to put their bodies on the line as human shields for protesters, Assistant Army Secretary for Civil Works Jo-Ellen Darcy announces that alternate pipeline routes should be evaluated. It is a pivotal, if short-lived, victory.

The presence of thousands of veterans sworn to "support and defend the Constitution of the United States against all enemies, foreign and domestic," affects the public image of the DAPL demonstrators. Veterans publication *Task & Purpose* posits, "A potent new political force had emerged as if out of nowhere: veterans mobilizing en masse to draw national attention to the failings of the government they once served." The public showing by veterans happens almost simultaneous with the Obama administration decision to shut down pipeline construction.

One month later, on January 18, 2017, the Army Corps announces it will perform what protesters consider a long overdue environmental impact study of the Lake Oahe crossing. Judge Boasberg declines an Energy Transfer Partners request to stop the study, which may take up to two years.

"WE ARE CONSTANTLY FIGHTING"

What was the high point for you? At what point did you feel most proud or fulfilled as an activist, as Lakota, as a woman living in this land?

"The minute I watched them shut down the pipeline the first time," reminisces Allard. "And when I watched the four women run out and stop the bulldozers. When I watched them put the dogs on people, and young men came to stand between us and the dogs. When I was at the front line and I brought supplies, this young man came and said, 'Don't worry about me, Grandma. The mace doesn't even hurt me anymore.'"

What about your lineage and the stories of men and women like Sitting Bull motivated or focused you?

"As you know, Sitting Bull represents resistance," responds Allard. "And it's always been with us. It is how we live. I personally come from medicine people. We are prayer people. That was our strength in everything we did."

What does that mean, to come from medicine people?

"My family, we're all spiritual leaders, they prayed. Tatanka Yotanka (Sitting Bull) was a medicine man. He prayed for the people. He was from the Cannonball River. That is my home. It is not someplace you move to.

It's not someplace that looks pretty. It's not someplace you came to camp. It is our lives. We can tell you where everybody's buried for 2,000, 3,000 years. Can anybody do that?

"I know exactly where Tatanka Yotanka is buried, because he was my great, great, great, great grandfather. Do any of the people who've came to my country have that knowledge? Do they know what happened on this land? They know where the medicine was put? Did they know what prayer and ceremony happened here? Do they know why we call that land sacred?"

What is Sitting Bull's significance to Standing Rock, the place where he lived and died?

"Sitting Bull was born down on the Grand River," says Allard, "he died just right up the river from where he was born. He lost the majority of his children during childbirth or within their first couple of years. He had two daughters that were able to live to adulthood, they died at 20 and 23. Soldiers killed his son. He became a symbol of a resistance. But for people here, he is a symbol of private ceremony. He was a spiritual leader. He prayed all the time.

"And so, within the tribe, we have stories of his medicine and how he prayed. 'Always put the children first. Stand up for the land and the water. Be proud of who you are.' We never stopped resisting. We don't want to be anything but what we are. So, as the desert cults (Allard's term for Abrahamic religions) come here and force assimilation, religions and conversions, they don't make sense to us because we already have a way of life that we understand.

"All of his frontline warriors were all my relatives. They fought hard. They went to the war prisoners' camps with him and, once released, got brought back here. So, we all have that background of resistance. Then if we are going back to 1910, to the 1930s, we are actually the first tribe to stand up for ourselves and declare that we are suing the United States for blackmail. We fought and fought and continue to fight. And we are the only tribe who refused money. This is the longest (Supreme) Court battle in the United States. We are constantly fighting."

During a driving tour of the reservation that includes the college, the tribal center, sacred burial grounds, the pipeline, and the river, Allard periodically jams on the brakes and pulls to the side of the road to emphasize a strongly-held view. When queried about political objectives with a $5 billion project fully operational and Donald Trump as president, she insists, *"That pipe is coming out of the ground,"* unequivocally, with confidence, while describing the unique perspectives her people have on the notions of time and sacred purpose.

The argument by ETP is that the DAPL reduces the need for rail and truck transport, providing a more environmentally-friendly mode of transport. The notion infuriates her.

"If a (tanker) truck rolls over, then it has an oil spill here, in a round circle. If the pipe bursts in the river, the whole river is gone. Where does it end? They have no plan on how to clean up this mess they're creating. And the land becomes unusable. So, you tell me which is worse: a truck rolling over here or a half million people dead?"

You drive by the pipeline site all the time and have a sense of pride and accomplishment, along with a sense of sorrow. You clearly don't feel a sense of failure.

"Oh, no. We've just begun," says Allard, shaking with emotion. "I am angry because there is no justice in

America. South Dakota just passed four laws against protesting, violating the Constitution to protect the Keystone XL pipeline (a separate project proposing to transport oil from Canada through Montana, South Dakota, and Nebraska). We were not violent, there were no riots, there were people mostly singing and praying. At the front we would sing and pray, and they would attack us. The security forces and all the camps would search the cars as they came in. No alcohol, no drugs, no firearms.

"I am a grandma. I don't care if I live or die. You come, go ahead. It's because my dad said, 'You are brave. You are better than anything walking on this earth, *you are Lakota.*' Even the youngest kid has this internal pride about who they are. If we had a choice, we would just close off everything. Because we're safe within our own. If the United States left us alone, we would thrive. But they come with their policies, procedures, trying to control us. And they still haven't been able to control us.

"We are the only people who took the United States flag in battle. Remember, we kicked their butts. They came and begged for a treaty from us. It cost them over a million dollars a day to fight us. And they could not fight us as we burned down every one of their forts, as we attacked from all directions. We don't do standing armies. We won't ever be an aggressor. But if you come at us, we will defend. Come at us and we stand stronger, committed.

"My grandmother was nine years old when she was shot at the Whitestone Hill massacre, the rest of our family was killed. She survived because a soldier decided to pick her up and throw her in back of the buckboard and take her to the prisoner of war camps.

"When they told us that the soldiers were on their way, our leader said, 'Well, we never had a treaty with them.

We've never fought them. We don't have a problem with them. So, it's not going to be an issue.' Some heard that the Americans had this thing about white flags; they made this flower sack and they went out there with it. And the soldiers surrounded them to take them off as prisoners, and then went and killed all the women and children. Our people wondering, why would they do that? Then we came to find out that we were the wrong Indians, we were simply in the way. Hence, they killed us because they couldn't tell the difference between the two tribes.

"As a child, she survived that, so that we are here. But we are told this story all the time about when she was in her 80s, with her nightmares, and the screaming, she would tell everybody to run, the soldiers are coming; it became so ingrained in our lives that we understood.

"We are the people of this massacre that live in Cannon Ball. We are the people who the Army Corps comes and floods our lands and takes our homes and moves us into the hilltops where we can't plant and destroys our economic base. And then we are the people who pay higher electric rates than everyone on the outside of the reservation. You get to a point where you say, 'What did I ever do? I have never been the aggressor. I've only been the defendant, what did I do to cause this?'"

Newly inaugurated President Donald Trump signs an executive order to advance the pipeline's construction on January 24, 2017, four days after taking office.

Twelve days later, the Army Corps of Engineers reverses its intention for further study and provides the necessary easement for completion of the pipeline. Drilling begins under Lake Oahe.

During February 22-23, the last remaining protesters are cleared from the camps. On April 4, the pipeline leaks 84 gallons of oil at a rural pump station in South Dakota. Federal reports in May reveal that the pipeline and a feeder line leaked more than 100 gallons of oil in North Dakota in separate incidents in March. The state environmental agencies confirm that the company cleaned up the spills, though activists remain skeptical.

The pipeline becomes fully operational on June 1, 2017.

THE FILMMAKER

"There was a media tent when you first got to camp," says Tina, one of the handful of activists who stayed behind to further assist the Standing Rock tribe. A filmmaker and social media producer, she first heard of the DAPL protests while working on a film in Los Angeles with Cherokee American actor and producer Wes Studi. She lives with other full-time supporters in the Water Protectors house, across the street from Allard.

"You had to learn about history and protocol, such as Native Americans not being allowed to pray until 1978. You don't record prayer, you don't record ceremony (unless approved). You had to go through a class and you had to get a media pass. There were hundreds of media people, but the bigger networks would only come out when there was blood in the water. Then you had all these mini-documentary people and kids with iPhones that just livestream any chance they get. I think livestreaming took off because of Standing Rock; that was the first movement that utilized it. People would record on the front lines to prove how the cops were treating people."

How that was achieved logistically? Was there connectivity available?

"Yes, mobile broadband until they started blocking us out. We got sabotaged left and right – people snuck into camp and cut the wires. There was a place called Media Hill, also called Facebook Hill, where you could get service.

"Once the cops rolled in, they took down the Wi-Fi with machines that stopped us from getting service. So, hotspots were really important. There was a lot of artistic stuff like those music videos that you saw, a lot of short form documentaries; we did daily updates. And livestreaming was great.

"A lot of people face jail time because of the livestream, since the cops were watching Facebook like a hawk," according to the filmmaker. "They were ripping footage left and right to make sure that they had proof (of events) because, while most people came to pray, there were a lot of angry people out there. Tiger Swan (the pipeline security firm) sent in a lot of agitators to be disruptors."

LaDonna said last night that National Guard from other states were specifically sent to infiltrate veterans to create a situation that could be exploited.

"That's why I tried to get people to put out video that's edited, versus a livestream, on a daily basis. That takes more discipline, makes you work differently as a filmmaker. Now, whenever I teach frontline media, we talk about when it's good to livestream versus producing an edited video to show what's going on."

Are there some key insights you gained for coverage of an event like Standing Rock?

"I would say to focus. The very first video that really came out of here was *ReZpect Our Water*. It was the kids talking about why their land is so important and why water is so important to them. My first video was Kendrick Eagle talking to President Obama. I would say creating content about the positive is more powerful than pointing fingers. Movies are emotion machines. They create and evoke emotion in people. As a filmmaker, I'm really good at finding the heart of a story and then tenderizing that to get people to care. That's the power of media and the power of the kids finally caring.

"And honestly, what really should have been done is a series of cultural educational videos for specifically Morton County and the cops. They were so culturally insensitive. Creating content specifically for the police (would have helped) to explain this is what it means when we drum and pray. They packed a pipe, not a pipe bomb."

Native American attitudes towards the earth seemed to resonate with people.

"We're mostly water," says Tina. "We live on a planet that is mostly water. Pua Case in Hawaii says, when the water is in trouble, the water spirits talk to each other. It was a molecular call from the water. The water was in dire need. There are things bigger than us. I think it's touching people whether they know it or not.

"Standing Rock was like a wave, or an earthquake, where the epicenter has so much history. Sitting Bull was one of the last chiefs fighting against colonization and he was murdered (by native agents working for the United States government) here, in Standing Rock.

"It has been happening specifically in North Dakota, in the center of the United States, the geographic center of North America. It sent out a ripple and it's touching the whole world. The United Nations reports that 80 percent of the remaining biodiversity exists on indigenous people's lands, so they have been protecting what's left.

"Over 500 tribes came together, the most ever gathered in one place. That's huge. And the prophecy was that the red man was going to be able to teach all the other colors how to live again, make peace with the earth, or the earth was going to be destroyed. I think what happened was indigenous people started communicating with each other again. It was an amplification. I've been going to the indigenous peoples' forum for the last two years, and they're all facing the same thing. Poverty, destruction, consultation without consent. I think of Standing Rock and, because of the power of the media, it's getting better. You can put out a video and it gets a million views in a day, and that wasn't a thing five, ten years ago."

On June 14, 2017, Judge Boasberg orders the Corps to do more environmental assessment of the pipeline's impact on the Standing Rock Sioux. On October 11, 2017, he rules that the pipeline can continue operating while court-ordered study continues.

THE HEADMAN

"There's an analogy that I've heard in the past," says LaMere.

"You see a baby floating down a river. And if you're a human being with some sense of compassion, you're going to dive in and save that baby. We've built our whole system around saving babies floating down the river. But not very many of us have gone upriver to see how the hell are these babies getting in the river in the first place. Some of us have done that and we see the solutions. We know what we need to do and we're working on that. But the whole reservation system is founded on just saving the babies floating down the river; they're not solving the problem upstream.

"But we failed," opines LaMere. "Oil is pumping under that river. So, no matter how much we say, 'Oh, it was you know it all it was a great thing,' we failed in what we were trying to do. There are other victories that have happened. It's a bit like the old days, where you go on the warpath to accomplish a certain mission. And you win some war honors but you lost the battle.

"Our people are familiar with the Battle of the Greasy Grass or Custer's Last Stand. We won that battle, but we lost the war and we barely survived it. America has broken the treaty over and over and over again. We remind them that the treaty is still valid, because we've upheld ours. How much longer does this have to go on?

"We just do what we gotta do to survive. We had to have the ceremonies go underground. Only since 1978 have we had the freedom to practice our own religion. I think that we were some of the last cultures on the planet to be beaten into submission. The elders who exist now usually come from the boarding school era that beat them, cut their hair, and did horrible things to suppress the language.

"I'm one of the leadership that lifted the horn in November. The horn is our traditional government structure. Many chiefs from the Sioux Nation had come together and said, 'We're going to put the horn up.' But none of the chiefs wanted to endure the winter because they were elderly. So, they appointed seven male leaders to take their place in those teepees that went around that fire."

Oceti Sakowin, the proper name for the Sioux people means, literally, Seven Council Fires. Each fire is a symbol of a nation. Lakota and Dakota are Sioux dialects, both meaning "friend" or "ally."

"The seven bands of the Sioux Nation," explains LaMere, "lit a fire with hundreds in attendance. The horn is symbolic of a buffalo horn. And we point our horns east, towards the threat. And that threat is Washington, D.C. A ceremony appointed seven men as chief, as headmen, and I am one of those.

"Two weeks later, I found myself in Bismarck with a document that states that I am defecting from the United States. And I am rematriating under the Sioux Nation of Indians of the 1851 and 1868 Laramie treaties."

The Great Sioux Reservation was established by the Treaty of Fort Laramie of April 29, 1868. In 1877 and again in 1889, Congress reduced the Great Sioux Reservation, into six separate entities, including the Standing Rock Sioux Reservation.[59]

"Bismarck is where Custer got his riverboat to start the military campaign to find Crazy Horse and the other rogue chiefs. That's where he started, at Fort Abraham Lincoln.

"I went in with my IDs to a state notary at a bank. He notarized it and signed it and then I went over to the Social Security office, and had them sign it. Federal and state agencies acknowledged my defection from the United States of America and read me the powers of the Sioux Nation. So not only was I headman, but I had also relinquished the federal jurisdictions that are placed over me."

How common is it for someone to do that?

"Well, there's about four of us that have done it," says LaMere. "But I'm the only one that possesses an actual passport of the Sioux Nation. Our elders have been attending treaty meetings for the last 60 years, and they haven't figured this part out. Upon my return to camp, I was already headman. But now I'm returning back to camp with my Sioux Nation status. I've placed myself back to the time when Red Cloud and Iron Shell and Mad Bear sign these treaties. I've heard elders say we're all Americans, so we need to figure out how to do this stuff as American Indians. We've been trying to. It ain't working. It ain't gonna work, period.

"My girlfriend, her last name is Iron Shell. One of the last times this happened was with her great, great grandfather, who became what's called a supreme owner, meaning full jurisdiction over the Sioux Nation. He and six other chiefs had become supreme owners and so technically, a seventh headman means that we became the authorities with full jurisdiction and powers within our own territories. And out of those seven headmen, I'm the only one that has true treaty status, within our own territory.

"I think the beautiful thing about being Lakota is, out of all the tribes on Turtle Island, we've maintained this sense of our independence."

"With all of these people that come here," muses Allard on the drive back to the Bismarck airport, "the first thing I tell them is they have to heal. And that you didn't come here to help us. We came here to help you. We want to see every American heal from the inside. And then we can heal the earth."

A sense of history permeates the Bismarck-Mandan
sister city area, specifically the history between the
Seventh Cavalry and the Sioux. Towns and parks named
after forts, streets and landmarks named after Custer.
Mandan is the name of a once great tribe before its
decimation by smallpox introduced at the time of the
Lewis and Clark expedition.

> "Every good western has a fort, and your western
> experience in North Dakota has plenty of
> them, too," promises the North Dakota tourism
> website. "From authentic buildings to faithful
> reconstructions, these North Dakota cavalry and
> infantry posts make it easy to envision life on
> America's last frontier."

"I can trace everybody's genealogy," says Allard. "I
know where the soldiers come from. It's right up here in
Mandan. I know that when I walk into the restaurant,
there'll be somebody walking up to my table saying, 'Go
back to the rez, you petty niggers don't belong here!'

"The racism is kind of covert. They don't wait on us at
restaurants. They don't like to have us in their stores.
Coming out onto the street, screaming at us, 'Did we kill
all of you yet?' Or 'I'm sick and tired of our taxes paying
for you.' Which they don't by the way," she laughs.
"Everybody pays for their homes, pays rent. We all have
to pay student loans. It's just propaganda to divide
people.

"When I was young, my stepmother took me go see a
friend, an old man, in a log cabin. She told me, sit there,
and she'd be right back. And her friend said, 'Come
here.' I walked over to him. And he said, 'You know
why we're still here? They done everything to us. They
gave us disease. They poisoned us, they killed us, they
took our children. But we're still here, because we have

a purpose. And I want you to know that. Our purpose and reason for living is to protect this earth. Remember that.'

"My grandma said, 'Indians are going to be here forever because God gave us a direction to care for the earth.' We're taught this all the time. We don't have any choice in it.

"And the prophecy says there will come a day when man will destroy everything, even the fruit he eats. And we must be able to be there to stand up to protect and save the Mother Earth. There are times I wake up and say, I don't want to do this. I want to stay home and take care of my grandkids and take care of my home and plants and do the things that I love, like researching. But this is what I have to do.

"I don't think I have any choice. My grandbaby – she has her right. And I'm going to make sure she has that right."

On July 6, 2020, Judge Boasberg rules that the pipeline must shut down and be emptied for a 13-month environmental impact analysis.

CONCLUSIONS

Twelve million people give up their weekend and march for hours to warn that the United States and United Kingdom are about to cause countless casualties in the pursuit of an unclear outcome in Iraq. The two governments ignore citizens' plea and go to war anyway. The demonstrators are ultimately proven right, but fail to hold leadership accountable in subsequent elections.

A decade earlier, a single legislative analyst from Texas does something achieved only 17 times since 1792 – he successfully leads an effort to amend the United States Constitution. It takes him a decade during evenings and weekends, showing that a persuasive argument, an understanding of the task at hand, and single-minded determination can surmount the insurmountable.

Between these two poles of a one-time engagement and a 10-year commitment lies an ordinary life for most people. Even the most apolitical citizens want to affect some change. Yet few are willing to maintain the discipline required to achieve those outcomes. Activism is daunting.

Citizens should not assume that a single march or demonstration, no matter how large, will lead to its intended result. An equally invalid assumption is that no change is possible.

Surmountable begins with an exploration of why certain men and women are successful in the arena and how that understanding could help make results more achievable for other activists. We are told by our interviewees that there is no checklist or universally applicable playbook but that there are stories and models for effective action.

Minds are rarely changed overnight. It takes patience to build consensus. Situations unfold that demand resourcefulness. And, as historian Stephen Schlesinger reminds us, "Every new generation has to refight the fight for democracy. You can't sit there and accept it as a given. You have to refight it all the time. Retrograde forces come back and try to grab that away from you."

Those forces predictably paint activists negatively, as unpatriotic or violent or as paid outside agitators. But assembly and petition are constitutionally guaranteed and civic engagement is an essential duty, required to maintain a functioning democratic republic.

The founders take inspiration from Jean-Jacques Rousseau's *The Social Contract*, where he reminds citizens, "The boundaries of what is possible in moral matters are less narrow than we think. It is our weaknesses, our vices, our prejudices that shrink them."[60] People limit opportunities to build a better country for themselves and future generations by believing achievable tasks to be out of reach.

Every movement documented herein is a subject worthy of its own book, so we hope readers will further explore the movements and movers that spark interest. Identify your own takeaways from each *Surmountable* chapter. As we review the stories gathered across four continents, we compile our own list of the 10 themes that impress us most, or recur as patterns over these 100 years of documented events.

Some may be a surprise while others will seem familiar. Activism is emotional, often sparked by transcendent revelatory moments. Movements are often ad hoc organizations that invent rules and structures as they go. Most begin with a simple passion to make the world a better place, without the resources, planning, or knowledge required to flourish. Some inherit decades of baggage and ineffective leadership that, for all of their optimism, have not made meaningful advances.

Surmountable documents the stories of inspired people who take on the challenge and move mountains. Here are some valuable lessons learned from their stories.

1. KNOW WHO CAME BEFORE YOU

Study the stories of past movements and the founding political ideas behind your constitutional right to assemble and to petition your government for a redress of grievances. Both first-hand experience and secondary research are invaluable in shaping strategy and avoiding the mistakes of the past. We publish this book to help future activists discover these ingredients of success.

Walter Waters and the Bonus Army distinguish between protesting and the civic duty of petitioning representatives directly for support on legislation. The Conservative Movement emphasizes that it is not highbrow magazine editors, but radio hosts who galvanize people to act during the Cold War. Gregory Watson researches similar scenarios from an entirely separate issue to identify the way forward for his objective. Ukrainian citizens learn from past demonstrations, using their media literacy to differentiate between propaganda and news while combatting disinformation. Standing Rock organizers realize that a single pipeline might not attract broader attention, but the issue of clean water affects everyone, while indigenous rights strike a chord with communities around the world.

2. CALCULATE WHAT IS REQUIRED AND WHAT SUCCESS LOOKS LIKE

Understanding the historical context and the stakeholders within each political moment can mean the difference between success and failure. Have a clear view of objectives and your measures of success.

Alice Paul calculates how long it will take to achieve suffrage with current tactics, and seizes the opportunity to start anew. Then she tasks Maud Younger to monitor the positions of individual representatives and senators as they change. Gregory Watson decides on a state-by-state basis if it is better to align with the majority or the minority party. Experienced supporters of the Internet blackout are critical to distinguish key players and understand how to navigate challenges. West Virginia educators know that many teaching positions are unfilled and use that as a bargaining chip to achieve their goals through negotiation.

3. EXPERIMENT TO REMAIN RELEVANT

Movements can lose creativity, as shown by the languishing suffragist movement before Alice Paul, Alva Belmont, and Lucy Burns become involved and change course. Experimentation in new methods keeps the media and public interested, volunteers engaged, and those invested in the status quo on their toes.

Suffragists learn new tactics from abroad and apply those experiments at home, such as the use of President Wilson's words against him to underscore his hypocrisy. Civil rights champions realize it is not enough to ask residents to boycott buses; they have to invent and manage a complex citizen-led network of dispatchers and drivers for their project to work. Internet activists encourage idealists to try new things with optimism and a dose of naiveté. Manape LaMere organizes an event for Lakota Sioux youth that is intentionally arduous to inspire awareness and empathy.

4. ADAPT TO UNEXPECTED EVENTS

Movements that do not adapt rarely succeed. James Madison believes in a right of conscience that requires constant vigilance to prevent despotism, and flexibility to adjust to the struggle against corruption. Dr. Paul Matzko, Kalle Lasn, and Dr. Kim Sun-Chul describe variations of political opportunity theory, the need to exploit and effectively respond to external events and forces.

The Reverend Dr. Martin Luther King, Jr. uses his time while wrongfully imprisoned to reflect on and publicize injustice. His partners in the civil rights movement turn what seems like a failure in the abbreviated march to the Edmund Pettus Bridge – Turnaround Tuesday – into a strategic success. Anti-Vietnam War activists enlist former political rivals when they become victims of offending policies, such as Admiral Zumwalt, who sees his son afflicted by the effects of Agent Orange. Tunisian citizens, long oppressed, react to the tragic self-immolation of a fruit vendor – and seize the moment to oust their dictator. Korean university students use their discovery of corruption to undermine presidential credibility, a first step in bringing down the administration.

5. SUCCESS MEANS GETTNG THE MUNDANE RIGHT

Those supporting the status quo often have vast, well-funded organizations at their disposal. The public sees the more visible public events but the logistical preparations and organizational networks make it easier for protesters to mass and have impact.

Police chief Pelham Glassford organizes sporting events for promoting the grievances of the Bonus Army by auditing veterans for talents. Conservative populists count on small donations in aggregate to fund momentum, which help them invest in media to affect long-term societal change. Occupy Wall Street co-creators coordinate for months to engineer a seemingly spontaneous event, despite their distance from the New York demonstrations. Local business owners provide pea soup and shoes to keep demonstrators warm in the cold of the Ukrainian winter; Korean unions provide buttons and flashlights for marchers. Social media groups plan valuable organizational infrastructures that enable West Virginia teachers to move quickly.

6. CRYSTALLIZE THE IDEA, LEVERAGE SYMBOLISM, BUILD A BRAND

Clear goals rally the masses. Vague notions can deflate the faithful and affect the ability to recruit support. Symbols are frequently powerful in our *Surmountable* stories, in communicating key messages or garnering sympathy. Social causes have learned something valuable from corporate marketers. Products rarely see success without investment in a brand to establish positioning and identity in the marketplace. Movements are no different.

Suffragists establish colors and branding for a
movement while rallying celebrities to the cause.
Civil rights organizations choose symbolic places
and memorable visual symbols to build support. War
resisters identify, utilize, and promote symbols such as
the burning of draft cards. London School of Economics
professor David Graeber concisely recognizes the
challenges of "the 99%," a meme that is widely adopted
by demonstrators and political leaders. Online
copyright activists use the draconian image of a blacked
out World Wide Web to generate publicity.

7. ESTABLISH CREDIBILITY TO BUILD CONSENSUS

Social movements require credibility to earn trust from
supporters and build integrity with those they need to
convince. Establish alliances across political positions,
industries, or communities rather than trying to stand
alone.

Walter Waters makes an alliance with fellow WWI
veteran, Washington, D.C. police chief Glassford who
helps champion his cause and welcomes thousands of
petitioners to the city to plead their case. The Freedom
Riders and white preachers marching alongside black
leaders are powerful allies for a united front. The
Electronic Frontier Foundation enlists corporate
supporters and elicits cross-party support. Movement
leaders in Kyiv formulate and vote on demands. Korean
citizens evoke support by shaming officials through
humility and sacrifice while showing their resolve by
marching in candlelight. Teachers cross West Virginia
county and union lines to discover they are not alone
and build popular support by keeping students fed to
avoid antagonizing the public.

8. BE RESILIENT IN THE FACE OF OPPOSITION

Committing potentially years of one's life and significant personal resources to a movement, when success is not guaranteed, is a difficult barrier to overcome. Movements have to be both persistent and resilient in the face of difficult challenges.

Lucy Burns' suffrage school prepares activists for the harsh treatment they expect and ultimately endure. World War I veterans remain stubbornly in place until they are forcefully dispersed, then return when their preferred candidate wins and still does not deliver. Advocates fend off rhetorical diversions ("whataboutism") with effective talking points and movement messaging. Watson uses his inadequate university grade to fuel his perseverance and prove his teacher wrong. Kyivites keep spirits high during demonstrations with musical performances and take refuge on holy ground when under attack.

9. MAINTAIN FOCUS AMID DISTRACTIONS

Set expectations, broadcast them, and stick to them. Well-meaning supporters often try to expand movement goals, unintentionally derailing momentum. External forces may try to sabotage groups, which necessitates caution even in the most inclusive of missions.

Walter Waters maintains discipline by rejecting partisan volunteers who threaten to distract the movement from its core goals. American citizens keep up the pressure on President Nixon even when an end to the Vietnam conflict is promised, skeptical after a decade of bipartisan deception. Tunisians maintain their democracy even after Islamists and allies of the deposed government threaten their newfound liberties. Hundreds of thousands of Korean citizens partake in weekly events for five months to see their objective through to the end. Standing Rock proves that the training of volunteers in nonviolence can de-escalate violent confrontations.

10. LEAD, SUPPORT LEADERSHIP, OR TAKE INITIATIVE

A hallmark of most successful social movements is inspired leadership. They may be unknown to the public, press, or authorities, and some may resist the label, but large groups of people rarely pursue a united path without smart guidance. Even direct democracies require someone to have a vision for a referendum, to garner support, and to follow through to ensure implementation. Otherwise, better-funded, better-organized interests may seize on indecision.

The civil rights movement establish a boycott leader and spokesperson who keeps supporters on message and executing unified tactics. Ukrainian parents respond in numbers to oppose brutality against their peacefully protesting children. Stephen Smith and Brandon Wolford reduce the risk of striking teachers by raising funds and ensuring loans are available. The efforts of LaDonna Brave Bull Allard underscore the need for initiative in handling the mundane details of a sustained mass protest.

ENTER THE ARENA, TOGETHER

A century ago, women had few rights. Veterans in the Great Depression had no hope of just rewards. African

Americans fought racism under the constant fear of reprisal. And yet they won their cause.

Fear peddled by the defense industry blocked America from ending the war in Vietnam, but citizens prevailed. Media monopolies tried to stifle voices, but citizens prevailed. Teachers were told to be happy with what had been negotiated by their own unions, but citizens prevailed.

The Reverend Dr. Martin Luther King, Jr. famously proclaims that the arc of the moral universe is long, but bends toward justice.

A less well-known corollary is that the arc does not bend toward justice on its own; it bends because people pull it that way.[61] Progress is not inevitable.

Those who crafted the Constitution formulated a way for citizens to stave off the power of corrupting influences.

We have promises to keep. Only civic engagement can realize the ideals the founders set forth, remaining vigilant against those who would wield power for personal gain. Only through continued activism can we keep the republic that the founders forged at the Constitutional Convention.

The movements recounted in *Surmountable* rarely attained success from a single event but achieved the seemingly impossible in 15 years or less.

There will always be someone invested in the status quo. Be invested in changing it.

It is not the critic who counts: not the man who points out how the strong man stumbles or where the doer of deeds could have done better. The credit belongs to the man who is actually in the arena, whose face is marred by dust and sweat and blood, who strives valiantly, who errs and comes up short again and again, because there is no effort without error or shortcoming, but who knows the great enthusiasms, the great devotions, who spends himself for a worthy cause; who, at the best, knows, in the end, the triumph of high achievement, and who, at the worst, if he fails, at least he fails while daring greatly, so that his place shall never be with those cold and timid souls who knew neither victory nor defeat.

– Theodore Roosevelt [62]

ENDNOTES

Introduction

[1] https://www.fairvote.org/voter_turnout#voter_turnout_101

[2] https://www.annenbergpublicpolicycenter.org/americans-civics-knowledge-increases-2019-survey/

[3] https://www.forbes.com/sites/daviddavenport/2017/12/13/a-growing-cancer-on-congress-the-curse-of-party-line-voting/#7e79958e6139

Chapter 1

[4] The Declaration and Resolves of the First Continental Congress. The Declaration of Independence. Philadelphia: Independence Hall Association. Retrieved from http://www.ushistory.org/declaration/related/decres.html.

Chapter 2

[5] Hansan, J. (2011). The women's suffrage movement. Social Welfare History Project. Retrieved from http://socialwelfare.library.vcu.edu/woman-suffrage/woman-suffrage-movement/.

[6] Hansan, J. (2011). The women's suffrage movement. Social Welfare History Project. Retrieved from http://socialwelfare.library.vcu.edu/woman-suffrage/woman-suffrage-movement/.

[7] Walton, Mary. A Woman's Crusade: Alice Paul and the Battle for the Ballot. St. Martin's Publishing Group. Kindle Edition.

[8] Walton, Mary. A Woman's Crusade: Alice Paul and the Battle for the Ballot. St. Martin's Publishing Group. Kindle Edition.

[9] Adams, Katherine H. and Keene, Michael L. Alice Paul and the American Suffrage Campaign. Urbana and Chicago: University of Illinois Press, 2008.

[10] Scutts, J. (July 11, 2016). The Society Girl Who Became a Martyr for Women's Suffrage. New York City: TIME Magazine. Retrieved from https://tinyurl.com/yb3ohsmn.

[11] Bort, I. R. Suffrage on the Menu: Traces of the Life and Legacy of Alva Vanderbilt Belmont. (April 6, 2017). New York City: New-York Historical Society, Behind the Scenes. Retrieved from https://tinyurl.com/ybh3y2ak.

[12] A Vote for Women. (September 30, 1918). Washington, D.C.: The United States Senate, Secretary of the Senate. Retrieved from https://www.senate.gov/artandhistory/history/minute/A_Vote_For_Women.htm.

[13] Walton, Mary. A Woman's Crusade: Alice Paul and the Battle for the Ballot. St. Martin's Publishing Group. Kindle Edition.

[14] Wilson, W. (1913). A New Freedom: A Call for the Emancipation of the Generous Energies of a People. New York City: Doubleday, Page & Co., 294. Retrieved from https://tinyurl.com/ycap3q8c.

Chapter 3

[15] Z., Mickey. The Bonus Army: History of the 1932 Bonus Expeditionary Force (BEF) or Bonus Army. Article. Zinn Education Project. Retrieved from https://www.zinnedproject.org/materials/bonus-army.

[16] Z., Mickey. The Bonus Army: History of the 1932 Bonus Expeditionary Force (BEF) or Bonus Army. Article. Zinn Education Project. Retrieved from https://www.zinnedproject.org/materials/bonus-army.

[17] Z., Mickey. The Bonus Army: History of the 1932 Bonus Expeditionary Force (BEF) or Bonus Army. Article. Zinn Education Project. Retrieved from https://www.zinnedproject.org/materials/bonus-army.

[18] Glass, A. (June 17, 2017). Bonus Army gathers at Capitol, June 17, 1932. Politico Magazine Retrieved from https://www.politico.com/story/2017/06/17/this-day-in-politics-june-17-1932-239562.

[19] Dickson, P. and Allen, T.B. (December 1, 2004). The Bonus Army: An American Epic. New York City: Walker Publishing, 162.

Chapter 4

[20] King, Jr., M.L. (March 25, 1965). Address at the Conclusion of the Selma to Montgomery March, State Capitol Steps, Montgomery, AL. Stanford, CA: Stanford University, The Martin Luther King, Jr. Research and Education Institute. Retrieved from https://kinginstitute.stanford.edu/king-papers/documents/address-conclusion-selma-montgomery-march.

[21] The Legacy Museum: From Enslavement to Mass Incarceration. Montgomery, AL: Equal Justice Initiative. Retrieved from https://museumandmemorial.eji.org/.

[22] Evans, Daniel. (May 23, 2015). "Forrest Bust Back at Old Live Oak." Selma Times-Journal. Retrieved from https://www.selmatimesjournal.com/2015/05/23/forrest-bust-back-at-old-live-oak/.

[23] Associated Press (March 26, 2012). "Bust of Confederate Gen. Nathan Bedford Forrest Missing in Selma." Retrieved from https://www.al.com/wire/2012/03/bust_of_confederate_gen_nathan.html.

[24] Robinson, Jo Ann. "Local Activists Call for a Bus Boycott in Montgomery," SHEC: Resources for Teachers. Retrieved from https://herb.ashp.cuny.edu/items/show/1140.

[25] Martin Luther King, Jr. Papers (Series I-IV), Martin Luther King, Jr., Center for Nonviolent Social Change, Inc., Atlanta, Ga.

Chapter 5

[26] America Has Been at War 93% of the Time – 222 out of 239 Years – Since 1776. (January 20, 2019). Washington's Blog. Montreal, Quebec, Canada: Global Research. Retrieved from https://tinyurl.com/y57aplu7.

[27] Lieberfeld, D. (Spring/Summer 2008). What Makes an Effective Antiwar Movement? Theme-Issue Introduction. International Journal of Peace Studies, 13(1), 3. Retrieved from https://www.gmu.edu/programs/icar/ijps/vol13_1/IJPS13n1%20Intro%20-%20Lieberfeld.pdf.

[28] Herring, G.C. (November 15, 2001). America's Longest War: The United States and Vietnam, 1950-1975. New York City: McGraw-Hill Humanities, 10.

[29] King, M.L., Jr. (April 4, 1967). Beyond Vietnam – A Time to Break Silence. American Rhetoric: Online Speech Bank. Retrieved from https://www.americanrhetoric.com/speeches/mlkatimetobreaksilence.htm.

[30] Quote. Brooklyn, NY: A Thought & Expression Co, LLC. Retrieved from https://quotecatalog.com/quote/muhammad-ali-my-conscience-w-vpZWE9a.

[31] February 1968 Gallup poll, https://www.pewresearch.org/2009/11/23/polling-wars-hawks-vs-doves/.

[32] Zimmer, B. (July 31, 2009). "Too Good to Check". On the Media. Interviewed by Bob Garfield. NPR. Archived from the original on August 4, 2009. Retrieved from https://web.archive.org/web/20090804011021/http://www.onthemedia.org/transcripts/2009/07/31/07.

[33] Pach, C. (2009). The Way It Wasn't: Cronkite and Vietnam. History News Network. Washington, D.C.: The George Washington University. Retrieved from https://historynewsnetwork.org/article/104635.

[34] Cronkite, W. (February 27, 1968). We are mired in a stalemate... Retrieved from http://www.ushistoryatlas.com/era9/USHAcom_PS_U09_tet_R2.pdf.

[35] Gitlin, Todd. Letters to a Young Activist (Art of Mentoring) (p. 170). Basic Books.

Chapter 6

[36] Matzko, P. (June 16, 2020). The Radio Right: How a Band of Broadcasters Took on the Federal Government and Built the Modern Conservative Movement. New York City: Oxford University Press.

[37] https://www.youtube.com/watch?v=4ssybQg1ZAY&t=10s

[38] McGirr, Lisa (2015-06-01T22:58:59). Suburban Warriors (Politics and Society in Modern America). Princeton University Press. Kindle Edition.

[39] https://www.webcitation.org/5uRU0fPQa?url=http://www.accessmylibrary.com/article-1G1-18396534/bold-grab-subs-murdoch.html.

[40] https://www.hup.harvard.edu/catalog.php?isbn=9780674185012

[41] https://www.npr.org/about-npr/520273005/npr-ratings-at-all-time-high

[42] http://www.talkers.com/top-talk-audiences/

[43] You say you want a revolution? Full Transcript. (February 19, 2009). Freedom Eden Blogspot. Retrieved from http://freedomeden.blogspot.com/2009/02/rick-santelli-tea-party.html.

Chapter 7

[44] Coleman v. Miller, 307 U.S. 433 (1939). Justia: US Law > US Case Law > US Supreme Court > Volume 307. https://supreme.justia.com/cases/federal/us/307/433/.

[45] A Record-Setting Amendment. (Apr. 11, 2016). Jessiekratz. National Archives History: Constitution, Bill of Rights. Retrieved Oct. 10, 2019, from https://prologue.blogs.archives.gov/2016/04/11/a-record-setting-amendment/.

[46] 27th amendment aimed at congressional pay. (Sept. 2, 2014). Rowley, Sean. Tahlequah Daily Press. Retrieved Oct. 7, 2019, from http://tinyurl.com/yjaz62n7.

[47] The Telling Tale of The Twenty-Seventh Amendment: A Sleeping Amendment Concerning Congressional Compensation Is Later Revived. (Sep. 27, 2002). Dean, John W. Findlaw, US Supreme Court Center, Legal Commentary. Eagan, MN: Findlaw. com. Retrieved on Oct. 10, 2019, from https://supreme.findlaw.com/legal-commentary/the-telling-tale-of-the-twenty-seventh-amendment.html.

[48] In October 2019, four states haven't ratified the Twenty-Seventh Amendment – Massachusetts, Mississippi, New York, and Pennsylvania.

Chapter 8

[49] Tunisia's Ben Ali sentenced to jail in absentia. (21 June 2011). BBC: News: Africa. Retrieved from https://www.bbc.com/news/world-africa-13850227.

Chapter 9

[50] Stiglitz, J.E. (March 31, 2011). Of the 1%, By the 1%, For the 1%. Vanity Fair. Retrieved from https://www.vanityfair.com/news/2011/05/top-one-percent-201105.

Chapter 10

[51] Speech at F2C: Freedom to Connect 2012 event in Washington, D.C. (21 May 2012) video as transcribed at "Freedom to Connect: Aaron Swartz (1986-2013) on Victory to Save Open Internet, Fight Online Censors" at Democracy NOW! (14 January 2013).

Chapter 11

[52] HOLODOMOR: The famine-genocide of Ukraine, 1932-1933. Retrieved from https://holodomorct.org/.

Chapter 12

[53] https://apnews.com/f26782acb46246a0835ecfc412ed7db1/How-sparks-at-S.-Korean-women%27s-school-led-to-anti-Park-fire.

Chapter 13

[54] Catte, E., et al., editors. 55 Strong: Inside The West Virginia Teachers' Strike. (July 5, 2018). Cleveland: Belt Publishing, 27.

[55] Catte, E., et al., editors. 55 Strong: Inside The West Virginia Teachers' Strike. (July 5, 2018). Cleveland: Belt Publishing, 52.

[56] Catte, E., et al., editors. 55 Strong: Inside The West Virginia Teachers' Strike. (July 5, 2018). Cleveland: Belt Publishing, 55-57.

[57] Bidgood, J. & Robertson, C. (March 8, 2018). West Virginia Walkouts a Lesson in the Power of a Crowd-Sourced Strike. The New York Times. Retrieved from https://www.nytimes.com/2018/03/08/us/west-virginia-teachers-strike.html.

Chapter 14

[58] Field Museum. (November 15, 2016). Facebook. Retrieved from https://www.facebook.com/fieldmuseum/photos/the-lakota-phrase-mni-wiconi-meaning-water-is-life-has-been-an-inspiration-for-p/10153869930357273/.

[59] History. Standing Rock Sioux Tribe. Retrieved from https://www.standingrock.org/content/history.

Conclusions

[60] Rousseau, Jean-Jacques (1762). On the Social Contract. (D. Cress, Trans.). Indianapolis, Ind.: Hackett Publishing Company.

[61] Eric Holder on the Arc of Justice. TuftsNow. Retrieved from https://now.tufts.edu/articles/eric-holder-arc-justice.

[62] https://perma.cc/T3HC-RQN6

ABOUT THE AUTHORS

This book has been a joint endeavor between co-authors Brian Gruber and Adam Monier Edwards over two and a half years. Adam was born and raised in Washington, Pennsylvania – home to one of the nation's earliest protests, the Whiskey Rebellion (1791-1794). He devised the original concept after becoming disillusioned by the passion that demonstrators put into their marches outside his New York City window when they failed to see any substantial political change. The *Surmountable* name came to him after months of mutual brainstorming with Brian while researching movements and developing hypotheses that formed the backbone of the work. Brian challenged assertions and clarified the objective, leading to the unified vision now found in this book. Together, they launched a successful Kickstarter campaign to fund Brian's travel by securing $15,000 from over 80 backers. He then traveled to 15 cities in four continents to interview over 40 activists, theorists, historians, and ordinary passersby, and ultimately wrote the majority of the preceding pages.

BRIAN GRUBER

Born in Brooklyn, New York, Brian Gruber has spent 40 years studying, leading, and developing new media companies and creative projects. He was hired by C-SPAN founder Brian Lamb to be the pioneering cable network's first head of marketing, where he hosted two live national call-in shows each week with politically prominent guests such as John McCain, Nancy Pelosi and Cesar Chavez. After years as a cable TV marketing turnaround specialist, he was hired as the first head of marketing for Australia's national cable television company FOXTEL.

While consulting for the San Francisco-based World Affairs Council, Brian founded FORA.tv, a global thought leader network presenting the world's leading public forums; it was named by *Time* magazine as one of the fifty best sites on the web. While there he interviewed numerous public intellectuals, writers and policy experts from Christopher Hitchens to Norman Mailer and Amy Goodman to Jim Lehrer. He also founded ShowGo.tv, which streamed hundreds of live concerts from elite jazz clubs in Brazil, the UK, Italy, and the United States.

Brian authored *WAR: The Afterparty*, a global "walkabout" to the scenes of a half century of U.S. military interventions. In additional to interviews on Fox News, C-SPAN, and public radio, he was widely praised in reviews for the book's vision and editorial style. Stephen Kinzer, former New York Times bureau chief and one of America's leading foreign policy authors commented, "Joining the army, according to an old proverb, gives you the chance to 'travel the world, meet interesting people and kill them.' In this book, Brian Gruber travels the world, meets extremely interesting people, and instead of killing them, tries to understand them. His book cuts through layers of propaganda and helps us see the world's problems – and ourselves – through the eyes of others."

Brian's last book, *Six Days at Ronnie Scott's: Billy Cobham on Jazz Fusion and the Act of Creation*, garnered uniformly positive reviews across the jazz community. Carlo Wolff of *Downbeat* called it, "... an unusual and welcome addition to the jazz bibliography." Geoff Nicholls of *Rhythm* magazine adds, "Well-written and thought-provoking... a challenging document of a half-century of cutting-edge musical exploration."

Brian is currently writing a history of his current home, the Thai island of Koh Phangan.

ADAM MONIER EDWARDS

In parallel to building a framework to document underdog activists' successes in *Surmountable*, Adam has helped turn the similarly underrepresented skillset of search engine optimization (SEO) into a thriving field during his 20-year career. He began as a freelance web designer and worked in-house at the leader in digital signage software before moving to Manhattan in 2004 to pursue SEO full-time with both startups and Fortune 500 enterprises. Most recently, Adam was promoted into his current agency's first ever global head for the discipline where he now leads over 250 practitioners worldwide. This role comes as the culmination of a journey punctuated by winning Best Large SEO Agency at the 2019 U.S. Search Awards and Best SEO Campaign at the 2019 OMMA Awards after rebuilding the company's U.S. department from the ground up with just one other colleague in 2012. He has spoken at events ranging from VOICE Summit to Onward to SMX Advanced, delivered the keynote at the IAB Forum 2019 in Montevideo, Uruguay, and judged entries for the inaugural 2020 Global Marketing Awards.

While building an award-winning marketing team, Adam has also been an executive producer of notable independent films such as *Refugee* (2018), hailed as "an extraordinary film … incredibly moving" by BBC World News, *Shooting an Elephant* (2016), official selection of the Tribeca Film Festival. He was also just named to the prestigious NationSwell Council after serving from 2010-2013 as a board member of Upwardly Global, where his events generated the nonprofit's first ever press coverage in the *New York Times* and *New York Daily News* for immigrant and refugee job placement assistance.

Adam is now applying his two decades of business insights to the stagnant analysis of civic engagement by showing how activist fervor and resilience can effectively lead to meaningful victories. He lives in New York with his wife.